CW00821570

'What a timely, scholarly yet accessible book on
following a substance-related death. A wealth
provided on so many diverse aspects. The emer
based on extensive clinical expertise and wisc
Not only healthcare professionals but those e..._ ..._.........._ ...._ ..... ./_ - --
grief have much to learn from reading this ground-breaking book.'

– Margaret Stroebe, Professor Emeritus, Department of
Clinical Psychology, Utrecht University

'A great gift to any counsellor dealing with grief or substance abuse. Cartwright's
book is solid – theoretically grounded yet eminently practical. Therapists will
find this book an essential tool for assisting bereaved family and friends in
coping with such devastating deaths.'

– Kenneth J. Doka, PhD, senior consultant, Hospice Foundation of America,
and author of Disenfranchised Grief: New Directions,
Challenges, and Strategies for Practice

'The response to loss is subject to many factors, cause of death being prominent
among them. In this book Peter Cartwright shines a light on drug- and alcohol-
related death, an epidemic that affects an ever-growing number of the bereaved.
This book offers abundant clinical illustrations, insight and information about
the complexities of grief in these cases, and will be of interest to experienced
bereavement therapists as well as those new to the field.'

– Phyllis Kosminsky, PhD, LCSW, FT, author of Attachment-Informed Grief
Therapy: The Clinicians' Guide to Foundations and Applications

'As Chief Executive of Adfam, England's leading organisation supporting
families and friends affected by substance misuse, I am very pleased to endorse
this book, which makes a very important contribution to practice around a
particularly difficult and sensitive issue…that of substance-related bereavement.'

– Vivienne Evans OBE, Chief Executive, Adfam

of related interest

The Creative Toolkit for Working with Grief and Bereavement
A Practitioner's Guide with Activities and Worksheets
Claudia Coenen
ISBN 978 1 78775 146 0
eISBN 978 1 78775 147 7

Grief Demystified
An Introduction
Caroline Lloyd
Foreword by Dr Jennifer Dayes
ISBN 978 1 78592 313 5
eISBN 978 1 78450 624 7

Responding to Loss and Bereavement in Schools
A Training Resource to Assess, Evaluate and Improve the School Response
John Holland
ISBN 978 1 84905 692 2
eISBN 978 1 78450 229 4

Supporting People through Loss and Grief
An Introduction for Counsellors and Other Caring Practitioners
John Wilson
ISBN 978 1 84905 376 1
eISBN 978 0 85700 739 1

Supporting People Bereaved through a Drug- or Alcohol-Related Death

Peter Cartwright

Jessica Kingsley Publishers
London and Philadelphia

Figure 2.1 reproduced with kind permission of Utrecht University.
Figure 3.1 reproduced with kind permission of The Guildford Press.
Table 3.2 reproduced with kind permission of Sage Publications.

First published in 2020
by Jessica Kingsley Publishers
73 Collier Street
London N1 9BE, UK

www.jkp.com

Library of Congress Cataloging in Publication Data
A CIP catalog record for this book is available from the Library of Congress

British Library Cataloguing in Publication Data
A CIP catalogue record for this book is available from the British Library

ISBN 978 1 78592 191 9
eISBN 978 1 78450 463 2

Printed and bound by CPI Group (UK) Ltd, Croydon, CR0 4YY

This book is dedicated to my father, John, who died during the writing of this book, and to his work as co-founder and phone volunteer of the Samaritans branch in south-east London, and at various times branch director, treasurer, trainer and secretary. His work lives on after him.

Contents

Part 2: How to Support Someone Bereaved Through a Substance-Related Death

Part 3: Examples of Good Practice

Acknowledgements

This book has been a truly collaborative effort.

First, I thank Bethany Gower at Jessica Kingsley Publishers for seeing the need for this book and Tony Walter, at the University of Bath, who proposed to her that I write it.

I thank my contributors: Jan Larkin; Jas Sahota; Zoe Swithenbank; Christine Valentine, with Jennifer McKell and Lorna Templeton; Roger Kirby, Stella Hurd and Michelle Michael; Carmen Joanne Ablack; Rual Gibson; Fiona Turnbull, with Jane Shackman and Oliver Standing; Pete Weinstock; Elizabeth Burton-Phillips; Marlene Taylor; Justina Murray and Scott Clements; Christina Thatcher; and Lorna Templeton.

I also thank Carol Seiderer, my counselling supervisor, for her ideas, support and review of the manuscript; my mentor, Jim Kuykendall, for his ideas and support; and Marian Harvey who proofread the manuscript and contributed her ideas.

I have been fortunate in having two fine peer reviewers of the manuscript, Dr Anne Cole and Dr Colin Murray Parkes OBE, both of whom provided many constructive comments that have improved the final book.

I'm also grateful to my editor, Elen Griffiths, and her colleagues at Jessica Kingsley Publishers.

In addition, my thanks to the following people who helped in so many ways: Dean Adams, the late Pamela Austin, Jessica Mitchell and Bereavement Care Journal, Paul Botsford, Elizabeth Burton-Phillips, Merle Cartwright, Michael Cartwright, Claire Chambers, Carolyn Cheasman, Dr Ross Cooper, Dominic Davis, Christine Duncan, Eugene Ellis, Jacqueline Wearn and the Gestalt Centre, Joanna Gibbs, Terry Gorski, Dr Gordon Hay, Hilary Hipps, Tracy Jarvis, Karunavira, Julita Levinson, everyone at Lewisham Bereavement Counselling, Jim MacSweeney, Dr Sangeeta Mahajan, Dr Andrew McAuley, Victoria McLaughlin, Anne Power, Tommi Raisanen, Stephen Robling, Bill Reading, Michelle Rose, Philippa and Graeme Skinner, Lorna Templeton, Fiona Turnbull, Professor Richard Velleman, and Marion Wilson. As well as my family and friends for their support and encouragement, despite my hardly seeing them for more than three years!

Last, and by no means least, I thank all the bereaved people who have taught me so much.

Disclaimer

The content of this book is provided by way of assistance, guidance and support only. The book does not constitute direction or instruction to act: it is purely for consideration by the reader. Related decisions and their consequences are the responsibility of the reader alone.

Introduction

Anyone who has lost someone they love knows the pain of bereavement. For most of us, a major bereavement is probably the most emotive life experience we have and the one that feels closest to 'madness'. Fortunately, we have the potential to come through it and most of us do not need specialist help to do so. Indeed, research demonstrates that psychological and emotional support for people with a straightforward bereavement often has no effect and they may be better off without it (Bonanno 2009; Hansson and Stroebe 2003; Jordan and Neimeyer 2003). Therefore, grief is not an illness, even if a minority of bereaved people are vulnerable to physical and mental illnesses (Parkes and Prigerson 2010).

However, there are some deaths, like those caused by substance use, that are often especially difficult to grieve. Therefore, these bereaved people *do* often benefit from support.

> Is there even any value in trying to put into words something so terrible, so visceral? ...[B]ut maybe the unbearable has to be borne in words as well as in real life, so that others who want to support friends or family members [of those who died through drug or alcohol use] may understand as far as possible why it is that it takes for ever for life to be normal again... [T]he best I can come up with is having a limb ripped off or an organ ripped out. 'Amputation' is too tidy, a word that carries images of clinical operating theatres and anaesthesia, and there was nothing clinical about this. (Skinner 2012, pp.36–37)

This description of severe substance-related grief is from Philippa Skinner, a mother trying to convey to us something of her experience of losing her son, Jim, to a heroin overdose.

Drug-related deaths (not alcohol-related deaths) have been referred to as 'special deaths', along with deaths by suicide, murder, the death of a child, etc. (Guy and Holloway 2007, p.84). These other deaths may also be related to substance use. Drug-related deaths have three characteristics that make them particularly difficult to grieve: stigma, the often traumatic circumstances of the death and the resulting disenfranchised grief[1] (Chapple, Ziebland and Hawton 2015; Guy 2004). Alcohol-related deaths, especially when the use was addictive,

---

1   A loss that is not socially sanctioned, openly acknowledged or publicly mourned (Doka 1989).

can similarly be stigmatised and disenfranchised (Walter and Ford 2018), and also probably traumatic when sudden, unexpected and horrific (Pearlman *et al.* 2014). These characteristics may inhibit, complicate and prolong grieving.

Additionally, substance-related deaths often evoke intense guilt for not preventing the death that can seriously impede grieving (Templeton *et al.* 2016). These deaths are existentially problematic for bereaved people, because they can damage their assumptions that their world is safe, familiar and predictable, which in turn can erode their self-trust and sense of purpose in life (Guy and Holloway 2007). Additionally, the social and media representations of such deaths are often sensationalised and stigmatised, which is often very different from bereaved people's own experience (Guy and Holloway 2007).

As many bereaved people experience the stress and strain of their loved one's addictive substance-using behaviour before the death, often for many years, they begin grieving in poor physical and mental health, and with much unfinished business[2] that remains to be worked through (Cartwright 2019; Valentine 2018). Also, people often misunderstand or feel confused about substance use, especially when addictive, and their own part in what happened, such as their inability to stop it. This can evoke seemingly unwarranted grief responses including enduring guilt (Cartwright 2019).

Grieving these deaths is often long, slow and exceedingly painful (Ross 1996; Valentine 2018). They can be experienced as a watershed in someone's life, from their life before to a completely changed life thereafter. However, alongside these common characteristics there is significant diversity in these bereavements (Templeton *et al.* 2018a).

Additionally, these bereavements often have many factors that typically make any bereavement difficult: premature death; a sudden, traumatic and/or unexplained death; the death of a child; personal vulnerability to an unhealthy trajectory for grieving, etc. (Parkes and Prigerson 2010). Also, in another way these bereavements are no different from any other – a loved one has died.

Generally speaking, the more of the above characteristics that are present, the more severe and complex the bereavement. As the number of these characteristics increases, it is more likely that someone's capacity to grieve successfully is overwhelmed and the greater their need of support. Fortunately, many of these characteristics are probably those most helped by support (Jordan and Neimeyer 2003).

These typically distinctive, severe, complex and disenfranchised bereavements are becoming more common as the number of substance-related deaths continues to rise.

---

2   Unfinished business refers to difficult situations and events that have not had a satisfactory resolution.

Despite all this, these bereavements have been 'internationally neglected in research, policy and practice' (Valentine and Bauld 2018, p.2). Also, the response of services to such bereaved people often falls short of what they need. They are more likely to experience help from any professional or other worker as a negative rather than a positive intervention, which adversely affects grieving and often prevents them seeking support (Valentine 2018). I could not find any research on the potential helpfulness of counselling for these bereaved people, and therefore conducted my own to inform this book (Cartwright 2019). I found that those who support these bereaved people seemingly often lacked the specialist knowledge and skills required. Subsequently, people had unmet needs associated with the substance-related characteristics of their bereavement, and also they could prematurely leave support.

I consider this happens for several reasons, reflecting the lack of specialist services and literature. Most bereavement support in the UK is provided by volunteers at bereavement services, who have limited training; some are not trained counsellors. Even when this work *is* done by trained and experienced counsellors, typically they lack experience of *both* bereavement and substance use and its impact on families. Also, working with substance use, especially when addictive, often provokes anxiety in workers unfamiliar with this work. Sometimes, bereavement support is provided by those in substance treatment services, including workers who support people whose lives are affected by someone else's substance use. However, they may not be trained and experienced in bereavement, and may be focused on the person who uses substances rather than their family. Finally, many of those supervising this work also may lack the specialist knowledge required for these bereavements.

This book is intended as a significant step towards redressing this situation. It continues recent work to describe and understand these bereavements (Feigelman, Jordan and Gorman 2011; Valentine 2018), and starts to establish how we can support this marginalised and high-need group of bereaved people.

Whom this book is intended to help

This book is primarily for those whose work is supporting a self-selecting group of bereaved adult people who see substance use[3] as a significant part of what led to the death of their loved one and their subsequent bereavement. This includes counsellors, psychotherapists and psychologists, family support workers, drug and alcohol treatment workers, those offering peer support, faith leaders, as well as family, friends and colleagues. Although they are not the primary readership,

---

3   Potentially this includes some deaths from smoking tobacco.

I have been mindful that people who have been bereaved in this way will be interested in this book.

Furthermore, parts of this book are relevant for supporting people who are not bereaved, but whose lives are still affected by someone else's substance use, as well as for supporting people bereaved in other ways.

How to use this book

The book is not a manual for how to do this work, because each bereaved person's experience is unique, as are the training, skills and experience of those supporting them. The book does offer knowledge about and ideas for supporting these bereaved people, and it is your responsibility to decide what seems appropriate for you to use when supporting someone. Inevitably, my training and therapeutic style influence this book and I have tried to keep it as accessible and jargon-free as is practical.

The structure and content

Part 1 aims to make sense of substance-related bereavements, with chapters on making sense of bereavement and on substance use, how addictive substance use affects a family, and substance-related bereavements.

Part 2 considers how to support clients bereaved through a substance-related death: Chapter 7 covers key considerations for everyone working with these bereaved people and introduces three fictitious clients who illustrate the work presented throughout Part 2. Chapter 8 offers ideas for non-specialists about supporting bereaved people. Then Chapters 9 and 10 consider what bereavement counselling is and how to provide it. Chapters 11–17 cover specific aspects of grieving a substance-related death. Potentially, this work can be provided by any trained and experienced practitioner, not just a bereavement specialist. The interventions presented are described for face-to-face, one-to-one work, and these can be adapted for helplines, group work, family therapy, etc.

Part 3 offers examples of good practice of supporting people who are bereaved through a substance-related death.

Key themes in this book
Challenging contemporary culture

Contemporary mainstream culture in the UK can stigmatise substance use, and often views any bereavement as taboo and expects bereaved people to 'move on' and 'get over it'. Also, the working culture in many support organisations is about problem-solving, and their help is often time-limited.

I regard these as unhelpful influences on supporting these bereaved people. Therefore, the book considers how to work with these stigmatised and disenfranchised bereavements, looks at what *is* effective bereavement work and states the importance of inter-agency working.

Working with difference and diversity
The importance of working across people's differences and taking full account of clients' diversity is well established (British Association for Counselling and Psychotherapy (BACP) 2018).

Joint working and referral
Effective joint working and referral are often needed, as any one practitioner or agency may well not be able to meet the variety and complexity of needs that many of these bereaved people have (Cartwright 2019). In particular, consider family therapy where it is advantageous to work with a whole family; medical help and supervision for someone with moderate to severe depression; and a substance treatment service where someone has difficulty with their own substance use during bereavement.

Good practice, not best practice
There is often no one best way of working that fits all practitioners and clients, and this is a newly evolving area of support. Therefore, what I offer is good practice as I know it, not best practice. I am interested to see how this work continues to evolve.

Terms used in this book

- **Bereavement** is what happens after a loss, and **grief** is how bereavement is experienced through all the emotional, cognitive, physical, behavioural and social experiences. I make no distinction between **mourning** and **grief**.

- **Family** is used for convenience to refer to the dead person's network of people, unless otherwise stated, and includes parents, partners, siblings, children, extended family members, friends, colleagues, neighbours, etc.

- **Substance** refers to anything people take, including drugs and alcohol, to change the way they feel, think or behave (UNODC 2017).

- **Addiction** rather than 'dependency' is used (despite the latter being used in the drug and alcohol field), because it is more familiar to bereaved people and probably to many readers.

- **Counsellor** has been used for convenience to refer to all people who provide emotional and psychological support.

The limits of this book

I have needed to hold the focus on substance-related bereavement, so it has not been practical to discuss working with other issues that are covered elsewhere. Therefore, the book does not provide comprehensive treatment of trauma and depression, and provides only minimal coverage of work on clients' childhood difficulties which can affect their bereavements as adults (including the impact of parental substance use on a bereaved person's childhood development – which would take another book). You will need to either refer someone on to others or have the necessary training and experience to work with these other issues, including being able to consider how grief may be affected by them. To help with this, further reading and referrals are suggested.

I hope this book helps you to have success and satisfaction in supporting people bereaved through a substance-related death.

Part 1

Making Sense of Substance-Related Bereavements

1

Making Sense of Bereavement

The exploration of substance-related bereavements begins with looking at bereavement in general to be clear about what happens and why. This is done by:

- defining bereavement
- considering the experience of grieving and why it happens
- a brief consideration of possible complexities and difficulties in grieving.

This describes bereavement following the untimely death of a person in the Western world. This is different from responses to the timely deaths of most older people in most societies (Parkes, Laungani and Young 2015), and even of responses to the death of young children in societies where parents expect many of their babies to die and show little grief (Scheper-Hughes 1992).

Defining bereavement

Bereavement is the process of adaptation that people go through following the loss of someone[1] to whom they have an attachment – that is, a loved one. 'Attachment' refers to the need for deep and enduring emotional bonds with others that provide security (Bowlby 1969), which evolved to ensure protection and enable procreation (Parkes 2009) (see Chapter 2). We receive this from an 'attachment figure', typically our parent; we can be an attachment figure to others, typically our child; and we can receive and provide attachment to someone, such as a partner, sibling or close friend.

Bereavement is the normal reaction to an abnormal life event. Whereas separation from loved ones is normally only temporary, in death it is permanent. This life crisis requires letting go of being reunited, going through a psychosocial transition to adapt to a new life without a loved one, and changing

---

1   Also, people can be bereaved for the loss of something, e.g. a home, role in life and even stopping addictive drug use.

the relationship with them from one with an actual person to a symbolic or internalised representation of them. Love and loss are two sides of the same coin, and inherent in loving someone is the risk of losing them (Parkes 2009).

> Imagine that both I and someone you love unexpectedly died in the same event. You might be interested that the author of a book you read had died and would probably give it little further consideration. In contrast, the unexpected and premature death of a loved one would result in a major bereavement for you. The difference is the emotional bond – the 'attachment' – that you have to your loved one and not to me.

The experience of grieving and why it happens

The following describes the typical experiences of a straightforward, uncomplicated bereavement, with an explanation of why they occur.

Where the death is anticipated, people may start to grieve before the death (see Chapter 4). Others, however, may deny what is going to happen, as psychological and emotional protection against the enormity of the future loss.

Parkes and Prigerson (2010), from many research studies, propose that following the death there is a process of grieving: 'numbness, commonly the first state, gives place to pining, and pining is often followed by a period of disorganisation and despair until, in the long run, this too declines as acceptance grows' (p.7). These are not a sequence of neat steps; rather, they 'blend into and replace one another' (p.7) and vary greatly between people, families and cultures.

Numbing happens soon after knowing of the death, although less often when the death was timely and expected. It is a normal way of blocking overwhelming pain and allowing time to take in the shock of the death (Parkes and Prigerson 2010).

As the reality of the loss becomes real, pining begins. This is the familiar pangs of grief, the painful yearning and longing for a loved one to come back, characterised by crying, feeling anxious at being separated, etc. At first, pining is frequent and seemingly spontaneous; it becomes less frequent and often comes in waves; then it diminishes over time so that it is eventually only triggered by reminders of the loss (which may still happen years later).

Pining is normal attachment behaviour; it attempts to reunite with a loved one by being preoccupied with them and the events leading up to their death – for example, restlessness, calling out to them, searching for them, returning to places associated with them (Parkes 2009). These attempts may even be experienced as successful by momentarily 'seeing', 'hearing' or 'smelling' them, talking to them and expecting an answer, dreaming of them, etc. This innate need to reunite happens despite people typically knowing it is futile, and is ultimately unsuccessful (at least in this lifetime). Pining also invites others to care for a bereaved person – that is, provide attachment in the absence of a loved one (Parkes 2009).

Another normal response is anger (Worden 2009), such as feeling irritable and bitter that nothing can be done and the world has become a seemingly insecure and dangerous place. Also, there can be attachment-motivated protesting aimed at reuniting with a loved one. Given this, it is unsurprising that family members can become bitter and irritable with each other. People can blame those they hold accountable for the death, as if this could have somehow prevented or rewritten what happened (Worden 2009). Blame can be turned inwards as self-blame and guilt, such as 'Did I do all that I could?' Sometimes self-blame provides an explanation for what is inexplicable about the death, reduces anxiety about the unpredictability of the world and/or somehow rewrites what happened (see Chapter 14).

Alongside this preoccupation with the person who died, people may avoid the difficult and painful reality of death in order to make it more manageable. For example, disbelief, experiencing themselves or the world around them as unreal, or avoiding places and reminders of a loved one can occur, although they tend not to last (Worden 2009). The stress and demands of grieving often lead to people getting physical illnesses and ailments. Also, at this time, people typically have an idealised view of their loved one (often encouraged by others) that seems to reassure them that their loved one is worth grieving; again, this diminishes with time (Parkes and Prigerson 2010).

Gradually, people experience periods of calm without grief. At first this may be momentary, but eventually a whole day can go by without wrenching emotion. This is an example of a much broader experience where people tend to oscillate back and forth between grieving and recovering from grieving, get on with living and creating a new life without a loved one. This 'dual process' is a normal way people self-regulate the enormity of the grieving (Stroebe and Schut 1999) (see Chapter 2).

An important theme through bereavement for many people is creating a 'continuing bond' with their loved one who died (Klass, Silverman and Nickman 1996). Although reuniting with a loved one is unsuccessful, a continuing bond is the rediscovery of the attachment to them that was feared lost, albeit in a new and internalised form such as talking to them and knowing what they would say back (see Chapter 2).

As pining subsides and people let go of being reunited with their loved one, they typically experience disorganisation and despair. Death happens quickly, but the reality of it is too big, too complicated, and its implications too many for people to adjust to it quickly. There are also secondary losses, those things lost a result of the primary loss of a loved one, to which they also need to adjust. It is therefore normal to adjust gradually.

Many practical adjustments need making. This includes everyday changes, such as one less place to set at the meal table, as well as more profound changes to find ways to meet all the needs that were met by a loved one – for example, companionship or tasks a loved one did such as driving.

An important theme is people making meaning of what has happened (Kauffman 2002a; Neimeyer and Sands 2011). This can take place throughout grieving and is associated with favourable adaptation to bereavement (Holland, Currier and Neimeyer 2006). In particular, this is sense-making, benefit-finding and identity re-formation (Kosminsky and Jordan 2016):

- Sense-making is forming an understandable narrative, or 'story', about the death, including explaining what may be inexplicable, often in philosophical or spiritual terms (Holland *et al.* 2006). This is particularly necessary where the death seems to be incomprehensible or unexpected and not prepared for. Sense-making also includes re-evaluating who a loved one was. This needs to produce a more complete and balanced view than the earlier idealisation of them, and resolves, as far as possible, what feels unfinished in the relationship with them.

- Benefit-finding acknowledges the significance of the loss and, paradoxically, identifies any positive gain from the loss (Holland *et al.* 2006), such as reordered life priorities or a desire for closer connection to loved ones still alive.

- Identity re-formation is re-establishing those aspects of who someone is that still 'fit' in their changed life, or creating new aspects of identity where the old no longer 'fits', e.g. 'we' has become 'I', and a person is no longer the deceased's partner/parent/child/etc., so that they have lost a significant aspect of who they are. In turn, this may prompt consideration of 'Was I a good partner/parent/child/etc.?' Also, others will now see them differently, and this in turn affects how they see themselves.

This meaning-making often requires people to update or even reconstruct parts of their assumptive world. This is all that they assume to be true about themselves and their world based on their previous experiences, which gives their life a sense of predictability, reality, meaning and purpose (Kauffman 2002a). For example, a premature death can challenge the assumption that the old die before the young, and perhaps also the assumption that the world is safe and stable. This is made harder when old assumptions are no longer accurate or relevant, and therefore cannot be used to help construct new assumptions; in turn, this makes it harder to create new assumptions (Neimeyer 2012).

Additionally, death invites people to face existential realities. This commonly includes facing their own death and the death of others they love, and even finding new meaning and purpose in life.

It is all these challenges that lead to psychological disorganisation. People can lose hope and start to despair, and this can lead to a period of depression (see Chapter 15). However, over time, people gradually form new assumptions and make meaning of events that finally 'fits' with their changed world. They can again feel hope for their future.

Over time a deeper acceptance is formed and enough adaptation occurs. However, there is no clear end and people do not 'get over it' or 'move on'. Rather, they have occasional upsurges of grief, even long after the death, that may come as a shock (and if they are in counselling, they may believe it is not working). They still reflect on a deceased loved one and associated meaning-making continues intermittently, often for many years. Most continue their relationship through a continuing bond. The loss is successfully integrated into the rest of who they are and their life going forward.

Determinants of grief

Bereavements vary enormously, even for any one person during their lifetime. Therefore, Parkes and Prigerson (2010) propose four determinants of grief that describe and explain this variation:

1. The bereaved person's gender, age and kinship relationship to the person who died.

2. The mode of death.

3. Personal vulnerability, due to previous mental health difficulties, and/or an insecure attachment style and associated difficulties in grieving and with the relationship with the person who died.

4. Social and cultural influences, including religion and the support of others.

Imagine, for example, the difference between a nephew grieving the loss of an aunt who died peacefully after a long happy life, and who has a lot of support from others, and a parent grieving the loss of their son who died by suicide after years of drug addiction, who feels isolated by the stigma of drug use and suicide, and who now has caring responsibilities for grandchildren.

> Consider how you would explain bereavement to a client. You might want to create an informal 'script' that summarises the three sections above and then rehearse how you would say it.

Complexities and difficulties in grieving

Although people are equipped to come through bereavement, some people's trajectories of grief are complex and/or difficult, which in turn impedes adapting to their loss. Therefore, the passage of time is not necessarily a healer of grief (Holland *et al.* 2006). This is due to complexities caused by characteristics of the bereavement and/or personal factors of the bereaved person. You need to recognise these and decide whether to work with them or refer someone on to specialist support. It is helpful to be familiar with the three theories presented in Chapter 2 and how these theories influence the following.

Substance-related bereavements are often complex, severe and long-lasting. As described in Chapter 6, this is because of five substance-related characteristics that potentially affect these bereavements (Cartwright 2019):

- substance use, especially when addictive

- unfinished business associated with the person who died and their substance use

- the death, including traumatic bereavement

- stigma, disenfranchised grief and a lack of social support

- coping with specific difficulties, such as an inquest.

Those bereaved by substance use are vulnerable to complexities and difficulties in grieving (Feigelman, Jordan, and Gorman 2011; Valentine and Templeton 2018).

Additionally, in common with all bereavements, personal factors can increase vulnerability to difficulties – in particular, an insecure attachment style (see Chapter 2); dependency on a loved one increases the risk during bereavement of severe depression, heightened anxiety and suicidal ideas (Parkes 2009). A further risk is a history of mental health difficulties (Worden 2009).

It can be difficult to know what is normal and will ease, and what is unhealthy or when grieving has become stuck. This is considered next and also in Part 2.

Difficulties in grieving

There are two main difficulties in grieving, reflecting the dual process model: problems in restoration through prolonging grief, and problems with loss through delaying or inhibiting grief (Parkes and Prigerson 2010). These difficulties are commonly, but not always, a consequence of an attachment disorder (Parkes 2009). Similarly, they can have separation distress at their core and also traumatic distress, often resulting from the shocking circumstances of the death (Holland and Neimeyer 2011). They can also be a consequence of an inability to make meaning of the loss (Holland *et al.* 2006).

Prolonged grief
Prolonged grief involves extended pining and often occurs with anxiety and depression (Parkes 2009). Being traumatised by the death often prolongs and may also complicate grieving (Holland and Neimeyer 2011).

Severe prolonging can be diagnosed as prolonged grief disorder (PGD) (Prigerson *et al.* 2009), characterised by intense and prolonged separation distress, as if someone is stuck pining for their loved one, as well as cognitive, emotional and behavioural symptoms.

Delayed or inhibited grief
Grief can be delayed by supressing and postponing it to protect against being overwhelmed (Worden 2009). Typically, someone responds to bereavement seemingly as if nothing had happened, although they may have panic attacks, experience persistent and intense guilt, or develop symptoms like those of their deceased loved one and become depressed (Parkes and Prigerson 2010). Also, grief can be delayed while waiting for the completion of prolonged official procedures such as an inquest and the hoped-for outcome they might provide (see also page 120).

Inhibiting grief can be linked to early attachment difficulties, particularly an avoidant attachment style (Parkes 2009). Where grief is too overwhelming, it can be 'masked' behind particular behaviours or physical symptoms (Worden 2009, p.144), such as delinquency, unexplained depression or psychosomatic symptoms, often in the same part of the body that was significant in the death; these often abate after grief is worked through. Also, grief can be masked by substance use. All of these can be seen as attachment responses: protesting, dissociating or clinging on through somatic identification with a deceased loved one.

Difficulties in grieving and addiction
Interestingly, a recent study found a higher frequency of complicated grief symptoms in bereaved people with a substance use disorder (34.2%) compared with bereaved non-addicted people (5%) (Masferrer 2017). Another study suggests that people with PGD and those who use substances addictively experience similar levels of craving, because both activities involve the activation of the nucleus accumbens in the brain's reward circuit (O'Connor *et al.* 2008). Both seem to keep searching for what they have 'lost': their deceased loved one or the effect of using substances. Despite the ongoing pain for those with PGD, there is seemingly the ongoing reward of keeping their loved one 'alive'

in this way (which also inadvertently reinforces the habits that prevent moving through grief).

These studies suggest that people who use substances addictively may be more vulnerable to difficulties in grieving, and these people are particularly likely to be bereaved through a substance-related death (see Chapter 16). Also I speculate, and have no evidence, that bereaved people who are genetically related to someone who died through addictive substance use *might* be more vulnerable to PGD. Although research is required, the *possible* implications for these people and for supporting them are profound.

Death following bereavement

There is evidence for an increased risk of death following bereavement (Stroebe and Stroebe 1993). The principal causes are cardiac events and strokes, suicide and liver cirrhosis that often originate before the death through heart disease, depression and alcohol dependence (Osterweis, Solomon and Green 1984). Studies show that the most stressful bereavements have the greatest risk of death, such as of bereaved mothers whose child of any age died unexpectedly and from unnatural causes, and bereaved partners who had high levels of caregiver strain before the death or whose partner died through an illness associated with risk-taking, such as alcohol dependence (Parkes and Prigerson 2010).

These characteristics can be found in substance-related bereavements (also see Chapter 4). Furthermore, those who use substances addictively often lose friends and acquaintances through substance-related deaths and can increase their use to cope with grief (Masferrer, Garre-Olmo and Caparros 2015).

Although suicidal comments are common in bereavement, and need to be taken seriously and worked with proactively (also see page 261), they are far less commonly acted upon (Parkes and Prigerson 2010).

FURTHER READING
Parkes, C.M. and Prigerson, H.G. (2010) *Bereavement: Studies of Grief in Adult Life* (4th edition). London: Penguin Books.

2

Three Useful Theories for Bereavement Support

This chapter presents three theories that are used throughout the book. They explain key aspects of grieving, offer guidance on how to help clients and can be integrated into a useful way of thinking about a bereaved person:

- the dual process model (DPM)

- continuing bonds

- attachment theory

- integrating the three theories.

However, to simplify the basic support work described in Chapter 8, this does not require knowledge of attachment theory.

The dual process model

Our purpose in developing the DPM was to provide a model that would better describe coping and predict good versus poor adaptation to this stressful life event, and by doing so, to better understand individual differences in the ways that people come to terms with bereavement… Coping refers to processes, strategies, or styles of managing (reducing, mastering, tolerating) the situation in which bereavement places the individual. (Stroebe and Schut 2010, p.274)

Stroebe and Schut's model proposes that grieving is dynamic and involves 'oscillating' between, and giving attention to, two different processes: a 'loss-orientated' process, focused on grieving, and a 'restoration-orientated' process, focused on recovering from a period of grieving or constructing a new life without the deceased, with both taking place within everyday life (Stroebe and Schut 1999, 2010). See Figure 2.1.

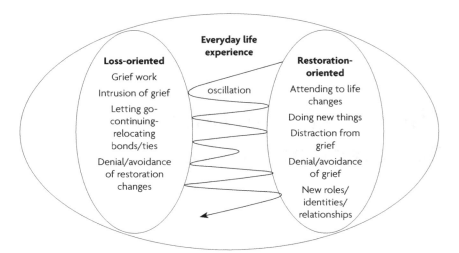

FIGURE 2.1 THE DUAL PROCESS MODEL
Source: Stroebe and Schut 1999

Healthy adaptation to loss occurs through both loss- and restoration-orientated activities, and flexibly oscillating between those activities to regulate the 'dose' of grief. However, as Figure 2.1 also shows, being in either orientation can be a denial or avoidance of the other; if not enough attention is given to one or both orientations and/or if oscillation is inflexible, adaptation to loss becomes harder.

There are gender differences: 'women appear to be more loss-oriented following bereavement, feeling and expressing their distress at their loss; men, more restoration-oriented, actively engaging with the problems and practical issues associated with loss' (2010, p.282). The model is cross-cultural and also offers some insight into cultural differences in grieving, such as the traditional British 'stiff upper lip', over-emphasising restoration.

How the theory supports bereavement counselling

- It offers a way to consider how effectively a client grieves. If needed, it proposes how they might grieve more effectively, both moment by moment (such as in a counselling session) and more generally in their life and over time.

- The idea of oscillating between approaching and avoiding grief can be employed both moment by moment in counselling, and more generally in a client's life, making grieving more effective and manageable.

- It provides clues to a client's attachment style and potential continuing bond.

- It can give clients the new and welcomed idea of having some control over grieving when typically it seems uncontrollable.

Continuing bonds

[T]he resolution of grief involves continuing bonds that survivors maintain with the deceased… [T]hese continuing bonds can be a healthy part of the survivor's ongoing life. Now the challenge for those who support the bereaved is about how to help them hold and adapt the continuing relationship in a new way, rather than separate from it. (Klass, Silverman and Nickman 1996, p.22)

A healthy continuing bond is some type of psychological and/or spiritual connection with a loved one who died that is not a denial of their death, lets go of future hopes and expectations with that loved one, and is compatible with existing and new relationships (Klass *et al.* 1996). Therefore, grieving is not about breaking the bond and detaching. Instead, it is a continuation of the attachment, which changes from an external relationship with a living person to that person living on internally through a symbolic or psychological connection. Like any relationship, a continuing bond can change and grow over time (Kosminsky and Jordan 2016).

The research is mixed and complicated about the role continuing bonds have in a healthy outcome to grief (Kosminsky and Jordan 2016). Forming continuing bonds may be adaptive or may not (Stroebe, Schut and Boerner 2010) and is likely to be 'more adaptive in a context where they are understood and culturally supported' (Bonanno 2009, p.180).

The functions of healthy continuing bonds include confirming the reality of the death, valuing a combination of contact with a loved one and getting on without them (which echoes the dual process model), grieving being about letting go of difficult and painful emotions rather than letting go of a loved one, and a loved one being lost but still valued and not completely given up.

A loved one can continue to serve as an attachment figure, often playing the same role as when alive (Kosminsky and Jordan 2016):

- a source of felt security, reassurance and comfort in times of stress or distress

- a resource to consult about making important decisions – for example, 'asking' them and knowing the 'answer' they would give if still alive

- a recipient of caregiving – for example, tending the grave and keeping who they were alive by sharing stories and memories of them

- for partners, a symbolic support to counteract any disloyalty about remarrying

- more abstract functions – for example, providing a new sense of purpose and inspiration in life.

In Western societies, ancestors are not generally publicly remembered (Walter 1999). Rather, the dead live on in more private ways such as sensing the presence of a loved one, through religious beliefs, consulting spiritual mediums, talking to a loved one; objects such as the grave, photographs and other mementos. Additional ways of maintaining connection (Rando 2014) are:

- adopting the attributes or views of a loved one

- personal and collective bereavement rituals

- maintaining certain routines that were part of the relationship

- purposefully using triggers to stimulate a connection such as listening to a loved one's favourite music

- daydreaming and fantasising as a way to symbolically interact with a loved one

- taking action on a loved one's values and concerns, and considering their perspective when making decisions.

However, some forms of continuing bond seem to be unhealthy. Signs of behaving as if a loved had not died include 'great distress at making changes to the deceased's belongings, active avoidance of triggers associated with the death (e.g. refusal to attend the funeral or visit the grave), and speaking of deceased in the present, rather than past tense' (pp.83–84). Although these are common in early bereavement, if they continue, they inhibit adaptation to the loss (Kosminsky and Jordan 2016).

A client's attachment style influences whether they relinquish or continue their bond and *how* it might be continued (Stroebe *et al.* 2010).

How the theory supports bereavement counselling

- It provides clues to a client's attachment style, how they oscillate between and attend to loss and restoration activities, and how they are adapting to their loss.

- It provides a way to start a 'dialogue' with the deceased that facilitates working through unfinished business.

- For clients, having their bond recognised and validated is often new, and can bring some comfort and hope, especially with distressing or premature deaths. Also, it potentially counters unhelpful cultural norms, such as traditional British norms of 'get over it' and 'move on' that imply breaking the bond.

Attachment theory

> We come into the world with an instinct to attach, and this instinct propels us to form connections that, if we are lucky, provide us with protection and nurturance in infancy, with solace in old age, and throughout our lives, with the gift of being known and belonging somewhere and to someone... [I]t is arguably only when we lose someone that the strength of our attachment becomes most fully, and painfully, apparent. (Kosminsky and Jordan 2016, p.3)

Bowlby (1969) founded attachment theory and inspired many others to extensively research and theorise further, confirming the theory. The following summarises the theory (Bowlby 1969; Kosminsky and Jordan 2016; Parkes 2009).

In infancy, the attachment behavioural system is activated when a child feels uncomfortable or afraid and care is not received. The resulting separation distress, such as crying, is designed to reunite and get care from its 'primary caregiver', usually (but not always) the mother, who has a reciprocal need to attach to and care for the child. As this care enables the child to return to a comfortable and secure internal state, the attachment behavioural system deactivates. Because separation from the caregiver potentially threatens the child's very survival, the need to reunite takes precedence over all other needs.

Ideally, children will experience their caregiver as calm, empathically attuned and able to respond effectively to their distress. Over the first 20 months or so of life, this experience of emotions being regulated through this interaction becomes internalised, involving both pleasant as well as difficult and painful emotions, to form a 'secure attachment' to the caregiver. This attachment gradually enables the child to become more independent, explore its world and withstand life's emotional ups and downs. The child is developing an internal working model, called a 'secure base', that provides the capacity to cope with separation, the capacity to self-regulate emotional distress, the cognitive ability to understand what is happening in its own mind and in the minds of others and differentiate between the two, called 'mentalising'[1] (Fonagy et al. 2004), and have trust in itself and others. Later, the child is able to go to school knowing

---

1   Mentalising is different from empathy, which is sensing feelings and emotions in others, and attempting to understand those.

its caregiver will be there at the end of the day, a young person can leave home, and an adult can form a partnership with another, have children and become an attachment figure for their child and partner.

However, some children do not experience their caregiver as attuned and effective, whether intended or not.[2] Then they use one of two secondary strategies to attempt to reduce their separation distress, and if this happens repeatedly, the child develops a form of 'insecure attachment' to its primary caregiver and is also possibly traumatised. This occurs in the following circumstances:

1.   Where a child repeatedly experiences its caregiver as unreliable, overly protective, or sometimes responsive but at others neglectful, the child adapts by habitually escalating its attempts to reunite and receive care, such as crying louder and, when the caregiver returns, clinging on, crying and protesting at any sign of further separation. Through internalising this early relational insecurity, the child develops an insecure 'anxious/ambivalent attachment' style with an internal working model characterised by remaining dependent on others, heightened emotion and difficulty regulating that emotion.

2.   Where a child repeatedly experiences its caregiver as emotionally distant, intolerant of its emotions or unavailable, the child realises that attempts at escalation fail, and so suppresses its discomfort and frustration at its caregiver's unavailability. Although the child may appear calm, this does not necessarily reflect their internal emotional state. Through internalising this early relational insecurity, the child develops an insecure 'avoidant attachment' style, with an internal working model characterised by attempting to be self-reliant and suppressing emotion.

These inflexible strategies are at least an organised way of coping with unmet attachment needs that work well enough for the child. However, some children are even less fortunate and experience their caregiver as frightening or as frightened of them, unpredictable and even abusive (often because the caregiver is overwhelmed and even frightened by their child's demands and vulnerability). They face an impossible dilemma: needing both to seek attachment from, and to withdraw from, their caregiver, who is the source of security and terror. This produces terror in the child that is likely to be traumatising. Usually, these disconnections remain unrepaired, so the caregiver becomes a source of fear and confusion, not of safety and security. The child is unable to find an effective strategy; its disorganised range of responses that attempt to seek attachment are an inconsistent mixture of both crying and clinging, and suppressing its

2   Parents tend to have experienced the same kind of parenting as their children experience from them; this explains the intergenerational transmission of attachment style.

distress and attachment needs, as well as freezing all movement and erratic and odd behaviour. This creates an insecure 'disorganised attachment' style, with an internal working model characterised by disorganisation and an inability to effectively regulate emotions.

Insecure attachment styles can have further lasting effects. A person's internal working model of relationships often includes ambivalence about others, formed through both needing their caregiver and anxiety about their response, and possibly a psychological dependency on others, particularly in those with an anxious/ambivalent style. Also, the ability to mentalise tends to be impaired by early attachment trauma, particularly in those with a disorganised style.

Their attachment style is a person's primary template for relationships with others and governs their expectations of future relationships. People may have a secondary attachment style, developed through another caregiver who responded differently to their mother, such as their father, grandparent or older sibling.

The advantages of a secure attachment are undeniable. However, attachment styles can be reworked (although never completely changed) and inner security 'earned' (Main 1996), such as happens through an effective counselling relationship. Through this, people can develop their capacity to mentalise, self-regulate emotional experience and to trust – all essential for effective grieving.

Adult attachment styles[3] parallel those developed in childhood, although one does not directly lead to the other, and exactly how this happens is under-researched. Put another way, adult love feels as it did the first time we experienced it with our primary caregiver (A. Sroufe cited by C. Siederer, personal communication).

Adult grief seemingly evokes the same childlike responses as when separated from a caregiver in childhood, such as crying, protesting and despair; for bereaved parents, a similar response is activated by their caregiving urge, and bereaved partners, siblings and friends are potentially responding to separation from someone who is both care giver and receiver. This continues until someone adapts to living without the person they are attached to. Attachment style is a significant determinant of grief (see Chapter 1), and people with insecure attachment styles are vulnerable to difficulties in grieving.

This need for attachment is found across all cultures. However, culture influences how parents relate to their children, and this in turn affects their children's attachment style.

---

3   The terms used for the adult correlation of childhood styles are not used in this book for the sake of simplicity.

How the theory supports bereavement counselling

- It informs counsellors how clients' present-day experience is influenced by past experiences of separation and loss, and how those were managed. Clients with insecure attachments often have childhood experiences of separation, loss and possibly trauma that often remain unprocessed, and have associated unmet developmental needs. Counsellors need to take account of this during bereavement counselling.

- It provides clues to how clients grieve, including how they might navigate the dual process model and continue or relinquish a bond.

- It provides clues as to how clients relate to others, including their counsellor. Counsellors need to respond in ways that take account of a client's attachment style, at least initially, without letting this blind them to a client's misperceptions of the world.

- Counselling needs to offer the client a 'secure base'.

- The counsellor needs to be a transitional attachment figure for the client. Rogers proposes that counsellors need to embody three core conditions – empathy, unconditional positive regard and being congruent – that are then actually experienced by a client (Mearns, Thorne and McLeod 2013). This is not unlike how an empathically attuned and responsively helpful caregiver relates to their child.

- The co-regulation of emotions in the therapeutic relationship parallels early secure attachment relationships.

- When needed, the counsellor helps a client develop their capacity to regulate their emotions and to mentalise.

- Counselling is an opportunity for insecurely attached clients to develop 'earned security'.

- Counsellors need to be aware of their own attachment style and how that can affect the way they relate to clients; where a client's way of attaching is different from their own, there can be a need for greater empathy.

- Counsellors need to have a good enough internal 'secure base' and be able to effectively regulate their own emotions. This enables them to be aware of their own inner experience and be empathically attuned to their client's experience; to balance being emotionally engaged with not being overwhelmed; and to be able to repair any strain or rupture in the therapeutic relationship in an open and non-defensive way.

- Counsellors need to consider how far they can help clients with insecure attachment styles and when to refer on.

Integrating the three theories

The dual process model, continuing bonds and attachment theory can be theoretically integrated by adapting the work of Stroebe *et al.* (2010). This provides a useful way to make sense of a client's way of grieving, how they relate to others, including their counsellor, and how their past experiences affect them now, as well as to propose ways to help them. However, it risks being an oversimplification because there is much individual variation; there are other factors that determine grief (see page 27), and this is no substitute for really getting to know an individual client, how they grieve and what they need.

Secure attachment
Potential adult characteristics

- Relationships have optimum emotional distance: they can be intimate and separate; co-operative; have mature dependency; can sensitively give and willingly receive care; and negotiate conflict.

- Can have a balanced and realistic view of parents, and generally were happy at school (Power 2013).

- Generally good self-esteem.

- Core attachment belief 'I am loved/I am loveable' (Power 2013).

- Can trust themselves and others (Parkes 2009).

Potential influence on grieving, counselling and the therapeutic relationship

- Probably grieve effectively.

- Have less distress than insecure attachment styles (Parkes 2009).

- Can access and describe in a coherent manner a full and balanced view of the loss and of relationship to deceased; self-regulate emotions; and separate from deceased. Grieving process relatively straightforward, unless complicated by other determinants, such as death premature, unexpected or traumatic, when more likely to access counselling (Kosminsky and Jordan 2016).

- Counsellor likely to experience client as trusting, forming an effective therapeutic alliance and making effective use of counselling (Power 2013).

Attachment-related work
Unlikely to be needed.

Dual process model
Can oscillate flexibly; can work through loss and restoration activities, including effectively expressing and regulating emotions (Stroebe *et al.* 2010).

Continuing bond
Can both accept the death and separate from deceased, maintain an effective internalised bond if they want to, and be bonded to a moderate extent. Can use continued connection to deceased to work towards acceptance of loss (Stroebe *et al.* 2010).

Avoidant attachment
Potential adult characteristics

- Can be subdivided into those fearful of being hurt and those dismissing of others to provide comfort and help (Bartholomew 1990).

- Relationships too emotionally distant: can avoid closeness by being independent, self-reliant, even seeming cold; avoid or dismiss attachment needs but can connect to others (although not deeply to attachment figures, and do so with anxiety they are unlikely to show); generally avoid conflict, although can be irritable and might angrily lash out. Can be caregiver, often in a controlling way, and even compulsive caregiver (through approval of it in childhood).

- Can be ambivalent about others. Can idealise parents. Probably performed well at school, but not close to teachers and friends. Can struggle to remember childhood accurately, and avoids reflecting on past (Power 2013).

- Can have defensive self-esteem: self-controlled, driven, perfectionist, or contemptuous of others who let them down.

- Core attachment belief 'I can be close so long as I keep my distress hidden' (Power 2013).

- Can trust themselves more than they trust others (Parkes 2009).

Potential influence on grieving, counselling and the therapeutic relationship

- Need to take account of whether avoiding is motivated by fearfully avoiding or dismissing of attachment (Kosminsky and Jordan 2016).

- Can avoid accessing, describing and feeling grief; has inflexible description of loss that lacks full and balanced view, with minimal amount of detail; ambivalent about deceased and dismisses significance of relationship to them; down-regulates emotions to avoid them; prematurely separates from deceased (Kosminsky and Jordan 2016).

- Can seem to cope well with bereavement. Lack of emotions can be because of coping well or suppressing, avoiding or delaying grieving. However, can be caught out by reminders of deceased and current bereavement can re-stimulate past grief that has not been expressed. Bereavement can bring home the extent of need for others (Parkes 2009).

- Can avoid turning to others for help, including counselling; may be sent for counselling by others or seek counselling if avoiding strategy no longer works – for example, unable to cope with emotions, physical symptoms, substance use, irritability in relationships with others. In counselling, can be reluctant to disclose; initially impressive ability to intellectualise about what happened; wary of being vulnerable or losing control of emotions and sensitive to exposure or intrusion; wants practical answers, advice and tools to cope, particularly to cope emotionally and get on with their life (Kosminsky and Jordan 2016).

- Counsellor can feel rejected, small, punished, deskilled in response to client implying 'I don't need you/I don't want your help/you're not important' (Power 2013).

Attachment-related work

- Initially match their attachment style, then gradually give disconfirming responses – for example, show warmth, keep connected, show interest, but not be insincere or give false praise (Power 2013).

- Pay attention to forming therapeutic alliance; work at their pace. Develop self and counsellor's support to consider beliefs about expressing emotions, raise awareness of emotions, and make connection to past attachment experiences to make sense of current grief and how they grieve (Kosminsky and Jordan 2016).

- Develop more trust of others.

Dual process model
Can be focused prematurely and dominantly on restoration activities and avoid loss experiences, and struggle to oscillate flexibly (Stroebe *et al.* 2010). Develop self-support and use of counsellor's support to oscillate and tolerate grief, so loss orientation can be approached and integrated.

Continuing bond
Can deny need to maintain any tie, trying to remain independent and to keep a distance from thoughts and reminders of the deceased. Can be unable to maintain useful symbolic bonds with the deceased. Need to acknowledge significance of bond to integrate the loss (Stroebe *et al.* 2010).

Anxious ambivalent attachment
Potential adult characteristics

- Relationships are too emotionally close: can be intimate but fear separation and cling on; intolerant of separation; co-operative; blurred boundaries with others; and unaware of own responsibility in current relationship problems. Can be either compulsive care-seeker, where attachment relationships are seen in terms of receiving care and expects attachment figure to assume responsibility for them, or compulsive caregiver, who places priority on needs of other, feels self-sacrificing and provides care whether or not requested. Can be ambivalent about and/or dependent on attachment relationships, with possible associated resentment, blame and jealousy.

- Can remain emotionally enmeshed with parents and family issues. School may have caused anxiety, learning suffered and may have been bullied (Power 2013).

- Low self-esteem; esteem of others is important.

- Core attachment belief 'I can be close so long as I cling on tightly' (Power 2013).

- Can trust others more than they trust themselves (Parkes 2009).

Potential influence on grieving, counselling and the therapeutic relationship

- Can have persistent and overriding pining (Stroebe *et al.* 2010).

- Can have difficulty down-regulating distressing emotions and that can compromise ability to reflect on loss. Can deny, ruminate, protest and despair, as if this will reunite with deceased. Dependency in relationship to deceased can produce high anxiety and difficulty believing they are capable of continuing life without them. Life devoid of pleasure, meaning or hope, and risk of depression. Can have an inflexible and possibly confusing narrative about the loss that is preoccupied with the loss, pain and recriminations, and can idealise deceased (Kosminsky and Jordan 2016).

- Vulnerable to prolonged grief (Parkes and Prigerson 2010).

- Can make excessive demands of others for reassurance and support, perceive that others do not understand their grief and despair, and can devalue help they receive; this can drive away others (Kosminsky and Jordan 2016).

- Can be more likely to seek counselling and the help of others and readily form a therapeutic alliance. Can have difficulty trusting own abilities, so hold on to their distress, hoping counsellor and others will meet their attachment needs. Can be open to suggestions that involve self-support, although may insist they do not have energy for exercise or social activities. Can cling on to their counsellor: see counsellor as having strength and insight they lack; fear being criticised, rejected or abandoned by counsellor; relieved to have someone who really listens; may be unwilling to end sessions or want more frequent sessions; and may struggle to separate from counsellor at end of counselling. Although can also be ambivalent towards their counsellor – for example, wanting their help and fearing losing them (Kosminsky and Jordan 2016).

- Counsellor can feel guilty, intruded upon, impatient, angry, deskilled in response to client implying 'I need more than you give me' (Power 2013).

Attachment-related work

- Initially match their attachment style, then gradually give disconfirming responses – for example, hold boundaries, acknowledge what is difficult while making appropriate challenges (Power 2013).

- Develop self-support to regulate emotions, consider how emotions of grief may be unhelpfully sustained, and make connection to past attachment experiences to make sense of current grief and how they grieve (Kosminsky and Jordan 2016).

- Develop more self-trust.

Dual process model
Can overly focus on loss-orientated experiences and struggle with restoration-orientated activities (Stroebe *et al.* 2010). Develop self and social support to oscillate and to regulate grief, so deceased is located in past and restoration activities approached (Kosminsky and Jordan 2016).

Continuing bond
Can cling on, bond may dominate and replace other relationships, and try to maintain lost attachment. Bond may need to be looser, more realistic and relocated to past (Stroebe *et al.* 2010). May need permission or reassurance to stop grieving.

Disorganised attachment
Potential adult characteristics

- Relationships too emotionally distant and too independent: socially avoidant, with poor social and support-seeking skills; can be defensive, experiencing 'fear without solution'. Current relationships complicated by past attachment experiences, loss and trauma, which are probably unprocessed. Can be compulsive caregiver. Attachment relationships can be deeply ambivalent and possibly dependent.

- Can be confused and incoherent about childhood experiences of parents. Schooling likely to have been problematic (Power 2013).

- Can both over- and under-regulate emotional experience, dissociate, have abrupt shifts in emotional state and be vulnerable to addictive substance use and other ways to avoid. Vulnerable to chronic stress, depression and low self-esteem (Kosminsky and Jordan 2016).

- Core attachment belief 'I can't be close, I want you and fear you'.

- Difficult to trust both themselves and others (Parkes 2009).

Potential influence on grieving, counselling and the therapeutic relationship

- Can be overwhelmed by grief, avoid it or dissociate; there is the risk of re-stimulated childhood anxiety, anger, grief and trauma, and insufficient ability to self-regulate emotions and use social support. Can have disjointed reasoning and fragmented narrative when describing the loss or trauma (Kosminsky and Jordan 2016).

- Prolonged silence, idealisation or angry recriminations reflect conflicted and confused nature of the attachment (Stroebe *et al.* 2010).

- Vulnerable to anxiety, trauma, depression, problematic substance use and complicated grief due to unresolved loss and probable trauma in childhood. Impaired emotional self-regulation, difficulty mentalising and low self-esteem (Kosminsky and Jordan 2016).

- Mistrust of others, turns in on self and does not use social support (Parkes and Prigerson 2010).

- Can be unsure whether to approach or avoid their counsellor; likely to attribute hostile and critical intent and be quick to react to counsellor; can have difficulty forming therapeutic alliance. Counsellor being hopeful and positive misses their experience and inadvertently leads to empathic breakdown (Kosminsky and Jordan 2016).

- Counsellor's experience can be that the client is hard to decipher, as if 'help me and go away' or 'I approach you, but I'm facing away', so may feel rejected, loved, confused, punished, idealised, angry, attacked, deskilled (Power 2013).

Attachment-related work

- Initially be reliable, predictable and kind, then gradually give disconfirming responses, e.g. hold boundaries, acknowledge what is difficult while making appropriate challenge.

- Develop self-support. Provide counsellor support to improve mentalising, regulate emotions and feel safe, and oscillate effectively, so deceased is located in past and true nature of relationship recognised. Make connection to past attachment experiences to make sense of current grief and how they grieve (Kosminsky and Jordan 2016).

- Likely to need to grieve and process past losses and trauma.

- Develop more self-trust and trust in others.

Dual process model
Likely to have difficulty with both loss and restoration activities; oscillate in a disturbed and ineffective way; and may oscillate between trying to continue bond and use it for guidance, and abandon it and move on (Stroebe *et al.* 2010). May need permission or reassurance to both grieve and to stop grieving.

Continuing bond

Most complex of bonds to deceased: difficulty finding coherent view of deceased that makes sense and then relocate them to the past. Confusion and uncertainty whether to continue or relinquish bond. May need to confront reality of relationship, find coherence and then relocate to the past (Stroebe *et al.* 2010).

Summary of the three theories and how they integrate (adapted from Stroebe *et al.* 2010)

Secure attachment style:

- Attaches securely and in an organised way, trusts self and others, and unlikely to have had attachment trauma as a child.

- Dual process model: effective at both loss and restoration orientations, and oscillates flexibly.

- Continuing bond: likely and probably healthy.

Avoidant attachment style:

- Attaches insecurely and in an organised way, trusts self more than others, and possibly had attachment trauma as a child.

- Dual process model: overly focused on restoration orientation and avoids loss orientation, and oscillates inflexibly.

- Continuing bond: unlikely.

Anxious/ambivalent attachment style:

- Attaches insecurely and in an organised way, trusts others more than self, and possibly had attachment trauma as a child.

- Dual process model: overly focused on loss orientation and struggles with restoration orientation, and oscillates inflexibly.

- Continuing bond: very likely and can be dependent.

Disorganised attachment style:

- Attaches insecurely and in a disorganised way, trusts neither themselves nor others, and likely to have had attachment trauma as a child.

- Dual process model: ineffective at both loss and restoration orientations, and oscillates in a disturbed way.

- Continuing bond: likely to be ambivalent and incoherent.

Consider a bereavement of your own and practise applying these three theories.

Consider your own attachment style and how that influences the way you relate to clients of all four attachment styles. For example, an avoidantly attaching counsellor might struggle to empathise with an anxious/ambivalent client and become frustrated by their demands and heightened expression of grief.

FURTHER READING

Kosminsky, P.S. and Jordan, J.R. (2016) *Attachment-Informed Grief Therapy: The Clinician's Guide to Foundations and Applications.* New York, NY: Routledge.

3

Making Sense of Substance Use

Substance use, and especially addictive use, can easily provoke confusion, anxiety and frustration in both people bereaved through a substance-related death and those who support them. Attitudes about substance use can often be controversial too, and tend to be polarised, seeing people who use as either tragic victims of a disease or making a selfish lifestyle choice and therefore being undeserving of help.

This chapter aims to provide a more temperate understanding of substance use. Its purpose is to help you if you need to build your confidence to work with the substance-use aspects of bereavement, by considering:

- What substances are.

- The range of substance-using behaviour.

- Theories of addiction, discussed by Jan Larkin.

- Substance use and co-occurring difficulties.

- How problematic and addictive substance use changes.

- Additionally, Jas Sahota shares his personal experience of recovery from addictive drug use to illustrate many of the ideas presented.

It is important to note that this understanding of substance use, based on psychological theory and research, may be different from the cultural and religious understanding of a bereaved person with whom you work.

What substances are

The United Nations define a substance as '[something] people take to change the way they feel, think or behave' (United Nations Office on Drugs and Crime (UNODC) 2007, p.11).

Throughout this book a 'substance' includes all legal substances including alcohol, tobacco and caffeine; all illegal drugs such as heroin, ecstasy and the novel psychoactive substances such as spice; all prescribed and over-the-counter medicines, such as diazepam and co-codamol, that are misused; and household products and volatile substances, such as cigarette lighter fuel, that are misused. Substances can be naturally occurring, such as magic mushrooms, and man-made, such as amphetamines. This does not include substances taken for purely medical reasons, such as antibiotics (although someone might misuse them hoping to change the way they feel, think or behave).

Viewed this way, substance use is a normal part of most people's lives, from having a cup of coffee in the morning to feel more awake to drinking alcohol in the evening to relax and socialise. However, some people's substance use becomes problematic. As the effects of a particular substance (or substances) on the person who died may have affected bereaved people in turn, this is covered next.

Different types of substances

There are many classifications of substances. This book divides them into three groups, using World Health Organization terms (1994). Each group identifies how a substance changes the way people feel, think or behave. People get to know the particular effects of substances, then choose what 'works' for them.

Table 3.1 Substance groups

Group	Affects neural activity by	Reasons to take are	Experiences people may seek include*	Examples
Stimulants (called 'uppers' because they lift someone's mood)	stimulating it	'I want to feel energised' 'I want to be more confident'	boosted confidence, improved alertness, delayed sleep, relief from boredom, exhilaration and energised	Caffeine, energy drinks, tobacco, amphetamines and cocaine Ecstasy in lower amounts
Depressants (called 'downers' because they calm someone's mood)	slowing it down or blocking it	'I want to feel soothed' 'I want to be less inhibited'	reduced anxiety, reduced inhibitions, relaxed muscles and mild euphoria	alcohol, heroin, fentanyl and minor tranquillisers such as diazepam Cannabis in lower amounts
Hallucinogens	interfering with it	'I want to escape reality' 'I want to enhance my senses'	changed sensory perceptions, relaxation, euphoria and hallucinations (known as a 'trip')	Magic mushrooms and LSD (lysergic acid diethylamide) Cannabis and ecstasy in higher amounts

* The experiences described are general and vary between substances in a group.

There are other effects that are common to all three groups:

- People often experience **unwanted side effects** as well as the effect they seek, such as slurred speech and nausea with alcohol.

- With use, someone's **tolerance** goes up so they need more of a substance just to get the same effect. When use reduces or stops, their tolerance comes down again.

- Someone can **overdose** by taking too much of a substance. This can lead to death, especially with opiates such as heroin and fentanyl, and when two or more depressant substances are used together. The risk is particularly high where someone's tolerance is lower than they realise or they use a higher than expected purity of a substance.

- Continual use of a substance risks developing **addiction**, where someone obsessively craves using and loses control over their use. In addition, physiological **dependency** can develop through continual use of depressant substances (see below).

- When someone stops using a substance they have become dependent upon, they go through a period of **withdrawal** where they **detoxify** and adjust back to normal. This experience is much more pronounced with depressant substances because the body needs to withdraw as well as the mind, e.g. going 'cold turkey' when stopping heroin use.

For sources of more information about substances see page 139.

The range of substance-using behaviour

There is a range of use from abstinence (not using at all) through to addiction, which varies both for any one individual and between people. Also, 'use varies with several social and demographic variables, such as age, gender and race' (Connors *et al.* 2013, p.14). What is the same for everyone, though, is that substance use serves a purpose, just like any other behaviour (Clemmens and Matzko 2005). People therefore tend to try something or keep doing it because it 'works' for them, even if it is also unhealthy and does not 'work' in other ways. The nature of bereavement is greatly influenced by the stage of use the person was at when they died (see Chapter 6).

Table 3.2 The range of substance-using behaviour

Stage of use	Purpose of behaviour	Effect on someone
Abstinence	No motive to use, a fear of using, or wanting to use and no access to substances.	(Not applicable)
↑ ↓	↑ ↓	↑ ↓
Experimental use	Curiosity to try different substances to find out what is liked and what is not, how much to use and when to use.	If use is excessive, it is either accidental or intentional. Capacity to relate to others, manage money and work are not regularly affected, if at all.
↑ ↓	↑ ↓	↑ ↓
Substance use	Regular use for recreational, social or medicinal reasons, or for coping with emotions.	Excessive use is rare. Capacity to relate to others, manage money and work are not significantly affected, so using substances is just another aspect of life.
↑ ↓	↑ ↓	↑ ↓
Problematic use	Using to regulate how they feel: to avoid emotions and sensations and/or for pleasure and thrill-seeking.	Excessive use is more frequent and intentional, including 'bingeing' and misuse of medication. Capacity to relate to others, manage money and work are adversely affected, often regularly.
↓	↓	↓
Addictive use, drug dependency and alcoholism	What served as a way to regulate how they felt has become habitual and unhealthy, so no longer serves a useful purpose.	Compulsion to use excessively, eventually to the exclusion of all else. Capacity to relate to others, manage money and work are severely affected. Eventually, every other aspect of life is either adjusted around substance use or no longer happens.

Adapted from Clemmens and Matzko (2005, p.282). SAGE Publications. Used by permission.

Comments about substance use from Table 3.2

- Substance use often serves someone by regulating their emotional experience. However, this can progress to problematic use and for some people results in addiction and dependency, where it no longer serves them.

- Someone can move up and down the range of behaviours, but often there seems to be a 'point of no return' if they become addicted and it is very difficult to move back up (Clemmens and Matzko 2005). The only other option is abstinence, as using eventually results in addictive use again.

A few people can control their use and not become addicted again, although this is usually only after a period of abstinence.

- Substance-related deaths can occur at all stages (see Chapter 6).

Further comment on the stages

- **Experimental use** usually begins in teenage years, where it is part of the wider experimentation with the adult world, along with learning to drive, having sex, etc. (Robson 2009). However, it sometimes begins earlier and very occasionally even in early childhood when it is typically linked to adverse experiences. Experimenting often continues well into someone's 20s and for a few people continues beyond that. Three main reasons to experiment are 'the expectation of a positive outcome...to fit in with friends, or to medicate themselves' when experiencing difficult or painful emotions (Robson 2009, pp.6–7). The readiness to experiment is influenced by someone's peers and family, and their social, cultural and religious norms that may be followed or rebelled against.

- **Substance use:** While someone has control of their use at this stage, there are a few people who may be unaware of building a tolerance of and developing a dependency on a substance. This can happen with alcohol or cannabis, and also prescribed medication such as opiate-based painkillers.

- **Problematic use** is dominated by someone using substances to regulate emotions, as if they think, 'Why feel this way if I can feel that way?' Emotions can be up-regulated to heighten pleasure and excitement, as in binge drinking[1] and chemsex.[2] Alternatively, substances are used to self-medicate overwhelming difficult and painful emotions, e.g. alcohol to dull the symptoms of trauma caused by childhood sexual abuse, or the confidence boost from cocaine to alleviate enduring shame. This can be seen as a form of attachment behaviour where someone feels 'better' through their pseudo-relationship with the substance, rather than with an attachment figure (Flores 2004) (see Chapter 2). As the effect is controllable, nearly instant and fairly reliable, it can easily become preferable to an attachment figure. However, in problematic use someone still has some control over their use and has at least short periods of abstinence between using.

---

1   The consumption of an excessive amount of alcohol in a short period of time.
2   Chemsex is the term for when men who are gay or bisexual use drugs to facilitate sex with each other, i.e. chemical sex.

- **Addiction** is a complex phenomenon where *someone feels compelled to use* substances excessively, despite the negative consequences, to the point where they effectively *lose control of their use*; therefore, they *persist in behaviour that is unhealthy*, potentially to the point of death. This can be seen as attachment behaviour (as described above) that has now become habitual and unhealthy. Someone is in an altered state, as can happen with (and is also significantly different from) severe anorexia and depression, where they are no longer able to think straight and make rational choices about their wellbeing.

Theories of addiction

Section by Jan Larkin

For centuries we have tried to make sense of how the drive to use substances can be so powerful in the face of physical and psychological harms that are detrimental to individual and social wellbeing. The language used to describe this process gives us some insight into the belief systems about substance use and how they have affected treatment and attitudes to the use of alcohol and other drugs.

During the 18th and early 19th centuries the moral model of addiction prevailed, with use of substances viewed as a spiritual weakness and recovery requiring willpower and development of morality. Treatment therefore involved an element of punishment and religious teaching to reorient the person to a way of life culturally and spiritually valued by that society.

As the 19th century progressed and physicians became more numerous, it was noted that long-term use of alcohol and other drugs resulted in physical harms, and the disease model of addictions began to develop. This model emphasised the way in which physical effects of substances on the body directly affected a person's ability to exercise control over consumption and ultimately affected their social functioning; they were seen as a victim of the disease process. The founding of Alcoholics Anonymous in 1935 further reinforced the idea of addiction as a disease. Addiction was seen as incurable, severely disabling and life-threatening, with abstinence bringing an improvement in wellbeing, just like being in remission from cancer. Treatment was therefore focused on maintaining this abstinence by getting social and spiritual support from others in recovery, working through a programme of 12 steps, including celebration of milestones achieved.

Since the second half of the 20th century there has been an explosion of research into how people become addicted to substances and what may influence their continuing to use, controlling use or stopping it. A number of models and theories have arisen from research and these show how complex and contradictory addiction can be. The only consensus seems to be that there is no single model of addiction that will explain all addictive behaviours – we are talking about complex individuals who are influenced by their genetics, environment and neurobiology, all within a social and cultural space.

However, the influence of the medical model has led to repeated efforts to arrive at a definitive description of addiction. In 1964 the World Health Organization replaced the term 'addiction' with 'dependence'. This was used to refer to both psychological dependence (impaired control over substance use and it having a higher priority than other behaviours) and physical dependence (needing more of the substance to get the same effect and suffering withdrawal symptoms on stopping use). In the United Kingdom, the *International Classification of Diseases* describes dependence as: 'a cluster of physiological, behavioural and cognitive phenomena in which the use of a substance…takes on a much higher priority for a given individual than other behaviours that once had greater value' (World Health Organization (WHO) 1992, p.69).

Emphasis is on the overpowering desire to use, with return to use after a period of abstinence often leading to a rapid return to dependence, with difficulties in controlling use and loss of interest in other things, and persisting despite harmful consequences.

More recent descriptions of dependence therefore point to a range of factors, rather than solely the spiritual, moral or medical. Use of the term 'addiction' may still be useful in referring to the process in its broadest sense, while 'dependence' often refers to a diagnosis indicating need for medically supported detoxification from a substance. By using the word 'addiction', we are not judging or labelling the person who is addicted, but instead referring to the process of how behaviour becomes more frequent, more difficult to resist and more all-encompassing to the extent that their life becomes governed by it.

So, what are some of the factors that contribute to becoming addicted to a drug? We will take a brief look at a number of findings that have come from a huge body of research, moving from the individual to their social and cultural context.

Discussion of genetics features largely in addictions research, characterised both by adoption and twin studies. Through the 1980s, a number of Scandinavian studies showed that alcohol addiction in biological parents was a strong predictor of alcohol addiction in their children, even when those children had been adopted into other families very early on. Twin studies helped to further clarify the role of genetics; because identical twins have all their genes in common and non-identical twins have only half of their genes in common; these two groups can be compared to see whether one or both of the twins share the same disorder. One hundred per cent heritability means that a condition is entirely genetic. The further below 100% one goes, the greater the contribution of environmental as well as genetic factors. Twin studies for alcohol dependence show a heritability of 50–60%, with a greater range of heritability shown for use of other drugs.

We grow up with differences in our ability to manage our impulses, termed 'STOP!', and to seek rewards, our 'GO!' brain circuitry (Childress 2006). Adolescence is particularly significant for changes in our reward systems: our 'GO!' system is fully developed, whereas our 'STOP!' system (located mainly in the frontal lobes and influencing decision-making) does not fully mature until well into our 20s. Adolescence is then a critical period where our environment and exposure to drugs could lead to experimental use becoming more frequent and prolonged. Studies suggest that environment is more important in influencing us to start and continue drug use past experimentation, while genetic factors may be more important in moving from use to dependence.

John Kelly (2016) describes how our genes can moderate how we respond to drugs – whether the effects are pleasurable, neutral or even aversive. So some of us may have a genetic predisposition to enjoy substances more than others do and, along with our environments and exposure to the drugs themselves, may be more influenced to choose to use them. Using drugs, and particularly alcohol, also produces structural and functional changes in our brain circuitry, particularly those areas that affect motivation, judgement, impulse control and memory. So our brains can become 'hijacked' by these changes, with the result that even when subjectively not wanting to use, choice and control become much more difficult. These brain changes contribute to people using drugs in a seemingly irrational way, even when there are many logical reasons to stop.

Clearly, our genetic make-up and brain chemistry are only part of the story and interact on a moment-by-moment basis with our social context and a myriad of other environmental influences. Jim Orford (2001) argues for a much more holistic model of addiction that takes account of our values, motivations, social networks and spirituality. All of these will set up a number of 'push–pull' factors on whether we engage in addictive behaviours that include not only use of substances but gambling, spending and internet use – where our focus becomes narrowed and addictive behaviours become both increasingly important and more difficult to control. Our internal motivations are fluid and we are often subject to a variety of conflicting goals and intentions, coming both from within us and the context we are in. We often hear about the idea of 'the addictive personality', with an implication of low levels of motivation and high levels of sensation-seeking. But there is no scientific support for this idea; the reality is much more complex: our motivations are often situational and not enduring, influenced both by current situations and people, and by memories and expectations. Ambivalence about changing our behaviour is a normal part of change – William Miller (Miller and Rollnick 2002) describes an intention to change as being triggered by what we perceive as a difference between what we are now and how we want to be. Our social influences affect our judgements about what is acceptable or desirable and we may face practical challenges and situations that make change more or less likely. All this will be embedded within our cultural context and prevailing values.

A number of researchers have taken a 'life course' perspective on addiction – the journey into and out of addiction and how patterns of use are different for each individual. People move in and out of change for various reasons, and many change without help from formal treatment services. Temporary lapses back into using are common following a period of abstinence, and relapse (the return to previous patterns of use, see below) is a normal part of the recovery process. Marlatt and Gordon (1985) researched which factors commonly predict lapse or relapse and found 'The Big Three': negative emotional states, social pressure from others and conflict with others. People with addictions (and those around them) can sometimes be reluctant to think about lapse or relapse because it can feel as though discussion makes it more likely to happen. However, research indicates that talking about relapse risks can make people better prepared to deal with high-risk situations.

In summary, a number of models of addiction contribute to understanding this complex process and it is likely that certain models will appeal more to us than others. Perhaps the most important consideration here is that no single model can explain how we become addicted or what course that addiction will take. Becoming addicted to substances is a complex process that includes elements from all of these theories. What we do know, from a large body of research, is that addiction is not simply a lifestyle choice, a personality characteristic or the consequence of a lack of will.

> Consider how you would describe the concept of addiction to a client. You might want to create an informal script that summarises this section and then rehearse how you would say it.

Substance use and co-occurring difficulties

Problematic and addictive substance use are often an unintended consequence of what began as an attempt to regulate difficult emotional experiences by self-medicating with substances. This is more likely if someone regularly experiences difficult or painful emotions, as described next (although many people who experience these difficulties do not use substances addictively):

- People who use substances addictively appear to be particularly vulnerable to complicated grief symptoms when they are bereaved (Masferrer 2017) (see page 29).

- Research shows that mental health problems are experienced by the majority of people who access community substance use treatment services, in particular 70 per cent of those who use drugs and 86 per cent of those who use alcohol (Public Health England (PHE) 2017).

- There is a strong link between being traumatised and problematic and addictive substance use (Najavits, Weiss and Shaw 1997; Stewart 1996). Trauma can occur in infancy, e.g. a disorganised attachment style (see Chapter 2); through life events associated with substance use, e.g. being assaulted for non-payment of drug debts; and/or through life events not associated with substance use, e.g. being bullied at school (Idsoe, Dyregrov and Idsoe 2012).

- Addictive behaviours can be a way to cope with feeling shame (Lee and Wheeler 1996), e.g. being different from the majority, such as someone from a minority GSRD (gender, sexuality and relationship diverse)[3] group feeling ashamed for being 'weird' or 'odd' through internalising the associated social stigma.

- Being neurodiverse[4] increases the vulnerability to problematic and addictive substance use. For example, for people with autism, dyspraxia and particularly attention deficit hyperactivity disorder (ADHD) (College of Occupation Therapists (COT) and National Association of Paediatric Occupational Therapists (NAPOT) 2003; Kunreuther and Palmer 2018; Ohlmeier et al 2008); and there is a research study that found people with dyslexia were overly represented in a drug treatment service (Yates 2013). Also, a consequence of being neurodiverse is an increased risk of being traumatised, e.g. in people with autism (Fuld 2018) and dyslexia (Alexander-Passe 2015), which further increases their risk of problematic and addictive substance use.

The unintended consequence is that someone develops a substance-use difficulty in addition to their original difficulty. In turn, using substances often exacerbates mental health difficulties, resulting in a complexity of needs.

---

3   GSRD is used because it better reflects the universal, diverse, non-binary and interrelated nature of these aspects of people than lesbian, gay, bisexual and transgender (LGBT) (Barker 2017).

4   People who are not 'neurotypical', as a result of variations in the human genome, including autism, dyslexia, dyscalculia, dyspraxia, attention deficit disorder (ADD) and attention deficit hyperactivity disorder (ADHD).

Substance-use treatment services are often unable to meet all of someone's needs; other services often expect them to be abstinent before they will work with them; and often each service only works with the difficulty they specialise in and does not co-ordinate with other services. Furthermore, where present, trauma and neurodiversity are often unrecognised by services, so treatment can be inappropriate or lacking altogether. This often results in a 'catch-22' situation, where someone is expected to stop using substances without addressing their reasons to use, which often results in them relapsing back to using again.

How problematic and addictive substance use changes

Problematic and addictive substance use often seems unchanging yet in reality often changes in a cyclic way over time. This in turn will have affected a bereaved person's experiences before the death too, which then often affects their bereavement.

The Stages of Change Model (DiClemente 2003) is one way of thinking about a typical cyclic sequence of attitudes and tasks associated with changing a behaviour, including problematic or addictive substance use (see Figure 3.1). There is much variation in how someone moves through the stages, the time each stage takes them, and how many times they relapse. Deaths can occur at any stage (see Chapter 6).

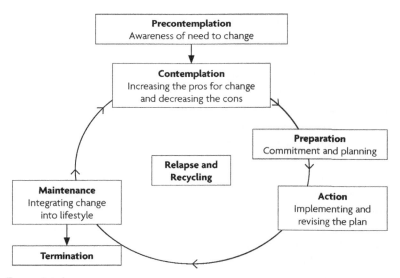

FIGURE 3.1 A CYCLIC REPRESENTATION OF MOVEMENT THROUGH THE STAGES OF CHANGES
Source: Clemente 2003 (p.30). Copyright Guilford Press.
Reprinted with permission of The Guilford Press.

Probably all substance use begins at **Precontemplation**, before someone is thinking about change. They want to use, see no reason to change, are unaware of any problems or are aware but unwilling to change (despite any pressure to change there may be from others). If someone can stay in the experimental, recreational and occasional problematic stages of use, described above, they may well not enter the cycle.

However, when someone becomes concerned or distressed by their use, starts evaluating it and is willing to consider change, they then move into the cycle at **Contemplation**. This change happens in response to difficult experiences associated with using substances, such as surviving an overdose, deteriorating health, financial problems, difficulties with people who deal drugs, involvement in the criminal justice system, relationship difficulties, losing their home, job or place at college, or becoming a parent.

Typically, someone is ambivalent at Contemplation, both considering change yet still wanting to use. The latter wins out; they still use and are not ready to actually change. A person often stays here for a long time.

At some point they stop contemplating and make a decision to change, and move into **Preparation** for actually changing. The motivation for this move is typically a response to the same kinds of difficult experiences that motivated them to start contemplating. They need to feel ready and committed, prioritise change, set a date to stop and have a realistic way to do it. This ideally involves the help of professionals, although they are not essential. Successful attempts often involve the support of family and friends.

However, as the person is still using, it is not until they actually act on their decision to stop that they reach **Action**. Doing this requires certain things to happen. They need to be motivated, often after having hit rock bottom through the kinds of difficult experiences already described. They need to have enough hope of success and of a better life without using substances. They need to have a strategy, enough confidence in their ability to change and enough support from others. Often at this stage they feel self-doubt about their ability to change and can feel the loss of substance use.

There is a difference between stopping and staying stopped, so after Action needs to come the **Maintenance** of change so that abstinence becomes someone's normality. This is often referred to as 'recovery' (as in recovery from substance use). Although someone may think substance use is now over, as can their family and friends, for them to stay in Maintenance many things need to happen. These include:

- developing the self-support to soothe themselves and regulate their emotions

- being aware of triggers to use substances and having effective strategies to manage the cravings that get triggered, e.g. activities to occupy their mind, self-soothe, seeking support from others

- creating meaningful and satisfying ways of living without using substances, e.g. parenting, work, leisure activities

- resolving past difficulties associated with substance-using behaviour, e.g. saying 'sorry' and making amends

- managing or resolving, as far as possible, any underlying difficulty that substance use was an attempt to self-medicate

- developing self-trust and the trust of others in them

- new friends who do not use substances.

A person may not be aware they need to do all these things, or can be unprepared to do them all. Even when they do work at these, it is difficult, complicated and takes a long time. Therefore, it is common to **Relapse** into using. Triggers include someone testing themselves to see if they can use and stop again; rewarding themselves for not having used by using; meeting old substance-using friends; using substances again as a way to cope with difficult, painful or stressful life events, including bereavement; leaving prison or ending drug/alcohol treatment (because there are fewer external controls on their behaviour and potentially the loss of support from others); believing addiction is in the past.

Following a relapse, a person usually returns to Contemplation or Preparation rather than going all the way back to Precontemplation; and can often learn from having relapsed. Change is therefore a cycle of stages, where both stopping use and starting again are possible. Most people seem to need several goes at finding their way to securely stay in Maintenance and thereby reach **Termination** of the cycle. Sadly, some people never manage that.

Observations on the stages of change

- It takes all the changes involved in the five stages before someone stops using. Real lasting change is a process, not an event.

- A person's family, friends or colleagues can prompt the difficult experiences that often motivate someone to stop, e.g. not paying their debts. Alternatively, they may prevent someone from experiencing these difficulties through understandable attempts to help that unintentionally slow down change, e.g. paying off their debts.

- Either way, although change may be influenced by others, it can only come from within someone who uses. Therefore, it is important that bereaved people realise they could not have stopped their loved one's substance use (see Chapter 4).

Take a moment to think of a behaviour you have had difficulty changing, such as losing weight, getting fit or stopping smoking. Now apply the Stages of Change Model to that behaviour to see how it works in reality. Consider what happened each time you moved on to the next stage, and reflect on how real lasting change is difficult and probably took several goes.

My recovery after 20 years of crack and heroin use

Section by Jas Sahota

I am eight years into recovery from drug addiction. I started off smoking cigarettes at 14 years old. Then cannabis from 16; at that time, I was rebelling, curious to try it, and thought I would be cool with the other kids and I'd get noticed. In my group of friends, I was the first to try cannabis, so when they started smoking it, I had to try something else – it was one-upmanship. There was the party drugs scene from the early 1990s, and heroin use came about in my early 20s, when I started selling drugs at a really low level. I enjoyed taking drugs, I enjoyed being cool and seen to impress other people. Then heroin got a hold of me for a long time.

I didn't have a normal upbringing. At five I heard my mum crying and rushed to her. She had been hit in the head with an axe by the man I was to find out eight years later was my real dad, who I did not see again after that day. That moment is still vivid in my mind: her on the floor in a pool of blood. Now I can understand I was self-medicating with drugs, masking this trauma and my anger by feeling numb and enjoying the buzz, but back then I didn't do this consciously and didn't even know about self-medicating. I was angry and rebelling about other stuff too: having to go into a children's home for nine months after mum was assaulted; her being paralysed down her left side after the assault; having to do housework because mum was not able to; how my friends' lives were better than mine; wearing hand-me-down clothes; being hit by mum's boyfriend who I thought was my dad; and then angry when I found out who my real dad was. So I used drugs because I wanted to feel normal like other people did and because I enjoyed it.

My partner also used drugs and we depended on each other to keep using, like making sure we each had drugs or money for drugs. We had three children, but when you are in the midst of your addiction, you don't hide it any longer. Using drugs always came first and I didn't want to go into withdrawal. It took away all the rational thinking. I imposed this lifestyle on my children, which is what had happened to me as a child with my mum's boyfriend who was a drinker. I knew deep down all this is not right and felt guilty. So I stayed for my partner and the kids and tried to do the right thing. But I couldn't stop and got angry about that, so I shut down in my mind by using drugs. I was stuck, it became normal and I got a 'Fuck it' attitude as 'So what if drugs came first?' So our children witnessed us smoking drugs and dealers coming to the house. We made sure that they had food, clothing and everything like that, but they missed out on the emotional support, family holidays and on us actually being there rather than just physically there. This continued into and then through their teenage years.

It got to a point where I went to a detox clinic to stop, but came out and started using again. I had stopped using but I had not changed old behaviours in my head. I still thought it was cool and I enjoyed the whole thing: scoring drugs from my dealer, preparing to use them and then using.

I had been involved with the police and courts from around 17 to 18 years old. In my late 30s and early 40s, I went to prison twice for drug-related offences. The second time both the judge and my barrister said, 'I hope you use this opportunity'. Prison was my saving grace. I begrudged what drugs cost in that prison, so I only used them occasionally. This gave me time away from my partner and drugs, and I could see my situation more clearly. Then at the end of my sentence I was moved to a different prison; drugs were hard to get there so it gave me two months of total abstinence. Coming towards my release date, the only thing on my mind was 'Can I score?', but then when I got out and did score, I didn't like it in the same way any more. Something had shifted in me; I didn't want this any longer.

That is when I started my drug treatment. I had been through court-ordered treatment before, but only did so because it kept me out of prison. This time I really engaged and applied myself. The more I talked to my keyworker, the more I got back, could understand my situation and know what to do. When I had the odd lapse, I was wanting to mask the anger and pain again. But those feelings were still there afterwards; I'd feel guilty for using and didn't like how I felt in my body afterwards. So I started realising that what I hoped would happen wasn't what did happen. It didn't serve a purpose to me any longer, which is a mantra I use. Also I remember the bad experiences and how I actually feel on drugs. I truly don't enjoy it now and it's nice to be normal without using. Now I can understand what my mum went through and I see what happened to us very differently. Plus, I have new good things in my life; I deal with situations and have learned to become an adult – whatever one of those is!

My family has broken up and I don't live with my children's mother now. It was a difficult time for me as a parent, going through recovery from addiction. One of my sons started using cannabis and got involved in gangs, selling drugs; he got beaten up and he disappeared for a week. Now he is okay. What made him stop using I think was less about him and the cannabis and more about me becoming the father I never was. All the attention was on him, so we didn't have attention to give to the other two. We neglected them, and they felt that. My other son moved out and lived with a friend and his parents. Once someone has been in addiction for so long, they don't grow emotionally, so it took me a lot of hard work to get where I am today. My kids were good compared with me as a teenager.

My life is going in the right direction now that I'm abstinent. I'm a 'family champion' for Adfam, helping other family members cope with their loved one's addiction. I ran a half marathon to raise money for local charities that support migrants and homeless people. My daughter got married and the whole family were there; it was a happy day. Her husband was her saving grace; she was on the cusp of turning in the other direction and I'm grateful to him. Recently, I found out she is pregnant so I'm becoming a grandfather. I'm truly blessed and I worked truly dammed hard to get here!

FURTHER READING

Maté, G. (2009) *In the Realm of Hungry Ghosts: Close Encounters with Addiction.* Berkeley, CA: North Atlantic Books.

Orford, J. (2001) *Excessive Appetites: A Psychological View of Addictions.* Chichester: Wiley.

4

How Addictive Substance Use Can Affect a Family

This chapter offers insight into the kinds of experiences a bereaved person could have been through before the death, when their loved one was using substances addictively, by considering:

- key ideas for understanding families affected by substance use
- addictive substance use in a family – this describes, from the perspective of a whole family, how addictive use develops, is sustained and continues through to its end
- families' experiences of services
- the influence of attachment on how family members respond to addiction
- grieving before the death.

Key ideas for understanding families affected by substance use

To make sense of family relationships affected by substance use, it is necessary to understand the idea of co-creation (Joyce and Sills 2014):

- Whatever happens in a relationship is created by both people.
- Each person influences the other and is influenced by them (even though they may or may not be aware of this).
- Each person is responsible for their part in what happens and is not responsible for the other person's part.

For example, a son coerces his mother into giving him money to buy alcohol; she is coerced and gives him money; then he buys alcohol and drinks it. Notice how they both create what happens – the mother's behaviour is influenced by the son's coercion, and the son's behaviour is influenced by his mother giving him money – and how the mother is responsible for being coerced and giving money, and the son is responsible for coercing, buying alcohol and drinking it.

For coercion to succeed, family members, like this mother, often need to be unaware of how they are being coerced and controlled. This makes it difficult for them to accurately understand what happens in their relationship. Typically, someone who uses substances addictively does not take responsibility for their part and blames others, and family members take on too much responsibility for what happens. In the example above, the son might manipulate by saying, 'If you'd just given me the money, I wouldn't be so stressed that I have to drink now.' The mother, knowing she has withheld money for a time, might believe she caused him to drink – and is unaware she has been manipulated into taking responsibility for his drinking.

Alternatively, family members can notice that the person who uses seemingly neither takes responsibility nor feels guilt for their behaviour, and so assume *they* must be responsible and then feel guilty. In reality, family members usually have little or no responsibility and are more often victims.

Family member's influence can be helpful too, but again it is up to the person who uses substances as to whether they use this help or not. As the saying goes, you can take a horse to water but you can't make it drink.

While family members do have influence (whether they are aware of their influence or not), they are not responsible for someone else's substance use. They cannot cause, control or stop substance use; that behaviour is the responsibility of the substance-using person. However, it may be difficult to know how far an addicted person is realistically able to take responsibility for their behaviour when they are in such an altered state.

The 'bad' behaviour associated with addiction is symptomatic of how someone typically relates to anyone who either assists or inhibits their using, rather than them being an inherently 'bad' person. Therefore, although being on the receiving end of this behaviour feels very personal, it is typically not personal. Addictive behaviour may be intentional or beyond awareness when someone is so preoccupied by substance use.

A family typically copes with and cares for someone who is addicted in the ways that any family tends to do when a member is in difficulty. Therefore, although what happens seems inevitable, it is seldom because these families are more dysfunctional than others. Although their situation can be compounded by insecure attachment styles (see Chapter 2), this is not always the case, and insecure attachments can adversely impact families not affected by substance use. Any family seems vulnerable to these unhelpful dynamics when there is addictive substance use.

Co-creation gives an essential insight for clients to make sense of their relationship with their loved one who died, and can help them to reconcile unfinished business. It is a sophisticated concept which is probably unfamiliar to many clients, and using it requires the capacity to mentalise (see page 35). Consider explaining this concept to your clients and help them apply it to their situation. You can use your relationship with them to illustrate this dynamic, such as how you influence them in helpful ways but are not able to make them change – because they are autonomous.

Addictive substance use in a family

This section is largely based on my experience of working therapeutically with families where there is addictive substance use. Addictive substance use is not just a personal matter. It can profoundly affect every family member and, conversely, those family members can affect the person who uses substances. Social, political, cultural, religious and other influences play their individual parts too.

The beginnings of addiction

No one sets out to become addicted; as someone's problematic use increases and they start to become addicted, they are typically unaware of what is happening. This lack of insight is symptomatic of addiction, and the person only becomes aware of being addicted after it has happened.

At this early stage, the family usually does not appreciate what is happening either. This can be because substance use is kept secret, people are in shock or deny reality to protect themselves emotionally, or they do not fully understand the nature of addiction. Therefore, the family inadvertently has little helpful influence on substance-using behaviour.

As addiction progresses

A person gradually becomes preoccupied with substance use and uses in increasing amounts. This typically follows a cycle of increasing craving to use, using, losing control over using, feeling remorse after using, and then resolving to stop, until cravings increase again, and so on. Over time this cycle speeds up as the addicted part of them progressively triumphs over their rational part.

Addiction perpetuates itself through denial, self-deception and self-justification, so that continued use seems necessary and justifiable. Also, the physiological consequences of using affect their capacity to think rationally – for example, alcohol may intensify aggressiveness, opiates induce a state of detachment from the external world, or continued use is required to relieve unpleasant withdrawal symptoms. They become self-centred and irresponsible, and do not appreciate the full impact they have on themselves and their family. However, sometimes self-centred behaviour may predate substance use, such as someone having always got their own way as a child. Eventually, they lose control of their using, lack insight into this and are not open to reasoned persuasion by others; they are effectively in an altered state. This has become their new normality.

It becomes increasingly obvious to the family that something is seriously wrong, which often happens long before the person who is addicted realises it. However, because family members typically do not understand the nature of addiction, they continue to see that person as basically who they were – and therefore open to reason. This results in unrealistic expectations of both the addicted person and the help the family can provide.

Over time, addiction can take over every aspect of a person's life, including their morals and values. They can become increasingly secretive, deceitful, chaotic, reckless and irresponsible, and continue despite negative consequences that either they avoid facing or are unaware of. However, they can also often be subtly disciplined, organised, creative and responsible when it comes to ensuring they can use. This includes coercing and controlling their family to behave in ways that assist their substance use (see below).

The family typically experiences addictive behaviour as confusing, frustrating and frightening, and may be traumatised by what happens. Family members ask, 'Why don't they just stop?' and partners may say, 'You love your drug more than me.'[1] They become stressed and distressed and start to neglect their own needs because they are so focused on the person who uses. Trust breaks down. The family feels isolated, stigmatised and shameful (Adfam 2012a). Some family members may not be told about the substance use.

With addiction, other difficulties often co-occur, which also take their toll on the person who uses and their family – for example, physical and mental health difficulties, and an increased risk of suicide (PHE 2017); financial problems such as debt; homelessness; criminality including violence, drug dealing and theft. Substance use has an adverse effect on the safety and development of children of any age (Advisory Council on the Misuse of Drugs 2003, 2011). For example, children can become traumatised when they 'fawn', i.e. respond to the threat from their parent by appeasing, pleasing and meeting the parent's needs, which is often driven by the need to stay

---

1   There is some evidence for this observation given that addictive substance use can be seen as a form of attachment behaviour (see Chapter 2).

attached (Walker 2013) (also see page 200). Also, children's care often falls to the grandparents (Adfam 2011b).

Over time family members tend to take on a role, out of their awareness, as a way of coping with addiction in their family: caring for the person who uses (see below); bringing esteem to the family through achievement and external validation; being a scapegoat who is blamed for the family's problems; trying to reduce the family's stress through humour; or withdrawing from the family (see below) (Wegscheider-Cruse 1981).

Families often describe someone as being like Jekyll and Hyde, split between the altered state described above and glimpses of who they were before addiction. In turn, family members can become split between 'I can't live with you' and 'I can't live without you', as they struggle to cope with their loved one's difficult behaviour while feeling the urge to maintain attachment to them.

Family members respond to this awful reality in the ways any family tends to respond to a member who is struggling: hoping that help will change them, trying to make them change for their own good, and potentially giving up in despair if these strategies do not work. Individual family members' responses often differ and can change over time. These three ways of responding are described next.

Support, love and education

A family member motivated by worry, care or possibly guilt can believe: 'I'll help you stop, because you can't stop yourself.'

As a person becomes addicted, they are increasingly unable to sustain their substance use *and* meet their basic needs for a home, food, paying bills, parenting children they may have, etc. Typically, family members help meet these needs, often for many years, at great cost to their mental and physical health. A particular way family members help is by giving money. This often happens daily and over time can amount to thousands or even tens of thousands of pounds. However, such money is typically used to buy substances rather than to pay bills. Hence, families can unintentionally help a loved one to continue using. Also, by doing things for someone who is addicted, families unintentionally disempower them by implying that they cannot do these things for themselves, such as washing clothes and preparing meals. None of this means that family members are responsible for substance use; this is always the responsibility of the person who actually takes substances.

It is a tragic irony that families can inadvertently assist the very thing they are hoping to stop. Even if they become aware of this, they can still find it difficult to stop, for various reasons, explained next, as well as the urge for attachment explained below.

Misunderstanding addiction

Families typically misunderstand the true nature of addiction and assume their loved one is still open to reason. They do not recognise that the addicted part of them is not open to reason and has triumphed over the rational part of them. Hence, families do not understand that their help often assists substance use rather than inhibits it. Alternatively, families can have an overly simplistic view that 'they don't have enough willpower to stop'.

Coercion and control

A person who is addicted can coerce or control their family into assisting their substance use, particularly if they cannot fund their substance use. Coercion and control are a form of domestic abuse and family members may become traumatised, feel dehumanised and lose their sense of autonomy (Home Office 2013). Abuse from substance-using teenagers and adult children of their parents is common, despite largely being unrecognised (Adfam 2012c).

This is motivated by a preoccupation and compulsion to use substances that is either by intention or done without awareness of the impact on others, and is symptomatic of addiction. Strategies include being charming, creating enough uncertainty to be given the benefit of the doubt, apologising and promising to change, playing the victim, appearing helpless, pleading, lying, nagging, manipulating, borrowing money that is not repaid, stealing, using emotional blackmail, issuing threats, bullying and using violence. Different strategies are tried until they find what works, then they exploit it until their family member consistently says 'no'. This is followed by further trial and error to find another strategy that works, and so on.

A common strategy is manipulating family members into believing substance use is their responsibility, often by manipulating with fear, guilt or shame. For example, saying 'If you don't give me money, the drug dealers will beat me up' can manipulate a family member into taking responsibility for a drug debt out of fear.

The family member gets a pay-off

Despite the huge price family members typically pay for helping, some also can get a pay-off for giving their support – for example, giving in to demands for money so that the demands stop for a while; assuaging guilt by giving what is demanded; or letting themselves be coerced and controlled to avoid violence. In all these cases, a family member is probably ambivalent about their pay-off.

However, the pay-off can be sought-after or even attractive. A family member's self-esteem or identity can be overly tied up with parenting or caring, such as a mother caring for her adult offspring as if they were still a child to avoid losing the role of being a mother. Also, a family member can meet their attachment needs through caring (see page 76).

Control, blame and punishment

As it becomes clear to family members that their help does not change a loved one's substance use, they can try to make them stop using, which is often motivated by worry, resentment or guilt. This might include taking someone to a treatment service and demanding they be cured, buying substances to control the amount of use or organising activities to prevent use. A person who is addicted typically resents what they see as intrusions and becomes either more secretive or actively resists being controlled.

Again, this is a usual response of a family to a member who is struggling, often motivated by the urge for attachment. However, it typically fails as a strategy, because it does not take account of addiction and involves trying to take responsibility for behaviour that is not theirs.

Both helping a loved one to change or trying to control them becomes very stressful, and can become an obsession, as if 'I'm addicted to their addiction'. A family member's identity can become defined by trying to help or control, or be lost in confusion and inadequacy. Attachment explains why family members keep trying to save a loved one, despite the stress and strain. Parents (especially mothers), young children and partners tend to have the strongest attachments. If a family member does end their relationship, it is often to avoid the pain of being attached – and they may find this is replaced by grief (see below).

Withdrawing and accepting the reality of addiction

Eventually, some family members can become burnt-out, depressed or fatalistic. They give up because they cannot stop the substance use, and are often motivated by despair, resentment and self-preservation. They may still live with the person who uses but lead a completely separate life, or feel glad for the break if the person goes to prison. Friends tend to lose touch first because their attachments are often weaker. Family members (often siblings and, to a lesser extent, fathers) can cut off angrily as a way to cope with their powerlessness, resentment, guilt, shame and/or pain. Other family members may accept their powerlessness and take steps to protect themselves, such as excluding the person who uses from the home.

These actions may have no effect on a person's use, they may use them to justify using, or they may trigger 'rock bottom' and stop using (see page 60). However, for most families the idea that 'giving up' *might* prompt substance use to end is so counterintuitive that it only happens after all else has failed, if at all.

Family conflict and breakdown

Conflict often occurs between a person who uses addictively and other members of the family:

- They use 'divide and rule' to play family members off against one another, thereby deflecting attention from their substance-using behaviour. This often exploits existing disagreements about how best to deal with substance use (often between parents).

- There is a power struggle between them and other family members. Both try ever harder to control the other, yet each lacks insight into the other.

- Family members, especially partners and children, believe that someone chooses substance use before them.

Also, conflict can happen between the family members who are *not* using substances:

- There is disagreement about how to respond to substance-using behaviour and how to help.

- Children often become resentful towards their parents, because they get less attention than their addicted sibling, and often they see the reality of addiction before their parents.

- Some feel coerced into choices they do not want to take, e.g. a wife having to choose between her husband and addicted adult child when her husband threatens to leave if she does not exclude that child from the family home.

- Families can become split between those who know about the substance use and those who do not, and conflict can arise if the truth comes out.

As addiction tends to be long term, family conflicts often endure, become deeply entrenched and lead to relationship breakdown. Family members, as well as the person who is addicted, can potentially become violent – for example, when feeling abandoned, as an attempt to keep their attachment to the person leaving them (Renn 2012). Children are likely to experience stress, anxiety and emotional insecurity through family conflict (whether openly hostile or subtly discordant). Family conflict and relationship breakdown have profound developmental implications for children (Advisory Council on the Misuse of Drugs (ACMD) 2003).

Addiction over the longer term

Eventually, a person *does* become aware of their painful situation and their loss of control over substance use. Although, typically, they feel ashamed of who they have become and guilty for how they behave, these emotions are overridden by craving to use, using, feeling ashamed and guilty all over again, in the vicious cycle described above. They may find their way to stop using and maintain abstinence. Families are delighted and relieved if this happens, often believing using is over for ever. Relationships may be reconciled and forgiveness given.

However, some relationships seem to become damaged beyond repair. Sometimes domestic abuse may continue into abstinence, and families are often unaware of how to support someone in recovery. If relapse happens, it is devastating for families, especially the first time it happens; they can lose hope and give up when they do not know that change is often cyclic (see page 59).

Families find ways to cope as best they can. However, they also typically experience prolonged stress and strain, focused around the person who uses and the impact their behaviour has on them (especially any children), and on the disruption and decline in the quality of family relationships. This strain increases family members' physical ill-health (e.g. anaemia, headaches, back pain, hypertension, asthma, palpitations, migraines, diarrhoea) and/or mental ill-health (e.g. anxiety, depression, guilt). This can result in an increase or instability in their own use of substances (e.g. smoking tobacco and prescribed medication). Typically, their poor health is inadvertently made worse by neglecting their own needs. (Orford *et al.* 2013).

Family members often accumulate much unfinished business (Cartwright 2019). This includes what the person who uses said or did, especially if these were not acknowledged, apologised for and put right, such as stealing money to pay for substances, as well as what family members did or did not say or do, which are now regretted.

Substance-related deaths

If a person does not stop using, they either die through suicide, or more likely die, often prematurely, through the direct or indirect consequences of substance use (PHE 2017).

Where a person has an illness before their death, it typically creates further stress, strain and unfinished business for family members. For example, families often lack medical knowledge, are uncertain how to care and do not have appropriate help, which in turn impedes them in providing good care. Often family members are reluctant to discuss a person's deteriorating health to avoid repeating conflict about substance use, or they are unaware of the true state of poor health, and therefore do not recognise that the end of life is approaching and discussions about it are often absent or late (Templeton *et al.* 2018b).

Suicide

There is a three-way relationship between addiction, depression and suicide. Addictive substance use is closely related to suicide risk (Harris and Barraclough 1997; Wilcox, Conner and Caine 2004), and the strongest predictor of suicide is addiction to alcohol (Beck and Steer 1989). Poor mental health is also closely related to suicide (PHE 2017), especially depression, and also bipolar disorder, schizophrenia and post-traumatic stress disorder (Cavanagh *et al.* 2003; Harris and Barraclough 1997; Kessler, Borges and Walters 1999). Also, depression is strongly associated with concurrent addictive alcohol use (Conner, Pinquart and Gamble 2009), and the symptoms of depression can reinforce suicidal thoughts, such as an exaggerated perception of problems, a reduced sense of capacity to cope, and self-blame and guilt.

Suicidal thoughts can emerge in two similar ways. First, someone perceives themselves as defeated, humiliated and trapped (O'Connor 2010) – for example, 'I can't live with taking drugs, but can't live without drugs', or, similarly, after having stopped using, feeling overwhelmed again by emotions that have been self-medicated with substances, and so feeling compelled to use again to cope and then becoming depressed by being defeated and trapped. Second, someone perceives they are a burden to others, have a thwarted sense of belongingness and feel alone, and have acquired the capacity to override the innate urge to live and to enact lethal self-injury (Joiner 2005). For example, those at highest risk of suicide are middle-aged men, due to relationship breakdown, separation from children, job loss, lack of close friendships, loneliness and being unable to open up emotionally (Wyllie *et al.* 2012), which are factors common to long-term addictive substance use.

Either way, suicide becomes the solution to what someone perceives as an otherwise insoluble problem. Their suicide is then either an implosion of accusatory energy through guilt, shame and self-loathing, or, conversely, aggression that has often been suppressed previously, which is now 'communicated' towards others who are perceived as rejecting them, as in 'look what you've done to me'. Also, someone either makes an active choice to die or is more passive, not caring whether they die and acting in a reckless way that may be fatal (Jordan 2019) (see parasuicide below).

Furthermore, the effects of substances increase the risk of suicide. Self-medicating depression with substances may seem to help in the short term but usually exacerbates it over time. Some substances, especially alcohol or sedatives, can trigger symptoms of depression, and taking some substances, particularly alcohol, lowers inhibitions that may lead to enacting suicidal thoughts.

Both addiction and severe depression are characterised by someone being in an altered state. They are not as open to reasoned argument, are focused on themselves and withdraw from others, and easily lose sight of the impact their suicide will have on them. Suicidal people are usually conflicted about dying: one part wants to live and another part is self-critical and ultimately self-destructive. Many do not really want to die; rather, they are unhappy with life (World Health Organization 2000).

Some other deaths, termed parasuicide, can result from risk-taking behaviour where an apparent suicide attempt was made *without* the intention of it being lethal. Such risk-taking increases in people with depression (Spittle, Bragan and James 1976).

Additionally, a study suggests that an insecure attachment style, mostly where characterised by anxiety and unresolved trauma, is associated with an increased suicide risk (Miniati, Callari and Pini 2017).

Families' experiences of services

Families can be very effective at helping a person to engage in and benefit from treatment for addictive substance use (Copello, Velleman and Templeton 2005) when this route is taken to abstinence. However, where someone has co-occurring difficulties, such as severe mental health difficulties, families typically find it distressing, frustrating and isolating if services are unable to work together and provide effective help to someone so vulnerable. This may go on for many years, where a person's situation is seemingly too complex and difficult for services to help, and families can feel ignored – despite often knowing important information about a person's condition.

Most family members do not get help for themselves. This is because of stigma and shame, because they do not know there is help or it not being available in their area, or because they see the problem as entirely with the person who uses. Those who do access support often do so following a crisis, by which time their difficulties are often deeply entrenched and harder to deal with.

At its best, family support is very effective (Adfam 2012b; Copello *et al.* 2010). It can help a person to make sense of addiction and how it affects their family, provide guidance on appropriately supporting someone and coping with difficult substance-using behaviour, and encourage them to value and meet their own needs. Also, this may have a helpful influence on someone's addictive behaviour. However, this is complex, longer-term work that is often not available, and is seldom able to satisfy a family's primary goal of stopping someone from using. Support can fail because:

- It is too brief and basic to address a severe and complex situation.

- Families are seen as part of the problem, e.g. they are 'co-dependent' or 'enable' substance use (see page 130). As this usually reinforces family members' sense of being stigmatised as well as their sense of failure and guilt, they are inadvertently disempowered at the very time they need to be empowered.

- Family members feel stigmatised by services.

- Simplistic solutions, such as 'kick them out so they hit rock bottom', typically deny family members' attachment to the person who is addicted and may even increase risk in certain circumstances, e.g. if the person is suicidal.

- Families are treated as formal carers[2] for people who are addicted, and are expected to support them, sometimes because this helps the services that support addicted people (Adfam 2011a). Some family members are unwilling to become carers or feel coerced into it through guilt. Although others may be willing, typically it comes at a cost to their own health and wellbeing. Either way, family members are often not seen as a person in their own right, who has unmet needs of their own (including information, guidance and support for caring for someone who is addicted).

Such experiences of support can influence whether families will seek support in future for their bereavement.

The influence of attachment on how family members respond to addiction

The urge for attachment (see Chapter 2) provides an explanation for protecting and caring for a loved one who is addicted to substances; for continuing despite the stress, strain and distress of doing so; and for much of the guilt that is felt for the perceived failure to protect and care when a loved one continues using and worse, eventually died.

Where a family member is an attachment figure for a loved one who is addicted, such as a parent or partner, this urge to care is strongest and therefore potentially at greatest risk of being coerced and controlled into inadvertently assisting substance use (as described above). Many mothers and some grandmothers especially seem to be vulnerable and are often the last people left supporting someone who is addicted. Stepmothers may be less vulnerable if their attachment is weaker.

2   See www.carersuk.org

Some insecurely attached children find that caring for their caregiver is a way to meet their need for attachment – for example, an anxious/ambivalently attached child finding that caring is a successful way to cling on and feel loved, or an avoidantly attached child caring because it results in parental closeness for being 'good' and undemanding. Where a primary caregiver is addicted, their child is vulnerable to being manipulated, such as into caring for that caregiver or their younger siblings. Stepchildren may be at greater risk of manipulation if the step-parent's attachment is weaker.

This childhood attachment behaviour may become compulsive caregiving by adulthood. As those who compulsively care can seek relationships in which caring continues to be a way to meet their attachment needs, they may form relationships with people who are addicted and need caring for. Indeed, this potentially explains why some children of parents who use substances addictively go on to have partners who use addictively. Compulsive caregiving correlates with parental depression/psychiatric problems, parental rejection/ violence and childhood unhappiness, and is most likely in those with a disorganised attachment style (Parkes 2009).

Attachment style can also explain *how* an adult cares for another adult. Feeney and Collins' (2001) study of caregiving by partners supported and extended previous studies indicating that attachment style is a significant and important predictor of caregiving behaviour in adult intimate relationships: 'attachment security was associated with more effective, responsive forms of caregiving… attachment-related avoidance was associated with unresponsive and controlling forms of caregiving' (p.989) and 'anxious individuals appear to be ineffective caregivers in that they tend to be intrusive and overinvolved' (p.990).

In my experience, family members with an insecure attachment style characterised by ambivalence may be more willing to tolerate the difficult behaviour that can occur in addiction. Although family members with an anxious/ambivalent attachment style are more likely to maintain a relationship with an addicted person if that relationship meets their attachment needs, they are also more vulnerable to coercion and control, and to taking responsibility for a loved one's difficult behaviour.

However it happens, the outcome is typically the same: sadly, attachment responses that evolved to protect and care for loved ones are often inappropriate for addiction, so family members' urge for attachment can unintentionally assist substance use. Some family members are deeply reluctant to recognise this, often as a protection against their expected pain of losing a loved one who uses. This reluctance can continue for years despite the evidence against their way of caring.

Grieving before the death

Living with someone addicted to substance use, as described above, typically results in a deep sense of loss (DrugFAM 2013; Valentine 2018). This can be loss of who someone was before addiction, of hopes and expectations for their future and for family life as it used to be, as well as anticipating their premature death. Therefore, these family members have been grieving long before the death. This has been described as a 'living bereavement' (Templeton and Velleman 2018, p.22). However, this is typically grief others do not recognise, known as disenfranchised grief, and occurs when 'a loss cannot be openly acknowledged, socially sanctioned, or publicly mourned' (Doka 1989, p.4). As a consequence, family members do not have the validation, sympathy and support that would be usual during bereavement. This can shape their expectations of others when the death does occur.

One common way this grief occurs is through ambiguous loss (Boss 2000). This is a loss that occurs without end or understanding, which occurs in two ways. First, 'a loved one is physically present, but missing psychologically' (p.138); this commonly happens when someone is no longer who they were because they have become addicted. Second, the 'physical absence with psychological presence…[where]…a loved one is missing physically…but kept present psychologically because they might reappear' (p.138); this happens occasionally, for example, when losing contact with someone who was excluded from the family home because of their substance-using behaviour.

Although grieving before the death may be confusing, ambiguous loss is a normal response to an ambiguous and unresolvable situation. Seen from an attachment perspective, the bond persists despite someone not being there, because they *could* come back. Unlike a death, there is no certainty that the person will not return, so there is no 'ending' and it is not possible to recover. Therefore, as grieving is ongoing, there is preoccupation with the absent person, a loss of hope, and despair and helplessness that can easily become depression. Also, the ongoing powerlessness over the threat to the person's existence can be traumatic (Boss 2010).

With ambiguous loss, part of a family member is grieving and part of them holds the possibility of return. However, family members can lose hope of any possibility of a loved one's 'return' and then anticipate them dying. This is known as anticipatory grief (Worden 2009), which may or may not be warranted and occurs for many reasons: anticipation that previous overdoses or suicide attempts will reoccur; misunderstanding addiction and believing it will be fatal; giving up hope through being depressed; protecting themselves against having hopes of recovery dashed; trying to prematurely resolve ambiguous loss; accurately predicting the trajectory of someone's addiction, etc.

Anticipatory grief can be seen as 'worry work' that prepares for the death.

It is unclear whether it helps bereavement, although worrying to good effect does help to prepare for it: 'when the death occurs it is…one more step in a process of psychosocial transition which [is] prepared for' (Parkes and Prigerson 2010, p.202). It may include premature emotional withdrawal and wishing someone were dead to end the distress and waiting, which can elicit guilt. Conversely, it may involve being too emotionally close, over-managing someone's care, saying 'goodbye' and rehearsing for a future without them (Worden 2009).

However, these grief experiences do not complete grieving for the subsequent death (Parkes and Prigerson 2010). Indeed, the death is often experienced as a second bereavement (DrugFAM 2013).

FURTHER READING

Orford, J., Velleman, R., Natera, G., Templeton, L. and Copello, A. (2013) 'Addiction in the family is a major but neglected contributor to the global burden of adult ill-health.' *Social Science and Medicine 78*, 1, 70–77.

5

Substance-Related Bereavement

Chapters 5 and 6 focus on substance-related bereavement and assume the level of understanding of bereavement and substance use covered in the previous three chapters:

- Zoe Swithenbank provides an overview of substance-related deaths.

- Christine Valentine, Jennifer McKell and Lorna Templeton present a summary of their work on the first large-scale research project into these bereavements.

- The chapter ends with a father, a mother and a sister sharing their personal experiences of substance-related bereavement.

An overview of substance-related deaths

Section by Zoe Swithenbank

This section looks at the growing worldwide phenomenon of drug- and alcohol-related deaths, with a focus mostly on deaths that occur directly through using substances in the United Kingdom and other English-speaking countries in the Western world. Many other drug- and alcohol-related deaths in these countries occur indirectly, such as through accidents, mental ill health and physical illnesses caused through use. The World Health Organization (WHO) estimates that 3.3 million deaths annually are attributable to alcohol use; this makes up almost 6% of global deaths each year, and these deaths are increasing globally (WHO 2014). Alcohol-related mortality globally accounted for 4% of deaths among females and 7.6% of deaths among males; alcohol also kills more teenagers than all other drugs combined, although alcohol consumption is linked with an increased likelihood of illicit drug use (Foundation for a Drug-Free World 2017). Approximately 585,000 deaths worldwide each year are attributable to drug use, the majority of which are attributable to opioids[1] (United Nations Office on Drugs and Crime (UNODC) 2019). Globally, drug-related deaths have remained stable over the five years to 2015, but they are generally rising in English-speaking countries (UNODC 2017).

Increased prevalence of drug and alcohol use is one significant contributing factor to the rising mortality rate, but there are other factors to be considered. Also, it can be difficult to form an accurate picture of the number of such deaths, because recording and diagnostic variances mean that some deaths are not counted in the data despite being related to substance use, and definitions vary on what constitutes a drug- or alcohol-related death (DrugWise 2018). In addition, there can be a link between mental health difficulties and these deaths. For example, in the UK, a history of alcohol or drug use has been recorded in 54% of all suicides in people experiencing mental health issues (Public Health England 2017) and is a commonly reported theme in all suicides.

The United Kingdom

The UK overall has seen alcohol-related mortality rates stabilise since 2013, but they remain higher than they were in 2001. The age group with the highest mortality rate is 60–64. Scotland reports the highest rate of alcohol-specific death within the UK, despite seeing a significant reduction since rates peaked in the early 2000s. Mortality rates are on average higher for males than females, although 2017 saw the highest alcohol-related death rates on record for women. For both sexes, alcohol-related deaths were significantly higher in the most deprived localities. Alcohol is a significant factor in the deaths of young people and is associated with the three leading causes of death among 15–24-year-olds: accidents, homicides and suicides (Office for National Statistics (ONS) 2018a).

In England and Wales, deaths due to drug poisoning have risen steadily to 4359 in 2018, the highest number and the highest annual increase since data collection began in 1993: the mortality rate for all drug-poisoning deaths for males has increased from 51.5 deaths per 1 million population in 1993 to 105.4 deaths per 1 million population in 2018; and for females the rate increased for the ninth consecutive year, from 34.2 deaths per 1 million population in 1993 to 47.5 deaths per 1 million in 2018 (ONS 2019a). In 2017, the 40–49 age group had the highest mortality rate, overtaking the 30–39 age group (ONS 2018b), as also found in 2018 (ONS 2019a). Over half of all deaths relating to drug poisoning involved opiates, although the number of deaths involving all forms of cocaine has doubled in recent years, from 320 in 2015 to 637 in 2018 (ONS 2019a).

---

1   Opiates are naturally derived drugs from the opium poppy, such as heroin and codeine, whereas opioids include both opiates and synthetically produced opiates such as methadone and fentanyl.

Similarly, Scotland has the highest recorded figures of drug-related deaths since data collection began in 1996, with 1187 in 2018, an increase of 27% during 2018 and more than double the figure a decade ago, resulting in the highest rate of drug-related deaths in Europe (National Records of Scotland (NRS) 2019). Again, males accounted for most drug-poisoning deaths (72% in 2018), and opiates or opioids were implicated in, or potentially contributed to, 86% of all drug-poisoning deaths (NRS 2019). In Northern Ireland, recorded drug-related deaths have also been rising between 2007 and 2017, with deaths involving opioids most frequent (Northern Ireland Statistics and Research Agency 2018).

The opiate-using cohort are ageing and have the health consequences associated with long-term opiate use, such as hepatitis C, as well as the lack of available treatment and services for mental and physical health. Increased availability of street heroin and changes to drug treatment and commissioning of services in recent years, coupled with the deepening of socioeconomic deprivation following the financial crisis of 2008, have all contributed to the increased death rate of this cohort (Advisory Council on the Misuse of Drugs 2016). An increase in opiate-substitution prescribing (a treatment where a prescribed opiate, such as methadone, is substituted for illegal opiates, such as heroin) can also be linked to unintentional overdose deaths (Anderson *et al.* 2016), as can the increase in fentanyl and its analogues being found contaminating heroin (ONS 2018b). Between 2001 and 2013, 28 children under the age of four died from unintentional poisoning from a prescribed drug, 57% from methadone; methadone is the most common prescribed drug causing fatal poisoning in adults (Anderson *et al.* 2016).

There has also been a 16% increase in the numbers of deaths involving cocaine from 2016 to 2017, rising to 432 (ONS 2018b). Data from the Home Office (2018) suggests that cocaine is the second most commonly used drug in the UK after cannabis. This data does not distinguish between crack and powder cocaine, so some of these deaths will be attributable to crack cocaine.[2] The National Crime Agency reported an increase in the purity of both powder and crack cocaine in 2018, which may account for part of the observed increase in mortality (ONS 2018b).

The number of deaths attributable to novel psychoactive substances (NPS, or the former 'legal highs') halved in 2017. They had risen significantly prior to this, with 76 deaths being recorded as involving these drugs between 2004 and 2013. Although these numbers are relatively small, it is important to note that they tripled between 2011 and 2013 (ONS 2016b) and are likely to be under-reported because not all these substances are tested for during a post-mortem or are recorded by a coroner. The use of NPS in prisons has increased markedly over the last few years and the numbers of prison deaths where NPS have been

---

2   Crack is the most potent form of cocaine and provides a very short but intense high.

involved continue to rise (PHE 2015) (although most drug-related deaths are still caused by opiates in English and Welsh prisons (ONS 2019b)). Although links between the use of NPS and death are not necessarily immediate or causal, they should not be overlooked because their impact on deaths from suicide, drug toxicity, apparent natural causes or even homicide may be significant. NPS are widely associated with detrimental effects on both physical and mental health and may well have implications for future mortality. The Psychoactive Substances Act was introduced in 2016, which effected a blanket ban on importation, production or supply of most psychoactive substances, and may be responsible for the recent reduction in deaths.

Chemsex typically involves the use of crystal methamphetamine, mephedrone and GBL/GHB (Gamma butyrolactone/Gamma hydroxybutyrate) by men who have sex with men. In the last decade or so, these drugs have become readily available and commonly used in some gay scenes. There was a 119% increase in GHB-associated deaths in London alone between 2014 and 2015 (Hockenhull, Murphy and Paterson 2017). The ONS reported 20 GBH-related and 22 mephedrone-related deaths in 2014 (ONS 2015), although it is not clear whether these were related to chemsex practices. Data is not widely available due to this being a fairly new phenomenon and the sensitive nature of the topic, and men may not be seeking diagnosis or treatment for related issues. Also, chemsex practices carry an increased risk of HIV transmission due to the increased prevalence in this population and because of increased risky behaviours, such as sexual practices and injecting drugs.

Europe

The European region, including the United Kingdom, has both the highest rate of alcohol consumption and the highest rate of alcohol-related deaths. Average per capita consumption (APC) among adults was 11.3 litres in 2016. Heavy episodic drinking is also common, with 47% of men and 14% of women engaging in this practice (WHO 2018). Alcohol is the second-largest risk factor for disease burden in Europe (WHO 2014). Most alcohol-attributable deaths in this region are related to chronic diseases such as cancers (29%), cirrhosis (20%) and cardiovascular disease (19%), rather than acute harms; in 2016, however, 42% of all traffic-related deaths were due to alcohol (WHO 2018). Research suggests that socioeconomic inequalities account for some of the differences in alcohol-related deaths across Europe, with Northern and Eastern Europe seeing large differences in mortality rates between different socioeconomic groups (Mackenbach et al. 2015).

European mortality rates for drug overdose deaths, including the United Kingdom, are estimated at 22.6 per million in the population aged between 15 and 64 (European Monitoring Centre for Drugs and Drug Addiction

(EMCDDA) 2019), with drug overdoses typically accounting for between one-third and one-half of the deaths among those who are high-risk drug users (EMCDDA 2015). Most deaths are from opioids; methadone and buprenorphine (another heroin substitute) are regularly found in toxicology reports, and data from Denmark, Ireland, France and Croatia indicate that methadone-related deaths exceeded heroin-related deaths in 2017 (EMCDDA 2017).

The United States of America

Alcohol is the third leading preventable cause of death in the USA and kills an estimated 88,000 people each year (Centres for Disease Control and Prevention (CDC) 2018). Deaths are more common among middle-aged adults (35–64 age group) and of these around 76% are men. The number of deaths attributable to alcohol for Native Americans is approximately twice that of the general US population, and 68% are of men (CDC 2008).

The USA accounts for approximately one-quarter of worldwide drug-related deaths, including overdose deaths that have risen dramatically since 1999 from 16,849 (UNODC 2017) to an estimated 70,237 in 2017 (CDC 2019), the highest level ever recorded and four times the global average (UNODC 2017). From 2016 to 2017, deaths involving synthetic opioids increased by 45.2%. Possible reasons for this are an increase in the misuse of pharmaceutical opioids (powerful painkillers prescribed by doctors), increased availability of synthetic opioids such as fentanyl and the variation in their quality and potency, and the increased use of heroin.

Canada

Alcohol is one of the top ten risk factors for disease among all Canadians and the top risk factor for Canadians aged 15–49 (Public Health Agency of Canada 2016).

Canada's drug reporting varies significantly between provinces, making it difficult to accurately estimate the number of drug-related deaths. Despite this, it is known that deaths related to prescription opioids have risen sharply and now make up an estimated 50% of all drug-related deaths. The provinces that do report overdose deaths have all noted an increase over the last several years (Canadian Drug Policy Coalition 2013). In British Columbia, the death rate from overdose is even higher than in the USA (UNODC 2017).

Australia

Like many English-speaking counties, Australia has a culture where drinking is an accepted and celebrated part of daily life. A 2014 report estimated that alcohol-related deaths had increased by 62% in a decade (Australian Bureau of Statistics (ABS) 2015; VicHealth and Foundation for Alcohol Research and Education 2014), despite the proportion of the population consuming alcohol daily decreasing. Residents of Northern Territory are three times more likely to die from alcohol use than Australians from other regions, and the leading causes of alcohol-related deaths vary between men and women. Injury is responsible for over one-third of deaths in males, whereas for women the highest mortality rates are due to heart disease, with only 12% being due to injury. In 2017, Australian women had the highest rate of alcohol-related deaths for over 20 years, at 7 deaths per 100,000 (ABS 2018). In Aboriginal communities, alcohol consumption is increasing at epidemic rates, perpetuated by a cycle of poverty and a lack of access to health facilities, with alcohol contributing to 7% of all Aboriginal deaths, particularly suicide among men (Currie 2014).

The death rate from drug use is currently the highest on record, although the rate per capita of 7.5 per 100,000 in 2016 is lower than in 1999 (9.2 deaths per 100,000 people). The type of drugs and the characteristics of individuals dying from their use have changed dramatically, with prescription drugs causing the highest number of deaths in 2016. Deaths from methamphetamine use have increased rapidly, with the death rate in 2016 being four times that of 1999. As elsewhere in the world, the age group with the highest death rate is older than in recent years. Those over 45 have the highest mortality rate; this is likely to be related to prescription opiates and benzodiazepines. Younger people are more likely to die from heroin or methamphetamines (UNODC 2017).

The Philippines

No discussion of drug-related mortality would be complete without acknowledging Philippine President Rodrigo Duterte's 'drug war'. Duterte came to power vowing to wipe out crime within six months, announcing a policy that would target both those using and selling drugs. He urged citizens to kill suspected drug users and offered rewards for dead suspects. Since it began on 30 June 2016, estimates of the number of people killed have varied, but sources suggest as many as 12,000 have died (Human Rights Watch 2018). The majority of these victims have been male, unemployed and underprivileged (Amnesty International 2017).

Globally, drug- and alcohol-related mortality is steadily increasing, with a wide range of causes of death associated with their use. Despite some difficulties in accurate measuring and recording, it is clear that this is a growing issue that needs addressing on national and global levels in order to reduce the increasing morbidity and mortality associated with the use of drugs or alcohol, and to address the needs of the vast numbers of families affected by this issue.

Findings from the first large-scale research project into substance-related bereavements

Section by Christine Valentine, with Jennifer McKell and Lorna Templeton

Families and individuals bereaved by alcohol or drugs have been largely neglected in research, policy and practice. In addition to the distress of losing someone close in such typically difficult circumstances, these bereaved people have generally lacked the support and information necessary to respond to the death and their bereavement.

In conducting the first large-scale research project on this kind of bereavement, we had the privilege of listening to and learning from those closest to these deaths (yet whose experiences are rarely considered). Funded by the Economic and Social Research Council (ESRC), nine academics from two separate fields, bereavement and addiction studies, and a bereaved mother and founder of the Bereavement Through Addiction (see page 300) support group examined (through in-depth interviews) the experiences of 106[3] bereaved adults (including six couples) across England and Scotland. From these experiences we identified *four key factors* – 'the life', 'the death', 'the stigma' and 'the memory' – that may combine to make this bereavement particularly difficult to grieve; and a *diversity* of experience regardless of commonalities. We use these terms to organise our discussion of typical experiences encountered by these bereaved people.

The life

When describing their relationship with the deceased while alive, many interviewees reported the stress and strain of living and coping with the person's substance use, in some cases over many years. Their experiences confirmed findings from previous research on families coping with a member's or close friend's substance use (Orford *et al.* 2005). Interviewees made connections between how it was before the death and the impact of the death itself – for example, how they had already experienced grief for having lost the person to their addiction.

> I lost my mum when this [alcohol use] started. I always hoped I would have my mum back. So I grieved the loss of my mum [and then] I have a second grief for the person she became with her addiction. (Daughter)

Such connections suggest that studies of how people experience and live with another's substance use might help with understanding how people

---

3   One interviewee has since withdrawn from the study, reducing the original interview sample to 105 adults, though not affecting the overall findings.

subsequently cope with bereavement. Particularly, the 'stress, strain, coping, support' (SSCS) model of the predicament of families living with a member's substance use (Templeton and Velleman 2018) seems to reflect that of families coping with a member's death from substance use. Based on five elements of stress, strain, understanding, coping and support, the model suggests that levels of stress and strain are influenced both by how the family understands and copes with the substance use and the availability of support. Similarly, how our bereaved interviewees experienced these five elements suggested an extension of difficulties they had already faced before the death.

For example, some interviewees reported how isolated they felt when the person was alive:

> I'd been up a lot of the night because Mum had been drunk... I got to school next day and remember thinking oh gosh I just can't hold this all in and a teacher saying well so and so is going to be off school for a while because her Mum's got cancer and me thinking...I really wish my Mum had cancer because then I could talk about it...say to people I can't cope, I haven't slept, I had to cook all the meals...but I couldn't because I was completely embarrassed. (Daughter)

Some found relief for their stress through finding out more about substance use and, in some cases, going on to work in the field:

> [T]here's lots and lots of...young people going through that kind of thing, so I just really want to help them and be there so they can speak out, so they're not trapped and alone... [M]aybe speaking to...me on [helpline] will give them the confidence to change more about their life and...get out of the situation. (Daughter)

These and other examples from our interviews suggest the SSCS model can illuminate experiences of bereaved families as inevitable extensions of the difficulties they already faced before the death.

The death

Interviewees typically discussed the often difficult and distressing circumstances of the death itself, such as the deceased dying alone, away from home and in 'unexplained' circumstances. What was more, they also regularly recounted experiencing poor treatment from the various services involved in dealing with these deaths; because substance-related deaths may be considered 'unexplained', establishing cause may involve investigation by police and the coroner in England or procurator fiscal in Scotland, including searching the family home, conducting a post-mortem and inquest, and media reporting of the death. The bereaved person may therefore be faced with a range of different and separate services and procedures to navigate, often with little or no guidance. Indeed, we learned of how daunting, confusing and time-consuming this process could be and the often inadequate, unsupportive, off-hand and even stigmatising responses from service personnel at a time when the bereaved person was at their most vulnerable.

So soon after the death, responses of service personnel were likely to have a profound impact for better or worse and have long-lasting effects on people's grieving. The impact was evident in how upsetting it could be for interviewees to recall such experiences several years down the line.

> Her manner was terrible, there was no warmth in her... I felt as if we were the wrong ones. (Mother)

In contrast, compassionate responses were gratefully remembered, indicating the importance of these findings for raising awareness and improving how services support these bereaved people. Indeed, they formed the basis of practitioner guidelines (Cartwright 2015) developed towards the end of the project.

The stigma

Unkind, stigmatising responses from services reflect the wider social stigma faced by those bereaved by substance use, which was particularly evident in our findings.

> And it's just a horrible stigma...you are labelled, especially by the police... [I]t's as if when she died, 'Oh, another one bites the dust.' (Mother)

Rather than encountering sympathy, they are more likely to be viewed through stereotypical assumptions, pathologising or blaming the family for failing to prevent the death (Walter *et al.* 2017). What is more, such stigma may follow on from having already suffered stigma related to living with a family member's substance use (Orford *et al.* 2005). Sadly, stigma devalues a bereaved person's grief and limits possibilities for sharing with sympathetic others. Yet finding meaning in and coming to live with a loss has been found to depend on such sharing (Holland *et al.* 2006).

Interviewees' experiences of the stigma of substance use suggest that stigma linked to these deaths not only challenges cultural norms, such as the taboo on 'self-inflicted' death, but also reminds us of our own mortality. Stigma was a major theme in our interviewees' narratives, including both direct stigma from unkind, inappropriate and judgemental comments, and perceived or anticipated stigma, which could prevent the bereaved person seeking support. However, we found that not every substance-related death was stigmatised, or by everyone the interviewee came into contact with. Also, a significant number of interviewees found positive, even creative ways of managing, standing up to and surviving stigma (Valentine and Walter 2015), such as writing a book and making a film (see below).

The memory

Another consequence of the stigma of a death related to substance use can be the difficulty remembering and memorialising a life that others, and, in some cases, the bereaved person, may consider unfulfilled. From our interviews, we found that remembering the person involved a complex process, evolving over time and shaped by the circumstances of the life and the death (Valentine and Templeton 2018). Thus, the impact of having lived with the person's substance use and/or the manner of their death could evoke painful and disturbing memories of that life and/or death.

> [M]y mum is my mum but I have a lot of very disturbing nasty memories of her... I wouldn't say I have got a lot of good memories of my mum... It's sad... because...I would die to have a natural friendship, a mother and daughter bond... (Daughter)

However, how interviewees remembered the person, both publicly at the funeral and more privately, varied considerably. For some, memory-making was solitary, while others relied on other people's memories and support. In some cases, the bad memories outweighed the good, while others managed to salvage fond memories from disturbing ones.

> [F]or a long time it was really hard to remember...any good times because it was just so awful before he died... But I can remember now...we had holidays... [H]e was quite charismatic...if you walked into a room...you would notice him because he was quite sort of bright and bubbly...people did like him... (Sister)

For some interviewees, their fond memories of the person fuelled projects designed to challenge stereotypes and the associated bad press these deaths tend to attract. These included setting up a support group, making a film, and writing and publishing a book.

> By telling the story...then somebody else tells their story...and before you know it, it's no longer such an area for shame that people can be more open...and it's only by doing that that you can say...I'm proud of my son. (Mother)

Thus, notwithstanding obstacles to remembering, a significant number of interviewees acknowledged their continuing bond with the deceased person.

Diversity

Having identified core features of substance-use bereavement, it is important to emphasise the considerable diversity we found. Recognising diversity is crucial to countering the stigma by which those concerned are stereotyped. As well as the diversity one would expect to find between individuals, differences were evident across several dimensions, including the nature of the relationship, the pattern of substance use (ranging from singular use to long-term substance dependence), whether in treatment or recovery, the kind of substance used and the nature of the death. Thus, interviewees' experiences were shaped by their relationship with those who died (which included that of parent, child, spouse or partner, sibling, friend and extended family member). Some interviewees' experiences reflected their own substance use for which they were in treatment or recovery. Experiences were affected by whether the substance use involved alcohol, drugs or a mixture of the two, and whether the death followed one-off use of a substance or years of substance-use problems. Experiences also varied depending on how and where the death occurred.

These findings have implications for supporting these bereaved people. In addition to core difficulties related to the life, death, stigma and memory, support also needs to cater for diversity – that is, be more widely available for subgroups including those beyond immediate family (such as siblings, friends and extended family members), who felt very strongly there was insufficient support available for them. There is also scope for offering more bereavement support as part of or alongside packages of care for those who are in treatment or recovery for their own substance use (see Chapter 16). Finally, we stress, regardless of any shared features, that each bereaved person, as well as the person they are grieving, is an individual, and that for support to be effective, both must be acknowledged and treated as such.

FURTHER READING

For a more detailed summary of this project:

Templeton, L., Ford, A., McKell, J., Valentine, C. et al. (2016) 'Bereavement through substance use: Findings from an interview study with adults in England and Scotland.' Addiction Research and Theory 24, 5, 341–354.

The whole project is recorded and discussed in:

Valentine, C. (ed.) (2018) Families Bereaved by Alcohol or Drugs: Research on Experiences, Coping and Support. London and New York, NY: Routledge.

Experiences of substance-related bereavements

This section is written by three bereaved people who share their experiences of grief.

A bereaved father's experience

Roger Kirby

I met my first wife when I was 16. Ten years later we had had three children, but I was a very different person by then and we had very little in common apart from our children. I felt compelled to leave in search of new experiences and a greater understanding of life. I was never far away and saw my children often, but Ezra, the youngest, probably suffered the most from this separation.

By the age of 14 he began to smoke cannabis, and by his 30s he was a well-established, binge-drinking alcoholic. He was very difficult to be with at times and often spoilt the occasion. We struggled to cope with this as a family. It was painful for all of us and we were unable to help him find a solution. We were already losing him and were already grieving, without realising this. His long-term girlfriend tried for several years to cope with it, but eventually asked him to leave, and within four months he took his own life.

I didn't see this final act coming. He was getting help from the NHS, had joined AA[4] and had a sponsor, and was regularly talking to his mum and me on the phone. He did say that he felt suicidal, but I made the great mistake of thinking that if he was talking to us about it, he probably would not do it! The truth was that he was planning to hang himself in the house he could no longer be part of. I found out when the police knocked at my door to tell me.

The first few weeks after his death were a manic cycle of coping and sorting out practical things. I was in an anaesthetised daze. Once all the formal processes had been completed, I was left on my own to come to terms with this reality. I was retired, living alone, with few friends. I had a session with a psychic counsellor. She helped me to see Ezra was his own person, and by seeing the bigger patterns I felt less overwhelmingly responsible. I couldn't afford regular counselling and my doctor offered no help at all. I had to draw on my own resources and fortunately I had enough.

I come from a family that is used to being 'on the outside' a bit. I never expected nor received much from the 'authorities', so I don't have anything much to say about that. I soon realised that I was more able to cope with my son's death than the people I talked to. Again, I didn't expect or receive much support from

---

4   Alcoholics Anonymous. Peer-led groups that provide support to people who use alcohol, using the 12-step model.

most people, apart from my ex-wife, who is a counsellor, my family, and later the substance-related bereavement group I joined. I also have my own approach to social attitudes: in my paradigm, an individual's addiction is a symptom of an unhealthy society, which would rather reject and blame the addicted person than own the problem. Therefore I wasn't too worried about what others thought.

The best way I can explain my approach to bereavement is in terms of how I have learned to manage stress, the 'flight or fight' survival response: my whole being was in major stress mode. I had tried to 'fight' it and failed – that is, to help my son recover from alcohol and want to live – so I was left with 'flight', or, attempting to find a positive way to cope, a way to 'stay and play' with life as it now was. One of the hardest things was the finality, the loss of hope for his future, of an opportunity to make amends and to help him. I was confronted with all my feelings of inadequacy and guilt as a parent, but with no means to try to put it right – at least not for him. The only people I could help now were my family and myself. I knew that this event would either push me under or up. The choice was mine. Being pushed under would be supporting my son's decision to give up. This would not help me or the rest of the family. I was clear that I had to find a strong 'yes' to life to counteract his total 'no'.

The first thing I knew was that I had to face this pain and anger as fully as I could, and that this would be healthier in the long run. So I spent days with a pile of pillows on my bed which I was either bashing with a batten of wood or falling on to, sobbing my heart out. The rest of the time I was exhausted and buried myself in TV and the computer. Constant tiredness was the worst physical symptom. I tried to get help with fatigue from my doctor, but he just said come back in a year's time if you are still tired! I was offered no further support of any kind!

Between these episodes my brain was still re-running all the 'if only' scenarios it could think of. There were plenty of those since I was an absent and, in my mind, not very good dad. I see this as the 'flight' response – the attempt to escape by putting it all back as it should have been. Death is very hard to accept; my brain was going to great lengths to repaint the picture and put it all right. I even 'saw' him in the distance sometimes and often dreamed it had not happened.

Apart from relevant reading and courses, the most significant experience was some years earlier when I was living in solitude and meditating daily. On one occasion I was feeling very peaceful and blissful, when a knot of discomfort in my stomach turned into a knot of profound grief, with no obvious cause or focus. I didn't want to leave this peaceful state and chose to let the pain take its course. I started to cry, and it became so gut-wrenchingly intense that it was like being violently sick. I had never experienced such pain before. This happened for several days and was probably the most cathartic experience of my life. As a result I was not so afraid of pain as I had been and discovered that letting myself feel it fully is healing. I also learned from this that I can live a fuller life by embracing more of my feelings and learning to accept and embrace joy and pain at the same time.

The key elements that helped me to cope:

- I had a mental framework which gave me perspective.

- I know that stress is not what happens to me but how I respond to it. I can review how I respond and learn to change this.

- I had some stress-management tools and strategies to use.

- I had learned to feel rather than avoid pain.

- I had learned to express anger safely, without involving anyone else.

- Therefore, if I could 'feel the pain and live positively' – to paraphrase Susan Jeffers (2007) – I would benefit. I was aware that the desire to block pain and seek pleasure is a mistake, and that one positive I could take from my son's death was to embrace a fuller range of myself. This might make me a better dad and grandad in future. Ultimately, we may learn to 'end the struggle and dance with life' – again to paraphrase Susan Jeffers.

- Within the support group I felt held and accepted; I got a sense of my progress, and began to discover that I had a lot to offer by giving support to others and that also helped me to feel better about myself.

Another key element is ownership. I had to own that part of my behaviour and state of mind that had contributed to my son's unhappiness. I had to own and embrace my anger and grief, and allow myself to fully express those, without upsetting others. I also had to recognise his part in it: as a 39-year-old man, he had not only the responsibility for his own life but the right to live it as he chose.

A bereaved mother's experience

Stella Hurd

My elder son Daniel died in 2001 aged 29, of an accidental drug overdose. He had suffered from depression for many years but with treatment had overcome his problems enough to get a good degree and a full-time job that he found fulfilling. At the time he seemed happy in his work and excited about the imminent birth of his daughter.

He was found dead on a stairwell in a block of flats during the early hours of a Saturday morning. Our younger son was visited by the police and had to break the terrible news to us. I was working away. My husband drove down to tell me personally and we continued on to London to join our younger son and partner, Daniel's partner and her mother. I remember we stood in a circle without any preliminaries, trying to take in what had happened, not believing it while knowing it to be true.

We went to identify him as a family – seven of us. He lay there, white and still, beautiful, peaceful. I asked for a lock of his hair. He had wanted to call his unborn daughter Lily, so we bought lilies and left them with him. That was the last time we saw him. In the days that followed, we received a toxicology report which stated that Daniel had died from a mixture of alcohol, heroin and cocaine. We were told that had he been addicted, it is unlikely he would have died as his body would have tolerated the doses he took. I have never looked at the post-mortem report and remain unable to do so; it is still too painful to contemplate the idea of Daniel reduced to a collection of body parts.

We had a simple funeral in a church but without any religious rituals. The church was packed with friends and family. Around 60 of his work colleagues hired a coach and travelled up from London. We buried Daniel in a local cemetery – a perfect spot, by a hedge on the other side of which horses roam. Nothing seemed real, but I went through the motions of 'what you do'.

At first my husband and I found that we could not cope with noise or brightness. We took all the flowers to his grave as they started to become oppressive. We went away to Wales and read obsessively about grief and loss, trying to make sense of it all, trying to put some kind of order into the emotional chaos. I contacted The Compassionate Friends, an organisation for bereaved parents, and was comforted by those I spoke to. During the first year, I also found the Child Death Helpline enormously supportive.

The birth of Daniel's baby a month after his death was both traumatic and wonderful. She looked very like him, and I have to confess to wishing for just a moment that she was Daniel and all the pain of loss would instantly disappear. It wasn't a sustained, rational or developed thought, and I learned quickly to love her for herself.

The inquest was very well handled by a thoughtful and compassionate coroner, who asked the witness pathologist if Daniel would have suffered any pain: the one question I desperately needed answered. I imagined that he might have known he was dying, been in appalling pain, cried out to his partner or myself for help, but was assured that he would have died quickly and painlessly. I cling on to that.

The return to work after three months was extremely painful. I got cold after cold, couldn't sleep, felt utterly alone and unable to interact with my colleagues as I had before. The most supportive person was the workplace doctor who 'got it' in a way that nobody else did and went out of his way to help me, through writing to my line manager and referring me for counselling. Sadly, I did not get much from that experience. I found it hard to cope with the one-way nature of the process and kept wanting to ask 'And how about you?' But in retrospect it may have helped me to sort out some of my confused feelings and it was good to have space to talk. Grief can lead to a kind of madness because it is so hard to accept the death of your child. I also felt guilt: for a while I was constantly plagued by 'what if?' and 'why didn't I?' questions, even though I knew that there was nothing I could have done to change the course of events. I would have welcomed reassurance at some point from a parental bereavement counsellor that these feelings would pass and that I wasn't going mad.

The most important people in helping me get back to some kind of normality were my husband, my younger son and my sister. Their constant support, even through their own grief, helped me to recover a sense of purpose and enjoy life again. Together, we started to counter our grief with memories of Daniel's intelligence and commitment to justice, his quick wit and compassion for those in need. The pieces written by his workmates in their Newsletter and their Book of Memories were unbelievably moving and made me feel immensely proud. Later, working with a local sculptor from an organisation called Memorials by Artists to create a fitting tribute to Daniel in the form of a headstone engaged us positively and helped in the healing process. My grandchildren as they grow up have also been hugely instrumental in giving my life new meaning. The need to nurture does not vanish when your child dies, and grandchildren can help fill that gap and give you a fresh focus.

I do not believe there are stages to grief that you work through sequentially. The process is a jumble of denial, fury, guilt and resignation, with hopefully a final degree of acceptance – that is, you learn to live with your grief. I would contend, sadly, that there is a hierarchy of death, in that a fatal drug overdose is somehow a comment on the person and renders their death of less value. I still dread being asked how Daniel died, as if giving that information somehow diminishes him. What I miss from friends is talking about him. Not ever mentioning him feels as if he never existed. But their support in so many other ways continues to be something I value and they have been a crucial factor in my reintegration into the social fabric of life.

In the early stages, what helped most was reading about grief, articulating my feelings of loss through writing poems and other pieces about Daniel. Attending weekends where bereaved parents can share their experiences has continued to sustain me over the years. There is an instant empathy: you can say anything you like and will not be judged; a sense that each loss is unique but equal and that all our children are valued. As time goes on, it is also an opportunity to appreciate, in relation to the newly bereaved, how you have moved on in learning to live with your loss.

Finding a new emphasis at work was important in restoring my self-esteem. And finally, watching Daniel's daughter grow and change, and how proud he would be of her, is both a poignant, constant reminder of his absence and, perhaps paradoxically, a source of great joy.

Debbie and Maxine – a bereaved sister's experience

Michelle Michael

My mother had two partners, and had three white children with the first and two mixed-race children with the second. My elder three siblings' father was white Irish, and my youngest brother and I had a Black Jamaican father. My sisters Maxine and Debbie started using drugs at an early age. I believe this was because drugs and alcohol were normalised and were my mother's preferred coping strategy. Her poison was alcohol, benzodiazepines, marijuana and amphetamines.

I was about five when Debbie left home; she was 15. She was the free spirit, the sister that helped me aspire to be a gymnast, by flipping me around and doing acrobatics with me. The sister who had me in fits of laughter with her silly antics. The sister who would collect me from school, mostly in bare feet, and carry me home on her shoulders. At that time, my understanding of her leaving was that she had a boyfriend called Steve and they were taking drugs. I now know she ran away from home to get away. The grieving for Debbie started here!

I did not see her for several years. Then the woman I sporadically met up with years later was not the same spirit I once knew. Debbie and Joe (the father of her two children) were heavily into drugs; at the time I did not know which ones. Eventually, Debbie lost her children for adoption due to her drug use, I lost my niece and nephew, and we lost contact again. Five years later she came back into my life and I enjoyed getting to know her again. I was 15. I learned it was heroin she took, among other drugs, and remember her once begging me to help her find a vein, as we stood on the stairwell of a block of flats. Other times were a mixture of alcohol, heart-to-hearts, fun, adrenaline, crime, near misses, tears, laughter, pain, anger, and her overdosing and going back to prison.

I was 19 and lying on my bed when my phone rang. My eldest brother asked if I was sitting down and said, 'Debbie is dead.' My initial reaction was that he was mistaken. I couldn't wait to get off the phone to him to call the hospital morgue, but they just confirmed that she *was* there. She was 29.

I heard that my sister had died with her trousers down and a needle in her groin. She had been released from prison that day and had broken into her 'prison girlfriend's' flat, which had been boarded up with a metal door. This had obstructed the emergency services from reaching her sooner. Debbie's 'prison girlfriend' said she had taken heroin too, then 'gouched out'[5] and came around to find my sister had overdosed.

I visited Debbie in the morgue. Her lips had been sewn together a little haphazardly, pulling her facial expression into a grimace, her head had been tucked into her body and covered with a piece of cloth, and there was a proud V-shaped zigzag scar across her chest from the post-mortem. I wasn't forewarned. A far cry from how loved one's are normally shown to relatives in a funeral parlour, a luxury we never had due to her hepatitis. Despite all this, I kissed her face and stroked her hair and some of it came away and I took it home. Her hair was her pride and beauty.

She was left in the morgue for months, on ice like a piece of meat, cut up for the post-mortem and badly put back together, apparently so the coroner's court could investigate the cause of death. As a family, we attended the hearing. It ruled that she died due to a lifetime dependency on drugs. As a family, we obviously knew this and it felt a little insulting and like they had ticked a box. Her body was then burned when I had wanted her to be buried. There was no comfort in the thought of her being at peace! At the funeral I was filled with a white rage. Some of it at my own family, some at Debbie for abandoning me, and a lot at the 'prison girlfriend': she decided to make a show of her grief in the ceremony and tell me she had tried to pull Debbie's trousers up before the ambulance arrived to 'provide her with some dignity'. It all felt like some sick joke and that her memory and her body belonged to everyone but me. I felt invisible, insignificant, and as if grief was something that happened to more deserving families.

Debbie had been let down by our parents, by social services and later by the prison service, the mortuary and the coroner's court. In their ways, they had each expressed their lack of concern and treated her without any dignity. I thought to myself surely if they knew how much this hurt, they wouldn't keep twisting the knife. Everything about her death and funeral screamed that she was considered worthless. It felt indefensible because it mirrored how Debbie had treated herself.

I was broken, angry, felt judged, exposed, ashamed and dumped in a box called 'Junkie's relative'. I couldn't cope, felt lost and didn't know what to do. I came out in psoriasis. It helped to have a physical symptom, as it was real and showed me I was hurting, and validated my pain. I asked my GP for therapy but didn't get it. When I was 21, I attempted suicide, due to Debbie's death and other difficulties, I was seen by a psychiatrist and the home treatment team, put on medication, but had no help with my grief and what I can now see as trauma.

I collected my sister's ashes for my mum but was not ready to part with them

---

5   'Gouching out' is falling asleep under the influence of heroin.

for seven years. Healing from this experience took some time. I found out grief does subside, the time in between the tears gets longer, and its intensity does lessen. When I would think, 'What could I have done differently?' I would get a vision of Debbie's face smiling down at me, as if saying, 'It's okay, let go', and the guilt I longed for could never take hold. My song that captures Debbie's life is 'Candle in the Wind' by Elton John.

My sister Maxine was the eldest, more serious sister, who was a mother to me and my four siblings. Shortly after Debbie left home, she did also. She settled in Woolwich and had two boys with Tony. Later when she met Mick, who was heavily into drugs, she suffered domestic abuse and became more involved with amphetamines. After an incident that left her son disabled, he was taken into care, and Mick was given a long prison sentence. Maxine's drug use spiralled; she eventually lost her other two children for adoption, and later turned to heroin and alcohol.

I was 31 when I was woken by my mobile in the middle of the night. My other brother was crying down the phone and I knew before he spoke what he was going to say. I had spent years anticipating this call.

Maxine was 44 when she died in the flat of an older man whom she would visit when requiring a safe place away from the drug world. He would let her stay, she would do some cleaning and he might buy her a beer or give her some money. He would not allow her boyfriend or her friends to visit, so in some respects she was safe. However, having worked in the drug, alcohol and homelessness field, I am aware that vulnerable people who use drugs attract men like this who are looking for a situation to exploit, usually being drug-free themselves and after sexual favours. Maxine, in search for peace away from the violence and chaos, would seek solace at this man's house. Maxine also died in a state of undress.

Going through her belongings, I found a note called 'if and when', where she left a few words to each of us in the event of her death. She had a list of songs; they explained how she felt and were songs perhaps for her funeral.

When we visited Maxine in the morgue, her nose looked like she had been face-down for some time. We all pretended she looked fine. I wondered how it happened, but I didn't really want to know. Her boyfriend privately said to me that it was 'naughty' or sinister. I knew, he knew and the police who attended the flat probably knew that something wasn't right. She is said to have died of drug complications and pneumonia. I am sure this is the case, but there are also a lot of unanswered questions. I know, after losing Debbie in this way, it is futile to expect any dignity, respect or even justice, or to even hold on to a desire for it. It is better to just let it go. My song for Maxine's death is 'By Your Side' by Sade.

Maxine was buried, and I struggled at times with a kind of claustrophobia and a gasping for breath at the thought of her lying so deep and trapped underground.

Having lost Debbie and my dad a few years earlier, I knew what I was in for emotionally. I compare it to being shot several times in the chest. Despite this major injury, while still 'losing a lot of blood and my internal organs hanging out of my chest', I would have to carry on getting up every day and do mundane life stuff. I dreaded the feeling of grieving around people, keeping up the pretence, as if people could see I had been 'shot' but had to pretend they hadn't noticed. Or those who couldn't bear witness to my pain and avoided me. I felt deeply ashamed, to still be hurt by a death that should somehow be painless.

The death of my father from cancer was viewed very differently to my sisters' drug-related deaths. There is permission to grieve; it is a more legitimate, socially acceptable loss, and is validated. I was offered and received bereavement therapy from the hospice, which provided me with a space to reflect on my relationship with my father, his death and helped me go through the tunnel of grief. With my sisters' deaths, there were no bereavement leaflets handed to me or anyone suggesting to get help. These deaths were silencing, shameful and deserved, and it didn't even occur to me that I was grieving. There is a lack of compassion towards you, and to lose a loved one in this way is almost criminal. For example, I called several funeral parlours who all refused to collect Maxine's body from the mortuary until the funeral was paid for in full, whereas we were given a payment plan for my father's funeral costs that continued after the funeral. As a relative of someone who uses drugs, you are by blood infected with mistrust and considered the dregs of society, even in your moment of need.

I truly feel that most of my life has been a process of incrementally losing them both.

BOOKS BY PEOPLE BEREAVED THROUGH
A SUBSTANCE-RELATED DEATH

Burton-Phillips, E. (2018) *Mum, Can You Lend Me Twenty Quid?* (2nd edition). London: Piatkus.

Esguerra, D. (2015) *Junkie Buddha: A Journey of Discovery in Peru*. Much Wenlock: Eye Books.

Rose, J., Cowell, M. and Cowell, S. (2016) *Tenacity: The True Stories of Two Mothers Who Battled Their Sons' Drug Addictions*. Scotts Valley, CA: Createspace Independent Publishing.

Skinner, P. (2012) *See You Soon: A Mother's Story of Drugs, Grief and Hope*. Presence Books in partnership with Spoonbill Publications.

6

Making Sense of Substance-Related Bereavements

This chapter offers you a framework for thinking about these bereavements to inform your work, by describing five characteristics specific to substance use that can potentially affect these bereavements, which are in addition to the characteristics found in all bereavements (Cartwright 2019):

- substance use
- unfinished business associated with the person who died and their substance use
- the death, including traumatic bereavement
- stigma, disenfranchised grief and lack of social support
- coping with specific difficulties.

Each characteristic is a cluster of related experiences. Also, these characteristics are interconnected and influence each other (see Figure 6.1). They combine to create a complexity and severity to the whole bereavement that tends to keep bereaved people in loss orientation, inhibits restoration-orientated activities and complicates any continuing bond. All of this inhibits grieving. For example, a bereaved person who misunderstands addictive substance use is likely to have more unfinished business and find the death harder to understand, addictive use increases their risk of being stigmatised, and all these combine to produce an unexpectedly severe, complex and long-lasting bereavement.

Each of these substance-related characteristics can be redefined as a need that can be met through support, which in turn facilitates grieving. So, in the example above, support can meet the needs to understand addictive substance use, work through unfinished business, make sense of the death, develop resilience against stigma and cope better with a difficult bereavement.

Chapter 5 noted the diversity of these bereavements and how each bereaved person, and the person they are grieving for, is an individual. Therefore, in order to support a client effectively, you need to consider their experience of each characteristic, how these characteristics influence each other and what their associated needs are. This will facilitate working through the substance-related characteristics of their bereavement.

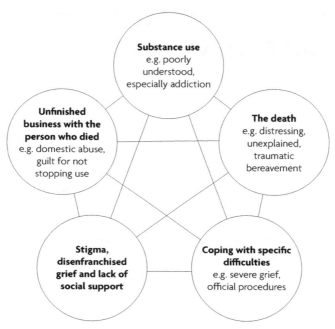

FIGURE 6.1 THE FIVE INTERCONNECTED, SUBSTANCE-RELATED
CHARACTERISTICS THAT POTENTIALLY AFFECT BEREAVEMENT

You can practise using this framework by identifying the substance-related characteristics and associated needs from the accounts of bereavement in Chapter 5.

Further consideration of these characteristics and how to work with their associated needs is offered in Part 2. In addition, you will need to consider the general characteristics found in all bereavements (see Chapters 9 and 10) and the determinants of grief (see Chapter 1 and below).

Substance use

Grieving is significantly influenced by the substance(s) used and the associated behaviour. They affected how someone died and also often affected bereaved people's relationship with them before they died. Bereaved people often experienced substance use, especially when addictive, as confusing, frustrating and frightening, and they can misunderstand or be poorly informed about it.

> [Substance use] is not something I have spoken about or explored, but…want to understand what he went through. (Mother whose counselling did not meet this need) (Cartwright 2019, p.27)

Therefore, they often need you to offer information about this and an opportunity to make sense of what it means (Cartwright 2019; Templeton and Velleman 2018) (see page 140). For any one death, the amount of available information varies. For example, some substances, such as heroin and alcohol, are well known and tested for in a post-mortem; this helps a bereaved person to make sense of what happened. However, others, such as some novel psychoactive substances available on the internet, are less well known and not tested for in a post-mortem; this inhibits making sense, leaves unfinished business (see below) and may even mean not knowing what the fatal substance was or what an illegal drug was cut[1] with.

It is important to know how a substance can kill. For example, an opioid overdose death kills by someone effectively falling asleep and not waking up.

> I said to the [pathologist] he didn't suffer did he? I wouldn't like to think he was lying there gasping for breath and he was paralysed and he couldn't move. She said no…he would have slipped away. (Mother) (Templeton and Velleman 2018, p.34)

People using illegal drugs are much more likely to have been involved with the criminal justice system, and their death is much more likely to involve official procedures and be more stigmatised (see below). Note that substance use may have begun legally and became illegal – an example is someone becoming addicted to prescribed opioid medication for pain relief and then using illegal opioids after their medication is no longer prescribed.

Chapter 3 described both the range of substance-using behaviour and the stages of change of substance-using behaviour. You can use these to help create an informed, accurate and compassionate narrative of someone's substance use and subsequent death.

Many deaths (including many substance-related suicides) occur through longer-term alcohol and opioid use, when a person is using in a problematic or addictive way and is at the precontemplation or contemplation stage. The death is often anticipated after the stress and strain of living with substance-using behaviour, and although it may come as a relief, in turn this can provoke guilt.

---

1   Mixing an illegal drug with other ingredients to give the impression of buying more of it.

However, other people may not have appreciated the risk and therefore experience the death as sudden and unexpected. For example, someone on long-term prescription medication might use other substances creating an unexpectedly lethal combination. Alternatively, a client might be naïve or misinformed:

> But to actually be told he had a drug addiction I was like how come, he is working…how can you hold up a full-time job and be a drug addict. It didn't make sense to me. (Friend) (Templeton and Velleman 2018, p.20)

When someone relapses and resumes using, there is a high risk of death from overdosing, especially with opioids, because their tolerance has dropped (see Chapter 3). Such deaths are typically sudden and unexpected for bereaved people. They shatter hopes of someone being free of substance use and there may also be the shock of discovering that someone was using again. It can be helpful to know that change is often cyclic, and that had someone lived, they could have stopped using again.

Alternatively, deaths can occur through inexperience at the experimental stage of use or through accidents at the experimental and recreational stages, such as drink-driving deaths. These deaths are often shocking, unexpected and possibly violent. They tend to be of younger people, who may be inaccurately labelled as a 'drug addict', to the distress of their family.

Deaths can happen even when someone is abstinent and in maintenance, resulting from long-term health difficulties stemming from earlier use – for example, from hepatitis C. The death may be protracted, distressing and/or re-stimulate unfinished business about past substance use. Even though the person did manage to stop using before they died, this may be small comfort to those bereaved.

Unfinished business associated with the person who died and their substance use

Substance-related bereavements usually include unfinished business from the relationship with the person before they died (Cartwright 2019; Templeton and Velleman 2018) – difficult situations and events associated with substance use that were not satisfactorily completed and/or deep ambivalence about the person that remains unresolved. This is part of people's relationship with the person who died, the 'back story', which is an essential part of making meaning during grieving (Holland and Neimeyer 2011). This can be highly emotive and even excruciating work (Rando 1993). However, there is usually less unfinished business where someone's use was at an experimental or recreational stage, and so had been unproblematic until the death.

As unfinished business can seem impossible to resolve after the death, it tends to keep a person in loss orientation, complicates any continuing bond and may risk inadvertently perpetuating attachment difficulties such as compulsive caring (see page 77). Therefore, you need to recognise unfinished business and offer to work it through (see Chapter 12), together with any associated emotions, commonly including blame and guilt (see Chapter 14) (Cartwright 2019).

Unfinished business from the impact of substance-using behaviour

The impact of living with substance-using behaviour, especially when addictive, typically leaves a lot of unfinished business (Cartwright 2019) (see Chapters 4 and 5). In addition, there may have been co-occurring difficulties, such as poor mental health, that bereaved people may also be confused and misinformed about; they therefore often need relevant information and an opportunity to make sense of these. Exposure to all these difficulties typically has a significant impact on bereaved people's health before the death; this can include trauma and depression (see Chapters 11 and 15). The emotions associated with the past can be 'so powerful that they block, replace or supersede normal grieving. Counsellors may need to help the bereaved person work through these blocks before grieving can occur' (Ross 1996, p.5).

Someone's unrealistic assumptions about what they could do can linger after the death, as they psychologically continue trying to control the situation and reconstruct their narrative with an ending different from the reality of the death (Ross 1996). This unfinished business is typically not resolved during the chaos of addictive substance use. Having your support for bereavement is often the first opportunity to meet this need:

> First time I'd spoken about what happened before the death, its impact and feelings. (Daughter of mother talking about her counselling) (Cartwright 2019, unpublished data)

Also, unfinished business often includes what bereaved people did or did not say or do, and their associated guilt. Possibilities include believing they caused substance use, failed to stop it or assisted it through buying substances, feeling guilty about their own substance use, or feeling guilty despite believing they do not need to. Guilt particularly affects parents and those whose loved one had used drugs as opposed to alcohol. However, their guilt often seems to be unwarranted and may occur through unrealistic expectations about what was actually beyond their control (see Chapter 14). Those who understand substance use and addiction are much less likely to feel guilty (Cartwright 2019).

> Guilt is a feeling that I had and still have in a big way. It really doesn't matter how much someone tells me that it wasn't my fault, I still feel bad about so many things. (Mother whose counselling did not meet this need) (Cartwright 2019, p.28)

Those who found caring for a loved one particularly stressful before any kind of death have more difficulties in bereavement (Parkes and Prigerson 2010). This is typical of caring for someone who uses substances addictively, and is usually greater for someone who was an attachment figure for their loved one, such as parents, someone who had caring responsibilities and those who care compulsively. Therefore, consider the impact of caring, including potentially a sense of failure and associated guilt, a feeling of relief that can provoke guilt, and loss of identity and depression.

Some bereaved people may have withheld from others some or all of what was happening, often motivated by shame and guilt. Following the death, it is often no longer possible to keep this secret and they then have unfinished business with others. Look for possible guilt, family conflict and feeling conflicted about whether they should have told them.

Another possible way unfinished business occurs is through bereaved people's struggle to get services to help their loved one, characterised by blame and possibly stigma:

> He had a different worker every time he had treatment and they were naïve about his lying. (Sister) (Cartwright 2019, p.28)

When the death was not prepared for psychologically, such as during a prolonged illness, it comes as more of a shock, and there is typically unfinished business and associated blame and guilt. For example, missed opportunities, key decisions that were taken and end-of-life conversations that did not happen (Templeton *et al.* 2018b).

> When he died it was the end of that hope, and more devastating than I could ever have imagined. For of course I *had* imagined and dreaded it, had lived with that fear for nearly fifteen years, but the reality, the absolute finality, was beyond my imagining. (Mother) (Lawton, Gilbert and Turnbull 2016, p.48)

A significant and complex form of unfinished business is the impact of parental substance use on a bereaved person's childhood, personal development and subsequent life. Potential difficulties to consider include neglect and unmet needs; physical and emotional abuse, and associated developmental trauma; caring for the parent; and, for some, being born dependent on a substance or with foetal alcohol syndrome.[2]

---

2   Foetal alcohol syndrome happens when a mother drinks alcohol excessively during pregnancy, resulting in mental and physical problems in the baby that can last into adulthood.

Unfinished business that is only apparent after the death

This often centres around the shock of discovering someone used substances or realising the true problematic nature of their use. Consider the impact this has had, such as an overwhelming need to make sense of what happened; not having known who someone truly was or losing who they thought someone was; and anger, blame, betrayal, exclusion and/or unanswered questions for those who *did* know and did not say. Additionally, there is often guilt and helplessness at being unable to tackle the substance use before it was too late (da Silva, Noto and Formigoni 2007).

Deep ambivalence

Another unresolved aspect of these bereavements can be people's deep ambivalence about the person who died and occasionally about the death. Their ambivalence often predates the death. Also, their ambivalence can complicate working through other unfinished business, as it can be difficult to have a consistent view of the person who died.

Potentially, people have happy memories, love the person and may be surprised by how much they miss them, yet also have difficult and painful memories that provoke anger, blame, guilt, hurt and even hatred, have lost hopes that the person will be abstinent and healthy, and experience stigma and shame (Valentine and Templeton 2018). Ambivalence makes it difficult to remember and memorialise the person who died (see Chapter 5). Also, people with insecure attachment styles can be habitually ambivalent about those to whom they attach (see Chapter 2). For others however, their mental health improves following the death of someone they had a conflicted relationship with (Wheaton 1990).

Generally speaking, difficulties in loving lead to difficulties in grieving. Deep ambivalence leads to conflicted emotions of love and hate, tends to result in more guilt and anger, and in turn increases the risk of problematic grief (Parkes 2009). Therefore, people need to resolve their ambivalence as far as is possible (see Chapters 10 and 17).

The death

The circumstances of substance-related deaths are often distressing, as discussed in Chapter 5, and form a significant part of grieving (Cartwright 2019). These deaths happen in many ways: anticipated after a long illness due to substance use, typical of the long-term complications of alcohol or intravenous drug use, or expected after previous overdoses or suicide attempts. Conversely, it may have been sudden and unexpected, sometimes also horrific, such as a road traffic accident. Other deaths occur far away or after losing contact, so may seem unreal; for others, the circumstances may be no more significant than deaths through other causes.

You will need to support a client to make sense of the death, or 'event story', and subsequent events related to it, such as an inquest, as this is an important part of making meaning during grieving (Holland and Neimeyer 2011), as well as recognise and offer to work through any unfinished business associated with the death.

Next, this section considers the characteristics of grief commonly associated with the death, traumatic bereavement, deaths by overdose and suicide, and ambiguous loss.

Common characteristics of grief

Despite the variation in deaths, there are shared circumstances of substance-related deaths, at least some of which bereaved people typically experience: usually premature and unnatural, and perceived as being preventable, needless and unfair.

These shared circumstances generate common characteristics of grief that you need to identify and consider.

Premature deaths often have numerous and significant secondary losses, such as parents not having grandchildren. Unnatural deaths can easily be disturbing; it can be distressing to know, or to imagine, how a loved one suffered or died in lonely or unpleasant circumstances. The more unnatural a death, the more that healthy grieving is interfered with (Rynearson, Schut and Stroebe 2013). There is often an overwhelming need to make sense of what happened, including to determine who is responsible.

How people find out about the death is also significant. Being informed by family members is very different from being informed by the police (who may have been stigmatising or insensitive). Although for those bereaved any death is uncontrollable, when substance use is involved, the helplessness at being unable to control someone's use and prevent their death heightens a loss of control. Any sense of helplessness and loss of control continues after the death when people are caught up in official procedures (see below).

Bereaved people may blame others for not preventing the death. More often they feel guilty for their perceived failings to prevent the death (Cartwright 2019). Their guilt is often a continuation of that felt while a loved one was alive, which is usually focused on believing that they had somehow failed them (Templeton *et al.* 2016):

> What did I do wrong? I must have been a horrible mum. (Mother) (Templeton *et al.* 2016, p.5)

Additionally, be aware that bereaved people are often blamed by others. Parents in particular are blamed for their perceived failings and this easily adds to their guilt; this is only found to the same extent in suicide deaths (Feigelman, Jordan and Gorman 2011; Templeton *et al.* 2016). The person who died can also be blamed, as well as the services helping them. Blame and guilt may be warranted or, more usually, seemingly unwarranted and occur in unexpected ways (see Chapter 14).

There is often uncertainty and unfinished business about the death. Where others were present when someone died, there are often suspicions, information may be withheld or there may be unanswered questions about their role (Ford *et al.* 2018). For example:

> He was wrapped in a carpet and put under a bed and left there to rot for three weeks. (Mother) (Ford *et al.* 2018, p.45)

Additionally, unsatisfactory outcomes to official procedures typically leave unfinished business (see below and Chapter 12).

Recognise how these deaths often undermine a person's assumptive world (see page 26), their belief that life is basically meaningful, benevolent, fair and just, that others are generally trustworthy, and that they and their loved ones are reasonably safe and secure. These assumptions shaped their identity and worldview/spirituality, which in turn can also be undermined. Additionally, they can have profound and disturbing existential realisations, such as how powerless they were over their loved one's behaviour (see Chapter 17). However, other deaths can come with relief, and this in turn may provoke guilt.

The death is often stigmatised, may involve official procedures and potentially receive media attention (see below and Chapter 13).

Traumatic bereavement

Substance-related deaths commonly traumatise those who are bereaved (Feigelman *et al.* 2011; Guy and Holloway 2007). Trauma is the normal survival response when someone's ability to respond to a perceived, inescapable threat is in some way overwhelmed, which results in debilitating symptoms in the aftermath (Levine 2008; van der Kolk 2014).

Traumatic bereavement happens when the way a loved one dies is so threatening that it traumatises the person who is bereaved, such as knowing a loved one suffered when dying. Thereby, trauma is inextricably intertwined with bereavement, such that both are *better considered and worked with as the single, inclusive entity of traumatic bereavement* (Pearlman *et al.* 2014; Zandvoort 2012). Therefore, it is important that you recognise and know how to work with a traumatic bereavement (see "'Grounding' an overwhelmed or traumatised client' in Chapter 7; see also Chapter 11).

Overdose deaths

It is important to recognise that bereavements from overdose differ from other substance-related bereavements (Templeton *et al.* 2016) and seem to be particularly disturbing and stressful (Da Silva *et al.* 2007; Templeton *et al.* 2016).

The death is often unexpected and horrific, and many are accidental, although some are intentional (see 'Suicide deaths' below). Trauma and grief complications have been reported as high in people bereaved by overdose deaths (Da Silva *et al.* 2007; Feigelman *et al.* 2011). However, where there had been earlier non-fatal overdoses, there seems to be a 'veiled preparation' for the possibility of death (Da Silva *et al.* 2007, p.301), although when it happens, it is still a shock and may be traumatising.

The circumstances of the death significantly affect grieving. Knowing or suspecting that others were involved in, responsible for or could have prevented the death negatively affects grieving (Templeton *et al.* 2016), as does any associated unfinished business. Alternatively, as many overdoses happen in the home, people may have responded to non-fatal and fatal overdoses, such as trying to resuscitate someone (Guy 2004), and can be traumatised. Recognise that families often lack awareness of the signs of an overdose and of how to respond (Templeton *et al.* 2016). The resulting deaths provoke intense guilt and self-blame, as well as the blame of others (Adfam 2012a):

> I moved out again and then it happened shortly after that and then I blamed myself that I wasn't there…that I'd caused it. (Sister) (Templeton *et al.* 2016, p.5)

However, grieving can also be characterised by relief (Da Silva *et al.* 2007) and occasionally there may be ambivalence about whether to resuscitate someone:

> I had had to do CPR three times in the past…and part of me wondered if I could leave him the next time. Because that thing about, he is your child, you brought him into the world and maybe you have a right to see them out of it. (Mother) (Templeton *et al.* 2016, p.7)

Such deaths are highly stigmatised (see below) and usually involve official procedures such as police investigations, post-mortems and inquests (see below). Finally, there are the substance-related deaths of public figures, such as Michael Jackson and Amy Winehouse, that get media attention; these can influence bereaved people's perception of these deaths.

Suicide deaths

This section covers suicide deaths that are substance-related, regardless of whether substance use was a factor in the death. Other suicide deaths happen through overdosing on substances but are *not* considered substance-related deaths by those who are bereaved, because the substances were not used problematically before the death.

Be aware that there are clear differences in how people grieve a suicide death (Jordan and McIntosh 2010). The death may have been sudden and unexpected, or anticipated after previous attempts and might even have become 'when, not if, they succeed'; either can be traumatic. People may feel relief that someone is no longer suffering and at being free of the demands of self-destructive behaviour. This in turn provokes guilt (Jordan and McIntosh 2010).

However, the death is typically perceived as horrific, frightening and disturbing (particularly if violent), and seemingly goes against our survival instinct. As the motive can seem inexplicable and the death bewildering and confusing, there is an overwhelming need to make sense of it and establish *why* someone chose to die (Wertheimer 2001).

> Is it me? (Sister-in-law, questioning herself about the cause of her brother-in-law's death through suicide) (Cartwright 2019, p.28)

Suicide deaths are often perceived as preventable, as well as being intentionally rejecting, betraying or punishing on the part of the person who seemingly chose to leave those bereaved. These perceptions bring a sense of being complicit and humiliated, and feeling intense guilt. Anger can be felt towards the person who died for what they did, which can elicit guilt or be suppressed after seeing how anger can lead to death (Jordan and McIntosh 2010; Wertheimer 2001).

Additionally, consider whether the following are significant. Bereaved people can question whether they really knew the person who died, and can doubt that the person would choose to reunite with them if they could somehow come alive again; these questions can result in deep ambivalence about them. There is typically unfinished business from life before the death and/or from the death that may never be fully resolved – for example, unanswered questions for the person who died and possibly uncertainty whether the death was suicide or accidental. Making sense of the death often requires being informed about addiction, depression and suicide (see Chapters 3 and 4) to gain insight into the likely frame of mind of the person who died. However, some people struggle to make sense and may not succeed.

Suicide notes may or may not be helpful for grieving. Typically, it helps if someone says they considered their death and saw no other choice, says that others are not responsible, acknowledges the impact, conveys love, etc. However, notes often say sorry and goodbye, rather than why, so may say no more than how a person felt at the time of death (Rando 2014 cited in Pearlman *et al.* 2014, p.88).

Suicide is often stigmatised (Feigelman *et al.* 2011; Wertheimer 2001), because, like substance use, it can be perceived as self-inflicted, selfish and dangerous (see below and Chapter 13). The person who died may be reduced to a label, such as 'stupid', 'coward' or 'loser'. Grief is therefore often characterised by shame, feeling an outsider in society, and as the death easily overshadows other aspects of who someone was, it distorts how they are remembered (Wertheimer 2001). This adds to the stigma of substance use and further disenfranchises someone's grief, so that they seldom seek support or disclose the full circumstances of the death. For these reasons, specialist support groups can be very helpful, so consider a referral.[3]

Be mindful that bereaved people *may* have suicidal thoughts and suicide *may* become an option in their family or peer group, as in 'I will follow you' or 'I'll reunite with you', which can be seen as distorted attachment behaviour, and even 'I'll punish you for punishing me'. This increases the risk of further suicide (Jordan 2019), which can cross generations and is learned and not inherited (Wertheimer 2001) (see also page 74).

FURTHER READING
Help is at Hand: Support after Someone May Have Died by Suicide, available at www.nhs. uk/Livewell/Suicide/Documents/Help%20is%20at%20Hand.pdf

Wertheimer, A. (2001) *A Special Scar: The Experiences of People Bereaved by Suicide* (2nd edition). Hove: Routledge.

Ambiguous loss
Where a bereaved person cannot verify the death, there is ambiguous loss, because 'a loved one is missing physically…but kept present psychologically because they might reappear' (Boss 2000, p.138). Real examples include:

- the body being so badly damaged by the death that identification is not possible, or the bereaved person being advised not to see it

- losing contact with someone when they become homeless who, when they die, cannot be identified by the authorities so has an anonymous funeral, the family only finding out later

- someone dying in prison and their body being 'lost' in the prison service's system for four months.

See pages 78 and 186.

---

3   See Survivors of Bereavement by Suicide (SoBS) www.uk-sobs.org.uk

Stigma, disenfranchised grief and lack of social support

As discussed in Chapters 4 and 5, and found by others, substance-related deaths typically stigmatise the person who died and those who are bereaved, although not everyone experiences stigma (Cartwright 2019; Feigelman *et al.* 2011). Also, there is often a continuation of stigma from before the death (Adfam 2012a; Orford *et al.* 2005). This section explains how stigma affects bereavement and creates disenfranchised grief, and the subsequent loss of social support (see Chapters 5 and 13 for why and how stigma happens).

The impact of stigma on bereavement

Stigma about substance-related bereavements adds insult to injury. Furthermore, it complicates an already difficult bereavement and typically inhibits people from seeking support (Walter *et al.* 2015). Stigma can potentially come from anyone in a person's social network, including those who would typically provide support during bereavement. When professionals and workers, including bereavement counsellors, involved in substance-related deaths stigmatise, this can have a profound, long-lasting impact on grieving, and can inhibit seeking support (Cartwright 2019; Valentine 2018).

Recognise how stigma may be explicit or implicit, intentional or unintended, and occurs through labelling, stereotyping, defining someone by their substance use, using language that excludes 'them' from 'us', and expressing emotional responses such as disgust or saying someone is better off dead (Walter and Ford 2018). Bereaved people may be shocked by stigma or, where they have lived with addictive substance use, they can anxiously anticipate it. Either way, when it happens, they can feel shame, anger, hurt and/or the urge to protect their loved one's reputation.

> I think it took five years before I could tell anybody. I could not say. I did not tell people how he had died. (Mother) (Templeton *et al.* 2016, p.7)

Also recognise that bereaved people can stigmatise themselves and their loved one (Walter and Ford 2018) (see Chapter 13). They may then project[4] their stigma on to others and perceive they are being stigmatised by them. Projections need a 'hook' on the other person to land on, which may not be intentional on their part, and therefore in reality others may or may not be stigmatising them. For some, the death contravenes their religious beliefs and is thereby stigmatised, such as someone dying through alcohol use in a Muslim family. Stigma can often define someone's identity:

---

4   Projection is a disowned part of the self that is projected, out of awareness, on to another person so they are experienced as being that disowned part (Joyce and Sills 2014).

[Substance use] defined me and my life was ruined, but it doesn't define me now. (Woman talking about the effect of counselling on her identity) (Cartwright 2019, p.28)

Stigma tends to be reinforced in the way drug deaths are discussed, managed and institutionalised in Western societies (Lloyd 2010). Often, the person who died is defined by substance use (Lawton *et al.* 2016), and this in turn devalues the way they are remembered (Doka 1989). They may no longer be spoken about, and this inhibits grieving. As the narratives people create about the life and death of a loved one are 'intimately bound up with socio-political narratives' (Guy and Holloway 2007, p.93), stigma can complicate, even contaminate, a continuing bond and how someone is remembered and memorialised (Templeton and Velleman 2018). Often, it is important to have dignity after the person's death, perhaps to counteract what is stereotyped as an undignified life (Walter and Ford 2018).

However, as discussed in Chapter 5, recognise that some bereaved people challenge stigma. They can feel resentment and anger at being stigmatised. Despite stigma posing a significant threat to a person's integrity, their memory of the person who died and their relationship to them, they can still have creative responses that rebuild their identity and form helpful continuing bonds (Valentine and Walter 2015).

Additionally, consider whether further stigmatisation is occurring. Possibilities include the person who died having a mental illness or being involved in criminal activity (Templeton *et al.* 2016); a sudden or violent death, including murder and suicide (Kristensen, Weisæth, and Heir 2012); the person having HIV/AIDS, being in debt, being involved in sex work, etc.

Therefore, potential needs you may offer support with are working through stigma and shame, developing strategies for coping with others' stigma, and finding ways to remember a loved one and form a continuing bond that are not defined by stigma (see Chapters 10 and 13).

Disenfranchised grief

As disenfranchised grief is a loss that cannot be approved socially, openly acknowledged or publicly grieved, effectively a bereaved person is denied the right to public grief and social support (Doka 2002a). This happens through others' failure to empathise with the bereaved person (Neimeyer and Jordan 2002). As many substance-related deaths are stigmatised, disenfranchised grief is common (Cartwright 2019; DrugFAM 2013; Valentine 2018) and it can happen in many ways. Possibilities to consider include the following.

Someone is perceived as not worth grieving for, especially when the death is perceived as self-inflicted (Doka 2002b) or when a bereaved person is seen as being complicit in or to blame for the death (Walter and Ford 2018). Also, the problematic aspects of substance use may be denied, particularly with alcohol as it is more socially acceptable, when someone might be seen as just 'a character' or 'a bit of a lad'. Similarly, those who do not stigmatise may still disenfranchise by withdrawing from a bereaved person through their uncertainty about how to respond to an unusual, emotive and difficult death (Jordan 2019).

You need to be aware that support services can disenfranchise if they do not recognise and work with the substance-related aspects of bereavement (Cartwright 2019):

> I needed to go into my depression and anger about the paedophile who'd abused my son [and was the cause of his drug use] but she avoided difficult stuff. (Mother talking about her counsellor) (Cartwright 2019, p.27)

Bereaved people may disenfranchise themselves: self-censor what they say, believe they are unworthy of support or even deserve to be punished (Kauffman 2002b), or believe the person who died is unworthy of grief (Guy 2004).

> I think the biggest thing with the way [our son] died was we didn't really feel entitled to grieve. Nobody said I couldn't…I felt that people felt, well, he was doing drugs. What are they upset about? (Parent) (Templeton and Velleman 2018, p.33)

In addition, any bereavement can become disenfranchised. Death can be taboo; others do not know what to say or over time assume grieving is over; or make well-meaning comments like 'Your poor mother, how's she coping?' and unintentionally disenfranchise the person being spoken to, etc.

Note that at as a result of being disenfranchised, grief is not expressed, so it may be intensified or repressed, elicit anger and guilt, complicate grieving and/or exclude people from social support and rituals (Parkes and Prigerson 2010). Indeed, being disenfranchised can intensify isolation at the time support is most needed (Adfam 2011a; Lawton *et al.* 2016). Additionally, it inhibits engaging with others to perform the many tasks needed after the death (Walter *et al.* 2015); can create a dilemma about revealing what happened and risking stigmatisation, or concealing it and losing support (Chaudoir and Fisher 2010); and may elicit self-attack and shame, which inhibit grieving (Feigelman *et al.* 2011). It may take years, if ever, to fully reveal what happened.

Lack of support
Recognise that as a result of being stigmatised and their grief disenfranchised, people often lack support. Although family and friends can be supportive,

something especially valued by bereaved women, they often struggle to comprehend the nature of a substance-related bereavement. Workplaces are often unsupportive, particularly people's managers, and can be less supportive of those bereaved through a drug- as opposed to an alcohol-related death (Cartwright 2019).

> My colleagues [doctors and nurses] were less than helpful and lacked empathy, that was surprising. (Mother) (Cartwright 2019, p.28)

Traumatic losses 'may elicit fear, dread, and a sense of impending danger that "it could have happened to us, too"' (Feigelman, Gorman and Jordan 2009, p.606) in the social network of those bereaved. Also, there are no clear-cut social norms for such bereavements and often people do not know how to support a traumatised person. In turn, bereaved people can assume that others are condemning them, act in ways that inadvertently elicit avoidance and rejection from their network, and experience 'harmful responses and strained relations' (p.591) with others in their network.

Doka (2002b) proposes that disenfranchised people can be enfranchised by being with others who are similarly bereaved. Specialist group support can be very helpful for people bereaved through substance use (Adfam 2011a; Cartwright 2019; Valentine 2018), such as groups for those bereaved through substance use or for bereaved parents:

> Meeting other bereaved parents was critical, they know how you feel. (Father) (Cartwright 2019, p.27)

However, be mindful that for some people group support may not be helpful (Cartwright 2019; Ford et al. 2018) – for example, being the only person who is gay. Some support groups for people whose lives are affected by someone else's substance use can find it too difficult to include a member whose loved one has died, because this represents the worst fears of other members. Bereavement support groups may produce a 'them and us' perspective that can hinder members' reintegration into society (Vlasto 2010), especially when they are traumatised (van der Kolk 2014). Also, few may find help from online communities (Walter and Ford 2018), although the anonymity of these helps people who fear stigma or discrimination.

Coping with specific difficulties

There are specific difficulties that people bereaved through a substance-related death can encounter that are often unfamiliar and may be unexpected, and these affect their grieving. These difficulties centre around the personal, their kinship relationship to the person who died, and/or official procedures and possible media intrusion. You need to recognise and offer to work with these difficulties, including developing someone's self- and social support to cope with them.

> [Counsellor] suggested helpful things…helped me quite a lot with coping with the demands of bereavement. (Mother) (Cartwright 2019, p.28)

Personal difficulties

Where there was difficult substance-using behaviour before the death, people typically start bereavement in a depleted state and have poor social support (Cartwright 2019) (see above and Chapter 4). This may include being traumatised and/or depressed. Lacking social support, psychological resilience and effective self-support increases the risk of trauma (Agaibi and Wilson 2005).

People differ hugely over whether to see the body and the impact of doing so on grieving. Some may feel relieved to see a loved one at peace, ensure they are being cared for, say goodbye, etc., and this can help them accept the death. Conversely, it may be distressing and even traumatic, especially if the body is damaged by a violent death or post-mortem (Pearlman *et al.* 2014). Therefore, people need to be informed about the condition of the body, time to consider and then choose whether to see it (Chapple and Ziebland 2010). Where the death was sudden, unexpected and traumatic, people typically benefit from viewing the body (even if it is badly damaged), have better outcomes to grief and are less likely to regret this decision (Chapple and Ziebland 2010). Occasionally, it is not possible to see the body, in which case it is important to establish the reason for this:

> They kept the body for eight weeks…and we couldn't see her because of decomposing circumstances… I phoned them every day for eight weeks and they said 'No, I'm sorry'. (Mother) (Templeton and Velleman 2018, p.31)

Be mindful of how substance-related bereavements are often unexpectedly severe, complex and long-lasting; that can be frightening, disorientating and distressing (Cartwright 2019). This easily contradicts someone's assumptions about bereavement, as well as potentially contradicting the assumptions of others around them, including you! This can include needing to return to work before being ready and not feeling supported at work (Cartwright 2019). There is a loss of normality. Over the longer term, look out for a greater risk of depression, a lower quality of life, relationships being conflicted and unsatisfying, feeling lonely and having difficulty in trusting others again, and being less likely to be in paid work. These are often normal and not necessarily a sign of poor coping, although still consider the possibility of problematic grief (see 'Complexities and difficulties in grieving' in Chapter 1).

Additionally, traumatic deaths can unexpectedly affect someone's whole family, so consider how this may negatively affect their grieving. Possibilities include worry about upsetting other members, clinging to each other and fear of further deaths, or, conversely, blaming and scapegoating, disrupted family roles and routines, loss of family cohesion and mutual support, and even family break down, as well as a collective narrative forming, such as 'our family is cursed' (Jordan 2019). Many of these characteristics often predate the death where the family was affected by addictive substance-using behaviour (see Chapter 4).

Also, consider how a substance-related death can result in practical difficulties (Adfam 2011a), especially when sudden and not prepared for. This can include poverty, legal and housing problems, and debts resulting from substance use (Ross 1996). These difficulties may make it difficult to pay for the funeral.[5] Some practical difficulties are life-changing and long-lasting, such as parents taking on parental responsibility for their grandchildren following the death of their adult child, facing significant financial and legal difficulties, and seldom receiving the support they need from statutory services (Adfam 2011b). There is a corresponding need for practical help, as having such difficulties while grieving tends to lead to poorer overall adjustment to bereavement (Parkes and Prigerson 2010).

Furthermore, substance-related bereavements present a particular challenge for people in treatment for or in recovery from their own substance use (see Chapter 16).

Difficulties through the kinship relationship with the person who died

The kinship relationship is one of the determinants of grief in all bereavements and also can have particular substance-related characteristics (see Chapters 1, 4 and 5). Both are briefly discussed below and need considering when thinking about a bereaved person.

Parents who lose a child through any kind of death have particularly long-lasting and distressing grief, associated with increased risk to mental and physical health, especially depression (Hindmarch 2009; Parkes and Prigerson 2010), and can be *the* most difficult bereavement (Riches and Dawson 2000). The death goes against the natural order of life and breaks the family line, and a parent can believe they are the one who should have died. Parents lose the part of their identity tied up in parenting, as well as their hopes for their offspring's future. Their grieving negatively affects relationships with any other children,

---

5   See www.gov.uk/funeral-payments for the Funeral Expenses Payment for those on certain state benefits.

who they may become overly protective of, which then adds to their distress and guilt.

Parents typically perceive they failed to protect their child, and therefore feel profound and intense pain, yearning, guilt, helplessness and anxiety about their child's wellbeing. Many have a 'more or less permanent state of yearning for their child that is relatively immune to diminution over time' (Kosminsky and Jordan 2016, p.78). This urge to provide attachment and caregiving stays activated long after the death and the 'gradual deactivation of it is a central component of the [parent's] grieving process' (p.80).

Although both parents have considerable distress, mothers tend to be at greater risk of a poorer outcome of bereavement as 'the loss seems to create a permanent vacuum in their lives' (Cleiren 1993, p.253). Marriages may experience conflict as both partners try to find their own ways of coping with overwhelming grief (Hindmarch 2009).

Regarding their continuing bond, 'the end of grief is not severing the bond with the dead child, but integrating the child into the parent's life and into the parent's social networks in a different way than when the child was alive' (Klass et al. 1996, p.199). This wise and desirable outcome can be problematic for parents who are stigmatised, disenfranchised and even blamed for the death. There is often greater stigma and less compassion in society for these parents compared with other child deaths (Feigelman et al. 2011). Additionally, parents can feel more guilt than other family members (Cartwright 2019).

> The death of a child changes one's life as profoundly as their birth and we can never be the person we once were. (Mother of son) (Lawton et al. 2016, p.48)

Adult children often find the loss of their mother harder than that of their father (Parkes and Prigerson 2010). They usually experience deep ambivalence towards a parent who used substances addictively. Alongside losing them, there are often long-term problems in attachment and lack of nurturing. The death means losing hope of ever having these, and they are less likely to have positive memories than other family members. They can perceive they failed to save their parent and feel guilty, especially if caring for their parent was a childhood role.

Partners' difficulties during bereavement may include loneliness, guilt, reflecting on their choice of partner, balancing grieving with raising any children, grieving for their children's loss of a parent, and difficulties with their partner's family:

> [B]ut his family refused to believe that he had a problem, absolutely refused to believe it. So I found that very difficult doing it all on my own. (Wife) (Templeton and Velleman 2018, p.21)

Husbands are at more risk of poorer outcomes of bereavement than wives (Cleiren 1993).

Siblings' grief is often not recognised by society and is therefore disenfranchised (Wertheimer 2001). They can conceal their grief to care for others, especially their parents; they can feel the need to reassure them that they were good parents. However, by concealing their grief, their parents may not see they need support and they may be frightened by their parents' deep distress. A twin is particularly vulnerable to a poor outcome of bereavement (Parkes and Prigerson 2010). As sisters can have a greater sense of connection and feel more responsible for their sibling who died, they can have poorer outcomes to grief than brothers (Cleiren 1993). Conversely, siblings often understand substance-using behaviour before their parents and feel resentful about the extra attention their sibling received, which can continue as their parents grieve.

Grandparents often grieve for their adult child who has lost a child as well as for their grandchild. Although bereavement seems to get easier with age, the death breaks the family line, it occurs when they are also probably losing their peers, and older people are often at greater risk of depression and social isolation during grieving (Parkes and Prigerson 2010).

Friends' and extended family's grief is often disenfranchised. They and others can perceive their grief as less significant than that of blood relatives, although they can still have a major bereavement. However, they are unlikely to be involved in official procedures and experience the associated stress and distress.

Additionally, traumatic distress is generally highest in the immediate family, followed by friends and then extended family (Holland and Neimeyer 2011); this is mirrored in post-traumatic growth that may occur after a trauma (Armstrong and Shakespeare-Finch 2011) (see Chapters 11 and 17).

Substance-related stigma tends to be more dominant for parents, partners and children than for others (Templeton *et al.* 2018a), and may be due to their stronger attachment and perceived responsibility for what happened.

Difficulties with official procedures and media intrusion

Official procedures can happen after a substance-related death, and there may also be media intrusion. Deaths that are sudden and unexpected, often in unexplained or suspicious circumstances, usually lead to official procedures. This tends to occur more with drug deaths as alcohol deaths are often expected and explained after prolonged deteriorating health.

It is impractical to cover all official procedures here. They may include the emergency services, hospital, a police investigation of where the death occurred (which may be a bereaved person's home), a post-mortem, an inquest and, where there are criminal charges, a court case, as well as the usual registering of the death and a funeral. Typically, the whole process takes many months and it may be years before everything is completed. This can delay the funeral, and delay and prolong grieving.

These typically create unintended difficulties for bereaved people, so you need to recognise and consider their potential impact.

As described in Chapter 5, bereaved people have to navigate this complex and fragmented system, and frequently encounter stereotyped, insensitive and stigmatising treatment in public settings. This system is often unfamiliar, daunting, confusing and time-consuming, and often navigated with inadequate support and information. Although they may be treated with sensitivity and kindness, have their wishes taken into account and be able to complain or lodge an appeal, ultimately they are caught up in procedures beyond their control. This is typically stressful, distressing and intrusive, and seems to take precedence over who their loved one was and their grief. There is often much frustration, anger and hurt about officials and their procedures, as well as towards the person who died for these consequences of their death.

Be mindful that the outcome of official procedures is very important for grieving. Commonly, public accounts of the death influence the meaning bereaved people make of the person who died and the death (Walter 2005). It can be a considerable relief and legitimise someone's narrative of what happened (Valentine and Templeton 2018), as well as providing answers, useful new information and a sense of resolution and justice. Conversely, it can undermine people's narrative, causing distress, anger and shame (Valentine and Templeton 2018), be hardly recognisable to them (Guy and Holloway 2007), and may be more distressing than expected.

Unfortunately, as outcomes are rarely definitive and may raise further questions, this adds to unfinished business. Typically, all this provokes anger, a sense of injustice and a heightened desire for revenge, and an increased risk of depression and anxiety. In turn, this can set back grieving (Pearlman *et al.* 2014).

> The Coroner started summing up and I [wanted to ask a question but]…he said that is outside the remit of this Court… I thought inquest means having the answers… I mean you might have more realistic expectations, but it's partly because I didn't get given any information. (Mother) (Templeton and Velleman 2018, p.34)

People therefore need information about official procedures, need to develop their self- and social support, and work through any unfinished business and associated emotions.

Possible media intrusion

Media coverage mostly happens in local newspapers and associated websites. It is more likely for drug deaths, and is often uninformed, sensationalised, stigmatising and insensitive (Adfam 2011; DrugFAM 2013; Guy 2004). There can be repeated coverage, which often occurs at particularly difficult times – typically when the death happened and again at the inquest. Bereaved people are typically distressed, angered and shamed, and lose their privacy. They can often find it better to work with the media and attempt to influence any coverage (Valentine 2018).

> [I said] 'I am not wanting to speak to the papers…it's a private matter and all the rest of it'… [T]hey said well you've got two choices, you either talk to us or you don't talk to us, we are writing something about it whether you like it or not. So my wife and I made a decision there and then to speak to the newspapers or at least try and control it somehow. (Father) (Templeton *et al.* 2016, p.6)

INFORMATION ON OFFICIAL PROCESSES IN ENGLAND AND WALES
Booklet on coroners and inquests:
www.gov.uk/government/uploads/system/uploads/attachment_data/file/363879/guide-to-coroner-service.pdf

Inquest, a charity providing expertise on state-related deaths and their investigation:
www.inquest.org.uk

Guidelines for those whose work brings them into contact with adults after a drug- or alcohol-related death:
www.bath.ac.uk/publications/bereaved-through-substance-use

For a death abroad:
www.gov.uk/government/collections/death-abroad-bereavement-packs

Media guidelines for reporting suicide deaths (many of which also apply to substance-related deaths):
www.samaritans.org/about-samaritans/media-guidelines

Part 2

How to Support Someone Bereaved Through a Substance-Related Death

7

Key Considerations

This chapter covers key considerations for supporting clients bereaved through a substance-related death, and includes:

- a summary of the research conducted for this book.

These clients often experience stigma, their grief is typically disenfranchised, and if they belong to particular social subgroups, they may experience further discrimination. Therefore, a key consideration for supporting these clients is working to promote equality:

- This chapter includes good-practice ideas for working with clients who are stigmatised and disenfranchised by a substance-related death.

- Carmen Joanne Ablack shares her experience of working with clients who belong to one or more social subgroups that can experience discrimination.

Next, consideration is given to key areas of practice:

- informing yourself about substances

- the need to educate clients and to offer them interpretations of their experiences, and how to do so ethically

- 'grounding' an overwhelmed or traumatised client

- seeing a client within the context of their family

- working with 'endings' in bereavement support.

The chapter ends by:

- introducing three fictitious clients used to illustrate the ideas in Part 2.

Research summary

The research I undertook for this book investigated how helpful counselling was for people bereaved through a substance-related death, and is referred to throughout the book (Cartwright 2019). The key findings, conclusions and recommendations were as follows.

The participants' bereavement-related needs were many and varied, and changed over time. Participants used many types of support to meet these needs and included one-to-one counselling provided by bereavement services, specialist helplines, their workplace and private counselling; and specialised group support for substance-related bereavements, for bereaved parents and for those affected by someone else's substance use. All participants had one-to-one support and over half also had group support. Group support was rated slightly more helpful than one-to-one counselling, with participants valuing being with others who had a similar loss because of the bond, mutual support and normalising[1] effect.

Participants valued being offered help to take up referrals, especially when the death had been unexpected. Also, they valued starting counselling when needed.

> My GP freaked out…said 'take this and call Cruse' [but the participant was too bereft to call]. (Half-sister bereaved by her half-brother's death through substance use) (Cartwright 2019, p.25)

Participants found long-term counselling the most helpful, although medium- and even short-term work could still be helpful, and support did not need to be continuous. Support with the general aspects of grief was helpful and, unsurprisingly, services specialising in substance-related bereavements were rated most helpful. However, significant needs associated with the five substance-related characteristics of these bereavements, described in Chapter 6, were often not recognised or worked through. For example, feeling guilty is a need to work on guilt, and misunderstanding addiction is a need to understand it better. Although most participants had these needs, their counsellors seemingly seldom recognised them. This implies that counsellors need to be informed about and know how to work with the particular characteristics/needs of these bereavements. When these needs *were* met, it was very helpful:

> See the bigger patterns than me, see the wood for the trees [which helped to reduce guilt]. (Father of son) (Cartwright 2019, unpublished data)

---

1   To normalise is validating, legitimising and humanising an experience that is normal for someone in a client's situation, while not inadvertently minimising it. This helps them make sense and breaks down stigma and isolation.

Unhelpful experiences of one-to-one counselling occurred through counsellors' apparent lack of knowledge or experience of working with bereavement in general and with substance-related bereavements in particular. Also, there was poor practice associated with the therapeutic frame,[2] such as cancellations, breaks and endings handled in distressing ways. Unhelpful group experiences involved other group members and included stigmatising comments, being inhibited as a result of being the only partner in a group of parents, joining too soon to be able to cope with hearing others' experiences, and participants unhelpfully comparing their progress with other group members.

Some participants prematurely disengaged from support. This was often for a combination of reasons, including a perceived lack of empathy or warmth from their counsellor; poor counselling practice as described above; practical difficulties, such as the location or timing; and especially perceived stigma from their counsellor or other group members. Participants did not report explicit stigmatisation from their counsellor; rather, they experienced it as inauthenticity or sensed judgement.

> I felt subtly judged; nothing was said, just that he didn't approve and was shocked. (Man who used drugs with his male partner who died) (Cartwright 2019, p.27)

In such a small study it is unclear how far the findings and conclusions about subgroups of participants can be generalised. The indication was that those participants who were from black and minority ethnic groups (BAME), as well as those who had experienced a drug- as opposed to alcohol-related death, experienced more stigma outside of counselling.

The research made the following recommendations:

1. Be informed about these bereavements.

2. Refer clients to other services, including local, national and the internet; suggest they consider what could help now and what could be for the future; and offer to help them take up referrals.

3. Consider allowing access to counselling when needed (not a set time after the death) and provide it for longer (it does not have to be continuous).

4. Consider counselling practice, both one-to-one and groups, particularly regarding stigma and the therapeutic frame.

5. Service providers consider having a counsellor who specialises in substance-related bereavements.

---

2   The therapeutic frame (Gray 1994) is 'how the work will be conducted' (p.6) and covers setting, times and duration, cancellations, breaks, fee, confidentiality, etc.

6. Recognise the needs in the five interconnected substance-related characteristics that potentially affect such bereavements and offer to work with these needs:

   • Make sense of substance use, especially addictive use.

   • Work through unresolved difficulties from the past, including any guilt and anger.

   • Work through difficulties associated with the death, including any blame, guilt, confusion and trauma.

   • Build social and self-support to cope with stigma and other specific difficulties.

7. Consider both the understanding of and how to work with difference and diversity:

   • Disenfranchised bereavements and associated shame.

   • How different relationships to the person who died affect the nature of bereavement.

   • Recognise both gender, sexuality and relationship diversity (GSRD) and BAME as umbrella terms for many different minority groups that may have different needs, not least in bereavement.

   • Consider how to counsel clients from these 'minority' groups if you are from the 'majority' group.

8. Group counsellors consider clients' readiness to join a group, and how to manage the stigma and comparison that may occur between group members.

9. Supervisors need to consider how best to supervise counsellors working with these clients.

This book aims to meet these recommendations.

Good-practice ideas for working with substance-related stigma and disenfranchised bereavement

Clients are aware of others' stigma about aspects of their bereavement. Therefore, they may 'test' you to see if you are safe. If they perceive stigma, whether intended or not, they could easily disengage (Cartwright 2019). Clients can project stigma on to other people (see page 113). As projections need a 'hook' on the other person to land on, you need to be aware of your hooks (which can be unintentional), such as appearing inauthentic, showing poor empathy or lacking emotional warmth; saying nothing can feel as stigmatising as saying the wrong thing. Also, clients are often not aware of feeling shame, probably would not say if they were, and can easily withdraw when feeling ashamed (see Chapter 13).

You need to earn these clients' trust and confidence, and your support has to create an accepting and enfranchising environment – one where they can truly be themselves and still feel that they can 'belong' with you. Put in terms of attachment theory, you need to provide a 'secure base'.

Normal good practice

- Use your empathy and validate a client's experience, as disenfranchisement occurs through empathic failure (Neimeyer and Jordan 2002).

- Create safety and trust through an effective therapeutic frame, e.g. confidentiality.

- Embody the core conditions of empathy, because clients can feel misunderstood; be non-judgemental, because they can feel judged; and convey both in an authentic way to your client (Mearns *et al.* 2013). Do not try too hard, because this can be perceived as being inauthentic.

- Show your humanity through warmth, kindness and compassion. These are necessary for effectively supporting people bereaved through a substance-related death (Cartwright 2019; Walter *et al.* 2015). Counsellors who lack these characteristics are typically experienced as unhelpful by any client (Browne 2008), and can cause these bereaved clients to prematurely disengage from support (Cartwright 2019).

Managing your risk of stigmatising and disenfranchising a client

Be aware of your assumptions and judgements about substance use and any other potentially stigmatising or disenfranchising aspects of your client's experience, as these are also potential hooks for their projections:

- Consider 'What do they represent for me?' Be honest and curious about any assumptions or judgements and the potential influence they could have on your work. Be aware of these and interrupt them in your work. This is usually more helpful than thinking 'I treat everyone the same' or 'I shouldn't think like that'.

- Consider 'What am I likely to represent to this client?' and whether they see you as understanding and safe enough.

Language

The language used with clients can perpetuate stigma, even among highly trained mental health professionals (Kelly and Westerhoff 2010). For example, someone with anorexia 'has an eating disorder', so is not a 'food abuser', whereas someone with a substance-related condition 'is a substance abuser', not 'has a substance use disorder'. The former happens to have an illness, whereas the latter is defined by their abusing behaviour, a difference that implies 'us' and 'other' (see page 222). Therefore, language can disenfranchise clients, whether intentional or not.

Your client

Use their name obviously. Use their way of describing themselves, unless it is potentially stigmatising or disenfranchising:

- Avoid the terms 'co-dependent'[3] or 'enabler'.[4] These have effectively become labels for people whose lives are affected by someone else's substance use. They are often experienced as stigmatising, as blaming for someone else's addiction, and imply a fixed aspect of who someone is that cannot be changed, rather than a behaviour that can be made sense of and changed.

- Avoid using 'carer', a term often used in the substance treatment sector for all people who are affected by someone else's substance use. Some clients will not have been carers for the deceased, so using this term can evoke guilt. Those who *were* carers may not see themselves as such; they may have felt coerced into it and are often ambivalent about this role, typically both doing it and resenting it. Carer implies a particular way of supporting another person (such as someone terminally ill) that is often inappropriate for supporting someone who is addicted. Many people who cared for someone who used substances did not get the

---

3   Co-dependent refers to someone who is in a relationship where they help another who is in difficulty, often for personal gain, such as feeling esteem or control, but 'help' in ways that inadvertently assists substance use. Therefore, both people are dependent on each other. This term has been popularised through self-help books (Beattie 1992) and 12-step fellowships such as Co-Dependents Anonymous, Al-Anon and Families Anonymous, which some find helpful.

4   Enabler refers to someone who enables another person's substance use by providing them with the means to sustain their use, e.g. giving money.

formal recognition and support that many other carers do. Also, the term implies that someone exists to meet the needs of the person they care for and not as a whole human being, with needs of their own.

- Avoid referring to them as a 'family member' or 'affected family member'. These imply they are defined by their relationship to the person who used substances and not as a whole human being. Also, some clients may not see themselves as a member of the family.

These are important because many people who have been affected by a loved one's long-term substance use *do* lose their own identity.

A client's loved one who died

- Use their name, or relationship such as child or partner, and see them as a whole, unique person. Avoid formal terms like 'the deceased'.

- Refer to them as having 'had a substance-related condition' (if relevant), and to all who use as 'people who use drugs or alcohol'. This avoids 'user', 'alcoholic' or 'addict', because these make them 'other' than the rest of us and define them by a behaviour that stigmatises and dehumanises them.

- Use 'abstinent' for not using substances. Avoid using 'clean' because it implies they were dirty when using, and is stigmatising.

- If they died by suicide, avoid using 'committed suicide'. This was the old term used for committing the crime of suicide, and is offensive and stigmatising.

Meeting across your differences

- Consider 'How can I work across our differences?' Say that experiences of stigma, disenfranchisement or being different can be part of your work together, e.g. towards the end of the first session, in a low-key and matter-of-fact sort of way, to allow space for a client to respond if they wish.

- Be mindful that many differences may not be visible.

- Validate your client's experience. Be open to what being stigmatised, disenfranchised or different means to them, because they may not follow the assumed norms of their group(s).

- Briefly research aspects of a client's experiences, while remembering they are a unique, whole human being.

- Explore other opportunities for a client to share grief and build social support. Specialist groups can be helpful (Cartwright 2019).

- Self-disclosure. People affected by substance use often ask those supporting them if they have been similarly affected, so you need to prepare what to say. The rule of thumb is not to share your own experiences, because a client may think that your experience is what will happen to them or they may feel the need to care for you – that takes the attention away from them. However, there can be a time when you consider it is helpful for a particular client, and offer to share a personal experience of substance use and/or bereavement. You can mitigate against the pitfalls described above by saying that you are not implying their experience will be like yours, that it is in the past and you are okay now, and then bringing attention back to them, e.g. asking about their response to what you shared. Appropriate, well-timed self-disclosure can create safety and trust.

- See Chapter 13 for working on shame and stigma.

Next, particular consideration is given to working with clients at further risk of stigmatisation and discrimination through being from certain social subgroups.

'Who am I, now they are gone?' Considering identity, culture and context

Section by Carmen Joanne Ablack

Here, I offer understanding several ways in which particular groups dealing with bereavement through substance use can be considered, how clients from these groups may think about themselves, and how you can support them to consider their identity in the face of bereavement. This is based on my decades of experience as a psychotherapist, trainer and supervisor, as well as on experiences of colleagues (much of which is not yet in the literature).

The multiple contexts of the person who died and those bereaved have a profound impact on grieving that involves social, cultural, familial, economic, mental and emotional circumstances. Our multiple contexts affect our sense of identity, provoking a questioning of 'Who am I now?' after a profound loss, and re-evaluating and re-forming our sense of self. For an example of this, see the vignette below. Bereavement generally can lead to self-questioning: 'Who am I now?' and 'Who and how do I want to be going forward?' Such questioning seems to be amplified when facing loss through substance use, potentially leading to deep changes in life and life direction, and leading to re-forming of identity and purpose for the bereaved.

This re-forming is a unique, ongoing and delicate process for clients and for others in their lives. How counsellors hold, understand and work with clients is central to reducing any anger, hurt, shame or trauma that arises because of mishandling of clients' bereavement experiences. Shame-based responses can arise from society's views on substance misuse, judgements about the deceased or the bereaved or about their relationship. Excessive levels of anxiety, problems with processing information or 'finding one's voice' and having lowered self-esteem (as well as feelings of guilt and inadequacy) can happen. A lack of being met with good enough care or understanding can be complex for clients and have a deep effect on their ability to function. They can become traumatically affected (psychologically, emotionally and sometimes physiologically unwell) by their experiences post-death.

Processes of re-formation of identity can be profoundly influenced when the bereaved or the deceased are part of a group that is not in the majority, as I describe next.

Differences, diversity and intersectionality

'Differences' and 'diversity' refer to all groups of people, not only race or ethnicity. They include social class, age, sexuality, disability, etc., and people who identify as being affected by problematic substance use. When thinking about differences and diversity, we are dealing with the *multiplicity of a client's identities and experiences*, and their intersectionality – an interconnected nature of social categorisations of an individual or group, typically creating overlapping and interdependent systems of discrimination or disadvantage.

These identities and experiences influence someone's unique ways of grieving and how they approach re-forming their identity. Clients need to experience being supported to find their own 'voice' in culturally and personally congruent ways in your work together; this includes how they 'listen to' and think about themselves in their grief, pay attention to how they might shame themselves, and how they may feel shamed by internalising others' perceptions and actions in relation to how they 'should' be.

People in socially excluded populations are less likely to receive good access to care and support, often made worse by social stigmatisation of substance use (see page 222). When it comes to majority cultures and minorities, there is a risk of counsellors' unconscious biases getting in the way.

Dave

At a time when the stigma attached to an HIV-positive status was overwhelming and unbearable, a client talked about the loss of a friend to a drug overdose taken because of his AIDS-related illness. The friend saw taking his life as his only option. Those left behind were impacted deeply by assumptions made about the death, and my client experienced a range of different 'senses of self' as he coped with changing feelings in response to their loss and to unconscious biases and prejudices they faced from others, including professionals. These profound processes of re-evaluation and re-forming his identity involved us reflecting together on the whole experience, including bodily, emotional and cognitive processes. We paid specific attention to the context of the client's identities (white, gay, middle class and British) and those of his friend (black, gay, working class and American). This raised issues of shame to do with internalised beliefs about his identity and later also his anger at how they were met or not met by others for who they were.

By working with awareness of my client's intersectional context, I was able to support him to appreciate his multiplicity of existence. I helped him move from a weak sense of intersectional existence, where the situation and contexts surrounding the death had the effect of marginalising and shaming, to one where he found a position of greater understanding about how he was impacted, having a greater sense of complexity of self and his place in the world. He could make sense of his shame (and, later, anger) in the context of shock, bereavement and when he felt vulnerable to his internalisation of others' judgements of his community. Anger played an important role in my client's development, especially when supported to harness this energy, helping him to notice and think about what he wanted now for his life. When supported to be present and expressed, his anger became an important vehicle for transformation, allowing him to find his way to accept what happened and incorporate this into his sense of self, going forward.

It is my responsibility to invite and undertake these difference, diversity and intersectional dialogues with my clients, and to make invitational spaces for them in our work together.

General considerations for working with differences and diversity

Use what works for you, adapt what seems needed and ignore what does not 'speak' to you or your client. I assume you work in a therapeutic setting and have appropriate training and supervision to work in alliance with your client.

Facilitated reflective spaces are a necessary part of ensuring our work with bereaved clients is well held.

Some groups are more identifiable than others and evoke more emotive responses from wider society. For example, being Muslim has a high profile at present, but others are more hidden and easily missed. For example, social class is often not acknowledged or recognised. Some differences can more easily be seen, such as race, and unseen, such as being from a minority GSRD group. Clients may choose to reveal or conceal parts of their identity (e.g. a black woman who is also bisexual) and commonly may risk-assess their counsellor before disclosing less easily identifiable aspects of themselves.

Differences in conceptualisations of death and bereavement are important across all populations. Religious, spiritual, community and/or cultural heritage dimensions, such as national/geographical origin, religious background or origin of family, need to be explored with sensitivity and openness to dialogue.

Differences between minority and majority ethnic groups can affect perceptions of anyone belonging or seeming to belong to the group in question. For example, praying at home regularly and in workplaces is generally seen as more common for Muslim groups and less so for Christian groups. How behaviour is conceptualised and how groups or communities understand and manage death are important considerations, such as collective understanding by a group of the psychological 'need' for self-medication (see page 53) through substance use by some members.

When someone identifies with a group that is 'different' from the majority, it can typically form a more significant part of their identity than for those from the majority. There is a risk of our pathologising in thoughts and deeds what is actually culturally consistent with our clients' identities. Also, we may have fantasies about other groups, based on previous negative and prejudicial experiences, including who 'they' are and who 'they' are not. We need to be willing to be vulnerable enough to ask for guidance without making this a responsibility for our client.

Appreciating dynamics of perceived and real power and influence that clients from each group have is a vital part of understanding intersectional effect. The prevalence of life stressors for minorities in all sectors of life needs to be part of our awareness, and is part of the intersectional awareness needed for this work. Also, be aware that family, community systems and institutions in the wider community may have a significant role to play in this.

We may hide behind interpretations and definitions of a client's behaviour when we remain unaware of how affected we are by the relationship and processes in the room, and also in response to not understanding enough about a group (which is often a clue to our own shame-based actions and attitudes).

We need to guard against what I term 'complexity effect blocking' – that is, the more there are perceptions of complexity of identity, needs or differences, the more this becomes a barrier to full engagement with our client. Complexity effect blocking by healthcare professionals is reported by BAME people in therapy sessions. It happens through attitudes, that imply 'you are/your situation is too complicated' or 'too different to my experience' for me to try to understand. Clients can experience this as 'I'm too difficult for you to take the time to consider my needs fully', thereby reinforcing perceptions of unfairness or inequity, and this is potentially re-traumatising. Preventing this requires us to think and act with contextual awareness, such as:

- Am I acknowledging the loss suffered and legitimising any pain that is experienced, whether *I* can see this or not?

- Am I willing to say I do not know what my client needs and ask them how they would like to be supported?

- Do I take the opportunity to check my understanding of what they are experiencing and are saying by both their words and their actions?

Paying attention to cultural differences during times of bereavement, seeing and naming possible related complicating elements and affirming clients' abilities to cope are important skills for you to develop (Laurie and Neimeyer 2008).

Consider how you can support a client to protect themselves from others' unintentional and possibly intentional judgements about their bereavement, and to exercise their right to grieve and have a voice in what happens with their dead loved one that is respectful of their cultural, heritage, religious, spiritual and other needs. Also consider where they may get additional specialist support, including helplines, peer support and therapy organisations such as Pink Therapy and the Black, African and Asian Therapy Network (BAATN).

A one-size-fits-all approach to working with difference is not effective. I describe next some ideas for working with three groups to further illustrate how to work with difference and diversity.

Gender, sexual and relationship diversity (GSRD)

When working with clients who identify as minority GSRD, attention needs to be paid to likely barriers and stressors specific to their group(s). Discrimination will be experienced differently within different groupings. Despite recent equality legislation for many minority GSRD people (such as gay marriage), there potentially remain some additional legal and financial hurdles during bereavement, as well as potential discrimination from healthcare professionals, police and others at the time of the death (see Chapter 6). Also, for clients from some cultural and religious groups, there can be the added burden of not having disclosed their true identity/relationship to the person who died, particularly if it was a sudden death and not prepared for. These kinds of experiences need to be part of our work. Consider:

- What was the quality of and access to healthcare for the person who died?

- What is the quality of and access to social support available to your client?

- Are there stigmas attached by others to the person who died and/or those bereaved? How can you moderate these? Where might you look to get better understanding of how this group can be affected?

- Is the intimate relationship a client had with the person who died known by their family, employer, etc.? Are they, and their friends, included in rituals and ceremonies associated with the death?

- How will you ensure you challenge any heteronormative[5] assumptions, without making your need for knowledge an added burden for your client?

It is important that we acquire holistic understandings and approaches to models of what a family can be, and do not limit understanding to heteronormative models (Bristowe, Marshall and Harding 2016).

Neurodiversity[6]

Sometimes people who are intellectually different or have learning disabilities (i.e. neurodiverse) are discriminated against when their sense of loss and grief is not recognised or acknowledged. Hence, previous deaths may not have been appreciated by others and grieved for effectively. Neurodiversity can be 'hidden', so we can be unaware of this aspect of our clients. People with learning and cognitive challenges do not need to have full knowledge of the concept of death to understand an important person in their life is no longer present. Whatever the views held about the individual's capacity to engage, attempts need to be made to include them in counselling, and funerals and other rituals, thereby allowing acknowledgement and validation of their loss and grieving.

---

5   Heteronormativity is a view that sees heterosexuality as a more normal or preferred sexual orientation.

6   People who are neurodiverse may be more vulnerable to addictive substance use (see page 58) and there is a research study linking the genes for different neurodiversities (Poelmans 2011). Therefore, there may be a greater likelihood of supporting a bereaved person who is neurodiverse.

Try to find ways to think about a range of awareness of death, loss and its meaning, from sensing loss and accompanying feelings, by seeing death and life as alternating, or realising death is final and irreversible in nature, to more abstract ideas about life and death.

Neurodiverse bereaved people also have feelings that are existential; their experiences can be varied and are often complex in nature. Be aware that time, space and routine should remain part of their care, including a continuity of forms of support, when they move to other environments (home, day care, new home, etc.), including consistent messages in new or different environments.

Be aware of challenges a client faces and potential frustrations in their daily life (such as cognitive, communication and learning experiences) that you will need to take into account. They may have reactions of fear, anxiety, frustration and anger regarding their loss and their changed circumstances – for example, where the loss is of their primary contact or carer, or where they have very limited social support networks (Gulbenkoglu 2007).

Therefore, pay attention to what I would term 'accumulating factors' of loss and grief. Where a client is in a residential setting, they may have experienced ongoing staff changes and other changes to their environment; these are compounding factors adding to their experiences of loss and affecting their sense of safety.

Culture, ethnicity, religion and heritage factors

In relation to any identity group, consideration also needs to be given to the ethnic, cultural, heritage and religious/spiritual life of both the person who has died and your client. Note the intersectional contexts and hold awareness of historic fears that some groups have about their expressions of grief when only seen through a white majority lens. For example, they may fear being described as 'histrionic', 'overemotional', or conversely as 'too stolid' for their grief to be seen as real. For many non-white groups, loss of extended family can have different meanings and significance; do not underestimate the impact of this loss.

With people who identify as Black or Asian, or other groups of colour, ethnicity and heritage, fairness and equitability in our work are achieved by paying attention to the specific needs of the individual and their socio-cultural, physical, economic and emotional contexts. This is not about treating people the same; good practice is the ability to identify and differentiate how your client, their family and community are approached and engaged with in order to take into account their particular needs. An understanding of possible secondary losses (see page 25) is also needed – for example, immigrant clients who have left behind social support systems.

Aim for an atmosphere of 'different and equal', where power is shared. As the work deepens, differences between counsellor and client become more a part of the person-to-person relationship process, rather than just what you represented to each other at the start. However, diversity and diversity of experiencing do not just go away.

FURTHER READING
Orford, J., Natera, G., Copello, A., Atkinson, C. *et al.* (2005) *Coping with Alcohol and Drug Problems: The Experiences of Family Members in Three Contrasting Cultures.* Hove: Routledge.
Parkes, C.M., Laungani, P. and Young, B. (eds) (2015) *Death and Bereavement Across Cultures* (2nd edition). London and New York, NY: Routledge.

Informing yourself about substances
In order to work effectively with the substance-related aspects of a client's bereavement, you need to know enough about the substances involved. This includes the substance(s) used by their deceased loved one, as well as potentially the substances used by a client and by other people in their life. In particular, you should learn the risks of using a substance and potential part in the death, and the potential effects on someone's functioning and behaviour, that a client could have been affected by before the death and/or a client may experience themselves during bereavement (see Chapter 16).

For alcohol and street drugs:

- FRANK – www.talktofrank.com
- Vital Info – www.vitalinfo.org.uk

For prescribed medication:

- The National Institute for Health and Clinical Excellence (NICE) guidelines for particular conditions include information on relevant medication, e.g. depression – www.nice.org.uk/guidance
- Rxisk – https://rxisk.org/drug-search
- Mind – www.mind.org.uk/information-support/drugs-and-treatments/medication/drug-names-a-z
- The British National Formulary (BNF), available at libraries and doctors' surgeries, details all prescribed medicines in the UK.

Offering to educate and interpret

Many clients bereaved through a substance-related death need to better understand aspects of their bereavement to be able to grieve more effectively. This includes making sense of what happened before the death – for example, of substance use and the associated behaviour, especially when addictive (Cartwright 2019; Valentine 2018); understand their experience of grief (Cartwright 2019); and, where relevant, making sense of particular aspects of grief, particularly trauma, shame, guilt and depression. As clients are often unaware of these needs, it may be unrealistic to expect them to work through these needs independently, and they may be unaware of how counselling can help them do so (Cartwright 2019). Therefore, be willing to raise a client's awareness of these needs, and offer to educate them and/or interpret aspects of their experience. This book aims to provide what you need to do this.

Although education is helpful for bereaved people (Simonsen and Cooper 2015) and clients cannot be expected to make complex psychological interpretations of their own experiences, counsellors are implicitly present in any information they give to clients. Hence educating and interpreting risks creating transference, such as 'It must be true because my counsellor told me'. This implies that you are an expert who must be right, reinforces the existing imbalance of power in the counselling relationship and could imply your approval/disapproval about what you offer a client.

Therefore, the ethical dilemma is 'How can my client become informed *and* I respect their autonomy?' An ethical way to resolve this is balancing the principles of 'beneficence' (a commitment to promoting a client's wellbeing, such as offering helpful information) with 'autonomy' (respecting a client's right to be self-governing) (British Association for Counselling and Psychotherapy 2018, p.11). Note that this section is written in a way that aims to model this balance.

As you work together, notice if there are things that are misunderstood, confusing or unknown by a client. For example, they misunderstand intense grief as 'going mad' and are needlessly frightened, or are misinformed about addiction and believe their loved one just lacked the willpower to stop using and feel needlessly frustrated about that. You then need to decide whether to invite them to inform themselves or offer to inform them yourself; in large part, this choice is defined by your training, experience and work role.

How to inform a client

The saying 'You can take the horse to water but you can't make it drink' is useful to have in mind. You can offer to educate or interpret, and then need to respect a client's choice. What matters thereafter is the subjective meaning a client makes of your information, rather than *your* meaning, opinion or hopes for them.

- Bring the need to a client's awareness, e.g. 'It sounds like you are confused about that and need more information' or 'I imagine that your feeling guilty might have a reason that you are unaware of'. Ask them if they are interested in that. If not, you need to let it go, although you might want to invite their curiosity about not wanting to meet their need.

- If they are interested and you consider it is realistic for them to inform themselves, discuss how they can meet this need, e.g. offering the sources of information about substances noted above. Alternatively...

- If they are interested and you consider it is unrealistic for them to inform themselves, or inviting them to do so would unhelpfully break the flow of the session, offer to provide this yourself, e.g. 'I could say something about that if you're interested?' If they are, provide general information, such as 'I'll offer general information about it and trust you to decide whether it applies to your situation'. Offer what you say tentatively so that they can reject it if it does not fit their own experience. Use everyday language, not jargon, and avoid your own opinions or appearing to be an expert. When necessary, normalise what you offer to them and/or explain how you imagine it relates to them. Check that they understand, particularly with complex or potentially confusing topics like addiction and trauma.

- Prepare how you would educate a client about commonly encountered topics. You might want to create informal 'scripts' for each one and rehearse how you would say them.

- Be mindful of a client's capacity for this cognitive work: they need to be 'grounded' and able to think clearly (see below). They may have a fragile, even shattered sense of themselves following being bereaved. Suggest that they take their time to consider what you say. Consider following up by offering them written information to take away and consider further, e.g. a handout explaining trauma. Note you may need to build their support first and leave educating and interpreting until later.

- Finally, invite them to decide what something new means to them, e.g. 'What it is like to know that now?' or 'What are the implications of knowing that?' As ever, such open questions invite exploration without directing towards a particular outcome. A client may be disturbed by what you offer, e.g. proposing they are traumatised or depressed. Also, be mindful of how their cultural background influences the meaning they make of what you offer, which may be very different to your psychological view. Respect their choices obviously, including their right to make the 'wrong' choice as you see it, unless they are at significant risk.

Through this approach, you model the limits of someone's influence on another. This is potentially helpful for a client who believes that they should have been able to make their now deceased loved one do things, such as stop using substances. Indeed, you may want to explicitly comment about this to illustrate how we cannot make others do something.

'Grounding' an overwhelmed or traumatised client

Broadly speaking, we encourage clients to express their emotions. However, occasionally this can be unhelpful, such as when a client is overwhelmed or seems too withdrawn from you. It is important to notice when this happens and know what to do to keep a client safe and their support feeling manageable.

A client needs to be able to regulate their emotional and bodily experience of grief and, if relevant, of trauma too, in a way in which they are still able to engage with you, and think about and process their bereavement. This emotional/bodily state can be seen as a client being within their window of tolerance (Siegel 2012) that is optimal for support work. Too much or too little emotional/bodily arousal is distressing for clients and reduces their capacity to engage with you and to think clearly. Therefore, a client needs to stay mostly within their window, and if they do move outside, to be able to come back in again. See Figure 7.1.

Outside of window
Too much emotional/bodily arousal for effective support:
Client too overwhelmed to engage with you
Emotionally reactive and racing thoughts inhibit processing grief
Overly upset, fear, rage, restless, disturbing and intrusive memories, flashbacks, etc.

Window of tolerance
Optimum emotional/bodily arousal for effective support:
Client can engage with you
Emotions and thoughts can occur simultaneously and are tolerable
Responses are appropriate to the situation

Outside of window
Too little emotional/bodily arousal for effective support:
Client withdrawn or disengaged from you
May be too numb or distanced from grief to process it
Overly numb, depressed, lethargic, amnesia about death, etc.

FIGURE 7.1 THE WINDOW OF TOLERANCE APPLIED TO GRIEVING
Adapted from Siegel 2012

The width of the window varies between people and is often narrower in trauma when someone is more susceptible to becoming dysregulated (Ogden *et al.* 2006).

A client may need us to help them come back into their window. This involves knowing when a client is either too overwhelmed or too disengaged. Cathartic emotional expression is typically characterised by the skin having colour, deep breathing and emotional sounds coming on the out-breath; whereas unhealthy expression is typically characterised by pale, sometimes clammy skin, rapid breathing that may be jerky and emotional sounds mostly on the in-breath (Rothschild 2000). If in doubt, check with a client:

> 'Right now, are you too overwhelmed/distressed/numb and need my help to change how you feel?'

If a client does need your help to become 'grounded' again – that is, regulate back into their window of tolerance:

- Ask them to turn their attention to the 'here and now' present moment with you. Switching attention away from emotional experience and associated memories, and towards bodily experience is often enough (Leahy, Tirch and Napolitano 2011), e.g. their breathing, being in their chair, being in the counselling room with you.

- If that does not work, be directive, use their name, make eye contact and have a firm, kind, calm voice:

> 'Emma, look at me Emma…you seem to be overwhelmed and you need to be calmer…breathe in…breathe in deeply…it's safe here…look around the room…feel your feet on the floor…look at everything in the room that is blue…'

and so on, until they are calmer (Rothschild 2000).

- Throw a ball back and forth between the two of you (van der Kolk 2014).

- Offer a breathing practice (page 158).

- You could add:

> 'Take your time…you don't have to do anything right now…just be with me in the safety of this room.'

See also developing support (page 152), regulating emotions (pages 167–9) and working with trauma (pages 207–10).

Seeing clients within the context of their family

Clients are part of a family and all family members influence each other. This can potentially affect grieving and your support in significant ways.

At best, a client's family is a source of support to them. Their family members are also those who are most likely either to encourage your support or undermine it.

As discussed in earlier chapters, some families have experienced much stress and strain through addictive substance-using behaviour before the death and/or through the circumstances of the death. This potentially results in stigma and shame, unfinished business and associated emotions such as blame and guilt, and even family conflict and breakdown, all of which needs to be worked through during bereavement. As these difficult aspects of a client's grieving may be associated with other surviving members of their family, these difficulties can negatively affect the support that family members can give them. Also, a client's family members may be too bereft and/or traumatised to provide them with support. Furthermore, aspects of a client's grieving can be confusing, demanding and worrying for their family, such as trauma, depression and the severity and long duration of many substance-related bereavements.

Any current problematic or addictive substance use, whether by a client or members of their family, is typically distressingly worrying for those not using substances, who are often also feeling blame or guilt about the substance-related death and can easily fear another death (whether likely or not).

Therefore, you need to be mindful of a client's family and the influences that members are having on each other. Be mindful that, sadly, some family relationships are seemingly beyond repair. Consider referral to and/or joint working with those who work with families. For example, a family support group to work on shame and stigma; or family therapy or a mediation service to work through unfinished business; or a substance treatment service for both someone who is using and to support their family members.

'Endings' in bereavement support

'Endings' occur throughout support work, such as the end of a session, as well as at the end of the work. Endings are particularly important during support for a substance-related bereavement, as a client comes about an ending – that is, the death. Each ending entails them also 'losing' you, even if only temporarily, and may re-stimulate grief at the very time your support ends. Poorly handled endings can contribute to clients prematurely disengaging from support (Cartwright 2019).

Therefore, each ending needs to feel satisfactory and not echo distressing aspects of the death, particularly not being sudden and unexpected. Pay attention to your client's attachment style and any history of difficult separation and loss that could make endings difficult for them. Ideas to help a client anticipate, prepare for and have some sense of control about endings include the following.

In time-limited work it is good practice to say at the start how many sessions are available. Then 'count down' the sessions as the end approaches to make the ending explicit and provide an opportunity to discuss it. Consider tapering the ending by offering to meet less frequently towards the end.

During each session taper the end, saying, for example, 'Just to let you know, you've got five minutes left'. If necessary, ask a client what will help them get ready to end so they can be emotionally 'closed up' by the end – that is, move to the restoration orientation. Then end on time so they know sessions do end when stated and can emotionally pace themselves accordingly. If they often want to go over time, sensitively end the session, by saying, for example:

> 'Sorry to butt in as that sounds important and we are out of time today. Rather than squeeze it in now, you can start with that next time if you would like to.'

However, be willing to go over time occasionally if a client is too emotional to leave; just sit quietly and do not re-open the session. This may be a way to avoid 'losing' you. If this happens regularly, explore it together and consider what will help them to end on time.

Inform them about breaks and holidays well in advance, offer to discuss any concerns and explore their other support options.

Raise the end of the work, particularly in time-limited work. Ask what ending means for them and how they feel about it. Invite them to decide how they want to end (the idea that endings can be chosen is often new and helpful). Consider together their support after ending. If necessary, refer on and do so before the end to avoid a 'cliff edge' of support.

In the last session celebrate what has been achieved, acknowledge what is unfinished and consider how they could meet these needs. Sometimes, a client can regress at the end, so consider saying:

> 'In your anxiety about ending you seem to have lost touch with your capability. I suggest we run through how you do cope, as a refresher; would you like to do that?'

Also, say goodbye and whatever else seems important.

Introducing three fictitious bereaved clients used in Part 2

Three fictitious clients are used across Part 2 to illustrate the work presented. They represent a variety of commonly encountered difficulties.

EMMA

Emma is 32 years old, white British. Her 44-year-old husband, Steve, died from health complications due to long-term alcohol addiction. She has two children and an anxious/ambivalent attachment style. Her father was addicted to using alcohol during her childhood, during which she cared for him as a way to feel special and valued by him, and this self-sacrificing, compulsive caring was modelled to her by her mother.

JOHN

John is 56 years old, white British. His 38-year-old daughter, Sarah, died of a heroin overdose after many years of addictive use. He is separated from Sarah's mother, Anne, and has an avoidant attachment style.

MAHI

Mahi is 45 years old, British Asian Sikh. Her 22-year-old son, Jake, unexpectedly died at a chemsex party following a drug overdose. She is married to Jag, has two younger children and has a secure attachment style.

Other contributors have referred to other 'clients' in this chapter and Chapter 16.

8

Supporting a Bereaved Person

In the UK, a diversity of volunteers, workers and professionals may support people bereaved through a substance-related death. This chapter proposes interventions that non-specialists can offer their clients, covering:

- what everyone can do

- bereavement support that can be provided by drug and alcohol workers, family support workers, faith workers, victim support workers, peer supporters, and those who recognise they are not yet ready for more complex bereavement work (to simplify this work, it does not require knowledge of attachment theory)

- a range of ways a bereaved person can develop their self- and social support.

You need to decide what of the above is appropriate for your training, experience and work role.

What everyone can do

There is free general guidance for everyone, whether they provide bereavement support or not: 'Bereaved through substance use: Guidelines for those whose work brings them into contact with adults after a drug or alcohol-related death' (Cartwright 2015). This guidance, produced by many people, was the final part of the research study summarised in Chapter 5.[1]

Bereavement support

Supporting someone who is bereaved can seem daunting, but in reality...

---

1   See www.bath.ac.uk/publications/bereaved-through-substance-use

Bereavement work is easy; all you have to do is be with someone. (Jacqui Love, 2000)

This quote from my clinical supervisor was made before I counselled my first client. She knew there was more to it than this and wanted to convey how the work is essentially to accompany a client in their grief, bearing witness to it and supporting them.

What you can offer

In my experience of training people to provide bereavement support, there are three helpful ways to support clients that those who are inexperienced in bereavement work can use. You may consider it appropriate to go further than this (as described in later chapters); conversely, you may refer on someone whose needs are beyond your current capability.

1. Give a client time and a safe place to grieve

Given how typically severe, complex and disenfranchised these bereavements are, offering a client time to grieve in a safe and confidential space is very valuable. It may be their only opportunity to do this.

Invite them to say how they would like to use their time; they often need to go over something many times. If they don't know what to say, suggest ideas (such as one of the themes in Chapter 10).

During your work together, invite them to slow down and become aware of what is significant and how they feel. Encourage them to pace themselves emotionally – for example, 'You are welcome to show how you feel here and you don't have to express it all this time.'

Sometimes there are things to 'do'. Consider particular difficulties, such as how to cope with attending an inquest or dealing with stigma, or offer the idea of a continuing bond and, if that interests them, explore what their bond would be like (see page 33 for ideas).

2. Help them make sense of their experience

Clients can struggle to make sense of their loved one's substance use, the actual death and other aspects of their grief. Also, they may have an inaccurate understanding of these, particularly if addiction played a part. Be willing to offer information about what you are confident to share; or consider together where else they may get information. Either way, invite them to consider, with you, what that information means for them. Where you can, normalise their experiences.

Also, invite them to consider their experience of grief and whether it makes sense to them. People experiencing a substance-related bereavement can be confused, disturbed and/or frightened by their grief (Cartwright 2019). Offer to inform them about grieving (see Chapter 1). Include consideration of what their emotions mean to them: sadness usually comes when we perceive we have lost someone or something; anger often tells us something is unacceptable, we have lost control or feel threatened in some way; anxiety and fear are felt in response to threat. Therefore, emotions provide information that needs consideration; this can lead to a realisation that a given emotion is unfounded, despite its feeling real, such as feeling anxiety but not actually being at risk.

The aim in this work is to help a client create a coherent narrative (as far as possible) about their loved one, the death and their adjustment to it that makes sense to them and 'fits' with who they are. This often entails a client updating their assumptions about life. You need to be realistic about how far you can help with this enormous, complex and long-term task.

3. Develop their self- and social support
Offer to explore together a client's support. You might need to remind them they are coping – if they are with you, they have got through their grief that far. Respect any resistance to engage in loss- or restoration-orientated activities; this is typically their current best way of coping with what feels unmanageable (and you could acknowledge this), and offer to develop further ways they could cope (see below for ideas).

How to provide this support
The intention you need to have is to 'be with' – to accompany – your client. We cannot 'fix' a client's grief. Paradoxically, change often happens when a client accepts what is, rather than by trying to be different (Beisser 1970); and this is true of much bereavement work. Therefore, being with a client – staying with however they are – creates an opportunity for them to grieve and thereby move a little through their bereavement.

If you usually deliver more task-orientated or outcome-led support, this can be a challenge, especially where there is organisational pressure to *do* something. It may help to see the task as 'being with' rather than 'doing something', as this reduces any implied pressure you might inadvertently put on a client to achieve something. Clients may challenge you to 'fix' something, so be prepared. You could say:

'I completely understand you want me to do that, and I don't know how anyone can do that. What I can offer you is a safe place to grieve, help you make sense of what's happened and help you develop ways to cope with grieving.'

'Being with' means finding your curiosity, compassion and willingness to engage and listen. Follow your client's lead, go at their pace, pick up what has energy and is significant for them, and hold the focus on that until you sense that energy has dissipated and enough has been said (at least for now). Or, if they are overwhelmed and skipping from one awful thing to another, ask what they would like to tackle first.

It helps to make statements rather than ask questions as statements help stay with what a client is talking about, demonstrate you have heard, witnessed and validated their experience, and offer back information that helps them to be aware of themselves. Statements also feel more conversational. Therefore, statements include:

- acknowledging anything significant a client says or feels, so that you witness and validate their experience

- reflecting back what you hear, see, sense and imagine, and what seems helpful for them to know

- sharing your own human reactions, such as a smile at the start, giving genuine condolences for their loss and occasionally even having a laugh with them at the right moment

- summarising your work together from time to time.

Questions, by contrast, tend to lead a client in your direction, don't convey what you think or feel, and do not offer information to them; clients can feel pressured to answer, and support can feel like an interview. You can usually find a statement in a question – for example, 'How do you feel?' is really 'I'm curious about how you feel'.

'Being with' entails sitting with their grief without you becoming overwhelmed or shutting down emotionally (so staying in your own window of tolerance – see pages 142–3), resisting the urge to find a false solution that gets you both out of their distress. This can be challenging and takes practice.

Use the terms 'dead' and 'died', because 'passed away', 'sleeping', 'passed on', 'resting', etc., can deny the reality of death. However, let clients use their own language and be sensitive to their beliefs, such as believing they will meet a loved one again in heaven.

Work together in partnership, where you collaborate on what a client wants to use their time for. A useful metaphor is a voyage: the client is the captain and you are their navigator. Navigators check where their captain wants to go, can suggest places to visit and how to get there, and respect the captain's choice – as long as the destination is realistic. Therefore, consider potential destinations:

- Ask a client what they want and consider whether their expectations are realistic. As you cannot make them 'feel better', be clear about what you can and cannot offer.

- Reframe the characteristics of their grief as needs that you can help with (see Chapter 6) and offer these ideas.

- Focus on what work is possible with you that is difficult for them to do elsewhere.

...and discuss possible routes to get to these destinations.

As the work progresses, consider whether both loss- and restoration-orientated activities are getting attention, as well as noticing what a client *doesn't* talk about that you imagine could be important. Regularly review and discuss your work together to ensure you are helping them.

> Recall a time when you were grieving, or going through another difficult and highly emotive experience, and remember those who helped you. Reflect on what they provided that helped and how they did that. If they were not helpful, reflect on what was unhelpful and what you needed and did not get. Consider what that means for supporting bereaved clients.

Example of bereavement support with Emma

Worker: Hello again, I've been thinking about you and how you're getting on.
Emma: Hi, I'm okay, thanks.
Worker: I'm interested to know how you'd like to use your session today.
Emma: Well I'm not sure... I'm not okay really...it's been awful.
Worker: Sorry to hear that... I'm curious what's been awful.
Emma: Well...I just can't stop thinking about Steve...I miss him so much. (Tears well up.)
Worker: Take your time. (Gives box of tissues, but after a pause so not to imply Emma should stop crying.) You really miss him.
Emma: Yes...yes. (Starts to cry.) I can't stop crying...
(pause)
Emma: ...and I'm so angry with him for drinking; he just wouldn't stop and I knew this would happen. I told him and he wouldn't stop...and now he's gone. (Continues to cry.)
Worker: I'm seeing tears for missing him and tears of anger for his drinking.
Emma: Yes...I shouldn't be angry.
Worker: Sounds hard to accept you're angry.
Emma: Yes.
Worker: I imagine it's normal for anyone to feel angry when someone they

love continues to do something that harms them, despite being told not to do it.

Emma: I can see that, and why didn't he stop?

Worker: I can't speak for Steve but I could say something about addiction if you want.

Emma: Yes, please.

Worker: I'm not an expert on addiction, although I understand a characteristic of it is that it is very difficult for someone to control their drinking... I wonder if that fits for you about Steve?

Emma: I don't know.

Worker: That's okay. Slow down and take your time to consider that.

(pause)

Emma: He wasn't well.

Worker: You miss him, you're angry with him and he wasn't well. I imagine all of those are true for you.

Emma: Yes that's it...and it's driving me mad...it's been going round and round in my head all week.

Worker: That sounds like grief rather than madness to me. I imagine it would help if we looked at how you might get a break from that.

Emma: Oh, yes.

Worker: Okay, I suggest I tell you about a way to manage grieving others have found helpful. If that appeals to you, we could practise it now, then see how you get on during the week and discuss that next time. Then we can either celebrate your success or put our heads together to think of something else. Would you like to do that?

Emma: Okay.

(Worker shares 'grief in a box' and Emma chooses Sudoku puzzles as an activity to distract her from her grief; see below.)

Developing a client's self- and social support

Effective support is essential for grieving, and developing it is a central and ongoing part of effective bereavement support. Many bereaved people seek help because their existing self- and social support are overwhelmed. Many people coping with a loved one's addiction neglect their own needs, so they start bereavement in a depleted state, with insufficient support, and often continue to neglect their own needs.

Although we are a source of support for our clients, in any counselling 'a substantial proportion of positive therapeutic outcome is due to factors outside the therapy room, such as supportive family, friends, spiritual groups, community activities, nourishing pastimes, self-care and so on' (Joyce and Sills 2014, p.83).

A client needs to be aware of their need for support, meet that need, and recognise when to support themselves and when to use the support of others, in a way that balances their needs with the needs of others. During grieving, a client may well need to receive more support than they can give. They may need and even want to support others too, and this may provide a sense of capability and control at a time when they feel helpless and their world feels horribly out of control.

Developing self-support is helpful for grieving (Cartwright 2019; Ford *et al.* 2018). However, some self-support may be unhelpful, such as critical self-talk, suppressing emotions and internet searches (Cartwright 2019):

Don't Google it, as it freaked me out! (Half-sister of brother) (p.29)

As discussed in Chapter 6, people bereaved through a substance-related death may have insufficient self- and social support for grieving, so it is often necessary to help a client develop their support. Start with exploring:

- what helped them during past bereavements and other life difficulties that is available now, including what they underuse and overuse

- how well they oscillate and engage with both loss and restoration activities

- what they themselves do to cope when feeling painful and difficult emotions, e.g. do they get overwhelmed; avoid their emotional experience; cope in ways that are also unhealthy, such as self-injury, dissociation or excessive substance use and other compulsive behaviours such as eating, gambling, internet use, etc.?

- whether there are additional difficulties or stressors that need more support

- whether any support they may currently provide to others is a burden or satisfies them.

Validate and encourage the use of existing support and whatever gets them through in a healthy way. This helps clients realise they coped before and that support may already be available.

How to develop support

A less-is-more approach is usually best, so offer one or two carefully considered ideas that meet a client's current needs and let them choose what they are interested to experiment with. Some, such as 'grief in a box', are better taught by you; where you do teach something, let them know they can stop at any time.

Other ideas, such as 'the support pyramid', could be given as an assignment[2] to do between sessions. Self-support strategies benefit from being practised with you in the session.

Say that what you offer is just an experiment, to see what happens, and be open-minded about the outcome. If relevant, add that they may feel self-conscious trying it and it may feel contrived, as happens when learning any new skill. After the experiment, reflect together on what happened. If an idea works for a client, they will need to take responsibility for practising and using it so that it becomes fully useful and available when needed; consider discussing what helps them do this, such as a postcard or polished stone to keep with them as a reminder. If an idea did not work, experiment with something else.

Return to developing support throughout your work: follow up how clients get on with the ideas you give; celebrate their successes and be curious about what does not work to find any learning for future support development. Notice when their needs change and offer new ideas. See also pages 208–10 for support with trauma.

Next is a menu of support ideas. Notice how the dual process model helps inform what to do.

Identifying and developing a client's support

The support pyramid (Kuykendall 2001) is a way to help a client identify and develop their support. It takes at least 20 minutes to complete this exercise. Ask your client to list all the support they have by the four sources:

1. **Self-support.** Talking to ourselves in a helpful way; empathy, compassion and forgiveness for our own experience; effective coping strategies; taking responsibility for ourselves; realistic beliefs about ourselves and the world; a strong sense of who we are; good physical health and taking care of our body, etc. See below for other ideas.

2. **Others who give emotional support.** People who will be with us at difficult or painful times; those who do not try to 'fix it' but let us talk and express how we feel; those with whom we can talk through a particular problem; those who love, validate and encourage us, and enjoy our successes.

3. **Others who provide a break from difficulties.** People we do pleasurable and fun things with; those who make us laugh; those we do a regular leisure activity with.

---

2   I prefer 'assignment' to 'homework' because the latter may have unhelpful memories for a client.

4. **Organisations who offer support.** This is where you fit in. It includes:

- Local bereavement counselling service, e.g. Cruse Bereavement Care.

- Other bereavement support, particularly groups for those bereaved in similar ways, such as DrugFAM, Survivors of Bereavement by Suicide, The Compassionate Friends, etc.

- Websites and social media groups. There are continuous and potentially anonymous communities of similarly bereaved people that provide and receive support. Online memorialisation of a loved one may feel like a connection or communication, and can be particularly helpful for those who feel disenfranchised or stigmatised (Pearlman *et al.* 2014).

- Religious and faith groups.

Next, ask them to draw a triangle where the size represents all of this support and then divide it into four parts, each representing the proportion of support from the four sources. Now explore their reaction to their pyramid:

- Is it enough support to help them cope with their bereavement? What is the balance between the four sources? Despite having this support, do they actually *use* all sources or just some? Invite them to imagine using support differently and what that would be like.

- Sometimes, others' support is not received by a client as intended: 'Anything you need, just call' may feel too difficult to do; and 'You're looking well' can sound like having to be 'well'. Allow them to be ungrateful! Also, encourage them to ask for the support they need, including being specific about their situation and what helps, so others are better able to support them. This might include inviting a family member to a session, when approved of and chosen by a client. However, some people in their network may be stigmatising and disenfranchising (see Chapter 6); therefore, evaluate which relationships seem worth preserving and which may need to be temporarily avoided or even discontinued.

- Be mindful how the nature of social support is influenced by culture, religion and bereavement customs and rituals.

- Support groups and online communities may inadvertently be unhelpful (see page 116 and page 127). Explore any unhelpful or inappropriate responses from others; these often stem from stigma, being unable to comprehend the loss, or from uncertainty, discomfort and/or anxiety about engaging with your client.

- Clients with insecure attachment styles can have fewer people to turn to and be less satisfied by any support they receive, and those with a disorganised style tend to have poorer social skills, which can make finding and using social support harder (Kosminsky and Jordan 2016).

You could suggest they draw a second triangle to represent all the support they believe they need at the moment. Then explore the differences between the two. If needed, consider together how they can develop their support.

Developing self-support

- **Supportive self-talk.** Explore how a client talks to themselves, particularly about bereavement. Many people are judgemental, intolerant or dismissive of themselves yet empathic, compassionate and kind to family and friends. Invite a client to consider how many friends they would have if they spoke to them as they do to themselves! Consider together how they can become a 'good friend' to themselves. Together, develop 'ASK' (Accurate, Supportive and Kind) self-talk (Crawford 1998).

- **Identify with their own experience** (Resnick 1990 cited in Joyce and Sills 2014, p.80). This form of self-talk provides self-empathy, compassion and forgiveness. It can include self-acknowledgement of strengths, capabilities and effective coping strategies, and prioritise their own needs at a very difficult time.

- **The evoked companion** (Stern 1985) is a 'companion' a client can imagine, 'hear' or recall connection to, e.g. an attachment figure, friend, faith leader, you, an imagined companion or perhaps the deceased. This is someone they can have an inner connection to who supports them at difficult times. It is particularly useful for clients who struggle with the first two above.

- **A positive worldview.** Studies show this tends to be associated with enhanced resilience and more flexible coping, e.g. optimism in believing that personal growth can occur through negative life experiences (Bonanno 2009; Zandvoort 2012).

- **Feel self-worth** (Pearlman *et al.* 2014). Encourage the client to do what they are good at; associate with people who respect and bring out the best in them; possibly help others if they are ready for that; acknowledge their competence in parental or work roles, etc.

- **Images, postcards and 'maps'.** Some clients find images better than words. Visualise a supportive image or 'daydream'. Have a stock of picture postcards, invite a client to choose the picture they find supportive, write self-supporting statements on the back and then keep their card with them for times they need support; consider whether it is more supportive for them to write their card and thereby develop self-efficacy, or for you to write it so they can 'hold on to' their attachment to you between sessions. Draw a 'map' of their inner world, with images and/or icons for parts of themselves and sources of support, and draw helpful connections between these. Their map can be used at difficult times to 'work out where they are' inside themselves and provide 'routes' to support.

- **Consider those helpful things that are easy to do but that are also easy not to do,** that get forgotten or not done, e.g. having a rest or watching a favourite programme on television.

- **Bodily support.** Reduce vulnerability to being emotionally overwhelmed through good nutrition, sleep, exercise, recreation and play.

Upsurges of grief can occur long after the death, often in social settings: cyclic events such as anniversaries; linear events that happen once, such as when the person who died would have graduated; and stimulus-cued events, such as a bereaved parent being asked how many children they have (Rando 1993). It helps to prepare for these using emotion regulation strategies (Gross 2014) to down-regulate painful and difficult emotions or up-regulate pleasant emotions:

- **Situation selection.** Choose to avoid particular people and places, e.g. where the death occurred or where people known to deal drugs operate.[3]

- **Situation modification.** Visualise in advance situations that are expected to be difficult, e.g. the inquest or Christmas Day, and prepare appropriate support. It can help also to prepare alternative strategies in case the situation is better or worse than anticipated.

- **Attentional deployment.** Choose to direct attention in a particular way, e.g. recalling pleasant memories of the deceased.

- **Cognitive change.** Reframe or modify how a particular situation is seen, e.g. recognising how habitual thoughts such as 'I can't cope' lead to habitual anxiety and acknowledging to themselves when they do cope.

- **Response modulation.** Directly influence a particular experience, such as described next.

---

3   Although visiting a hospice or hospital may be difficult, many feel better for doing so once they feel ready, and especially if the visit is planned and the staff provide a welcome and support (C.M. Parkes, personal communication).

Breathing practices

Breathing practices are quick and effective ways to self-regulate the nervous system (Porges 2011) and can improve symptoms of anxiety, depression and trauma (Gerberg and Brown 2016; Jerath *et al.* 2015). Generally, emphasising the in-breath increases arousal and energy, matching in- and out-breath maintains balance, whereas emphasising the out-breath decreases arousal and supports relaxation (Dana 2018; Ogden *et al.* 2006). Breathing practices can be potent and need to be used with caution (especially with a traumatised client), with an emphasis on experimentation and associated bodily awareness, and then reflecting on what happened (Ogden *et al.* 2006).

If a client has the need, offer an appropriate practice. If they are interested, show them how to use it and then invite them to try it with you – and be willing to have a laugh and say if you feel silly doing so! At the end, take time to feel the effects of the practice. If a practice helps, encourage them to use it between sessions and, again, take time to feel the effect afterwards.

- **To feel balanced in mind and body** (Schwartz 2019):

  Start with several long, deep breaths. Become aware of breathing. Use the diaphragm.[4] Then breathe with a count of 4 on both the in- and out-breath, counting silently in your head. Continue for several minutes. This can be developed to breathe in for 4, hold for 4 at the top of the in-breath, breath out for 4, hold for 4 at the bottom of the out-breath, and so on, as if breathing around a square.

- **To feel invigorated** (Schwartz 2019), such as when tired or depressed:

  Start with several long, deep breaths. Become aware of breathing. Focus on bringing the breath into the upper chest. Take a strong inhalation and hold the breath briefly at the top of the in-breath. Repeat three or four more times and then let the breath return to a natural rhythm. This can be repeated a few more times.

- **To feel calm** (Dana 2018; van der Kolk 2014), especially when feeling overly anxious, stressed or angry:

  Sit or lie comfortably. Become aware of breathing. Breathe in through the nose in a natural way, using the diaphragm. Then breathe out naturally, through the mouth, while also constricting the flow of air so it takes

---

4   Diaphragmatic breathing: in normal breathing this can be detected by sideways movement of the lower two ribs on both sides of the chest. Ideally, the abdomen and chest expand and contract rhythmically at the same time, and on the in-breath the lower two ribs move to the sides, down and back, the middle five ribs swing out to the sides and the upper five ribs lift upward (Rosenberg 2017).

twice as long to exhale by constricting the back of the throat, as when fogging a mirror. Pause momentarily at the end of the out-breath and then breathe in naturally. Count silently in your head, where the out-breath is twice the value of the in-breath. Continue for several minutes.

Some people can feel anxious when first using this practice (Dana 2018). Alternative ways to calm include:

- **sighing** (Dana 2018): one hand on the heart and an audible deep sigh, with a long slow out-breath and constricting the back of the throat (as when fogging a mirror), followed by a pause at the bottom of the out-breath and then feeling the effect

- **washing the face with cold water**

- **exercising** to 'burn off' over-arousal and induce calm.

A way to oscillate and thereby manage grieving – putting 'grief in a box'

Clients often feel they have little or no control over grief, such as crying at work but feeling okay when at the graveside. This visualisation technique enables choice over when to grieve and when not, thereby giving a sense of control and facilitating flexible oscillation (Kuykendall 2001). This is best taught to a client in a session so they can experience it; allow at least 25 minutes:

Briefly explain it is a visualisation and how it can work. They will need to signal when they have completed each step (e.g. give you a 'thumbs up'); there is no 'right or wrong' way of doing this, so that whatever happens is okay.

Invite them to close their eyes and turn their attention inwards. Using all their senses, they think of an object that represents their grief and signal when done. Next, using all their senses, they imagine a box or other container that can safely hold the object and signal when done. Then, using all their senses, they imagine placing the object in the box and safely closing it, putting the box safely on to the back of a shelf behind them, saying to themselves, 'I'm choosing to put you away for now and I'll choose when I take you down', and signal when done. Ask them to notice what that feels like.

Now invite them to imagine taking their box down, using all their senses, and saying to themselves, 'I'm choosing to take you down now'. They imagine placing it in front of them, opening it up and taking out their grief. Ask them to notice what that feels like and signal when done.

Then they put it away as they did before. When ready, they open their eyes and join you again.

Reflect on what happened, in particular how they felt when the box was opened up and when it was put away. Encourage them to adapt it so it works for them. Explain:

- During periods of acute grief, it may be less effective. They can still use this and can add saying, 'I feel my box behind me and I'm choosing to focus on this instead', and/or visualise gently putting their grief back in the box and up on the shelf again, until it stays there.

- This is not about putting grief away for ever. They need to take their box down, open it up and 'take out' their grief, and can now do so when they choose.

- Being with you is a time to take their box down and open it up.

Develop your own script to explain the visualisation and guide someone through it, and rehearse your 'lines' so you feel confident to use it.

Ways to engage with loss orientation

Clients need to engage with the difficult and painful aspects of grief. Below are ways to evoke grief, such as when a client takes their 'box' down:

- **A memory box** of photographs, objects and possessions that connect to the deceased (be aware that people who use substances addictively often sell anything to fund their use, and this potential lack of personal possessions can be distressing for clients who may only have basic items such as clothing).

- **Listening** to music that evokes the right mood.

- **Talking** to the deceased and possibly imagining what they would say back.

- **Writing** a letter to the deceased, or writing about them, and perhaps reading it out loud with you (see more on writing on pages 310–312).

- **Reading** other bereaved people's poetry or prose.

- **Turning their attention inwards** to become aware of their body, emotions, memories and thoughts. This could be developed into a meditation or visualisation, which initially may need to be guided by you (Levine 1986).

Encourage your client to slow down when using these, so they can better engage with their body, emotions, memories and thoughts. Afterwards:

- **Supportive self-talk:** 'I can endure engaging with my grief', 'I feel better afterwards, at least for a while' or 'Every time I grieve, I'm one step further in my journey'.

- **Arranging social support:** someone to phone or be with after grieving.

Ways to engage with restoration orientation

Clients need to take a break from grieving; below are ways to suspend grieving, such as when a client puts their grief away in their 'box'. There is a difference between choosing to temporarily distract from difficult and painful emotions and habitually avoiding them, which inhibits grieving.

- **Give themselves permission not to grieve.** It may help if you give them permission first.

- **Stopping crying** by accentuating the in-breath, sitting up, drinking something, deciding 'that is enough for now', etc. If these do not work, then knowing their body will stop crying when they get tired.

- **Calming the body** – see above.

- **Shifting their experience** from their body and emotions into their head and cognitions by doing something that requires concentration, e.g. Sudoku or crossword puzzles, computer gaming, knitting, etc. Or visualising a place, pet, activity or past experience that evokes a bodily and emotional experience of relief and wellbeing (Rothschild 2000).

- **Making a list of 20 enjoyable things** and doing three every day. These may be more effective if done with other people. Often, looking forward to something is as helpful as actually doing it.

- **Feeling positive emotions** (Bonanno 2009). Genuine smiling and laughter, such as when talking about the deceased, helps people cope better with bereavement by providing a break from grief and making it easier for others to be with them; people who feel positive emotions during later bereavement experience reduced grief.

- **Maintaining a gratitude journal** every day, however small, and lingering on feeling grateful (Emmons 2007), e.g. for not feeling as bad as feared or noticing the sun shining for the first time since the death.

- **Asking them 'What would you be doing now if you weren't bereaved?'** and encouraging them to start picking up the threads of their past life or creating a new life.

- **Medication and substance use** (see Chapter 16).

...and when nothing seems to work

Invite a client to remind themselves that no feeling lasts for ever, even if that takes time; emotions will not hurt them, even if they are difficult and painful; and they are getting help with you. Help them to develop a realistic, self-accepting and compassionate attitude towards themselves. If nothing seems to help, consider together whether continuing grieving serves them in some way, such as seeing it as a 'duty to the dead' or fearing they cannot adapt to a new life without their loved one.

> Supporting bereaved people is demanding. Consider these ideas to build your own support for this work.
>
> Have a go at ideas like the 'support pyramid' and 'grief in a box'. Having used them, you will probably be better at facilitating a client to do so.

FURTHER READING ON SUPPORTING BEREAVED PEOPLE

Worden, J.W. (2009) *Grief Counselling and Grief Therapy: A Handbook for the Mental Health Practitioner* (4th edition). Hove: Routledge.

9

Bereavement Counselling

The purpose of bereavement counselling is to facilitate all aspects of a client's grieving, through a counselling relationship where you are a transitional attachment figure (see page 38). Through this, the client can integrate their loss into who they are now and adapt to a changed world without their loved one. Grieving is an active process and the passage of time alone is not enough to adjust. Therefore, this chapter considers what needs to happen in bereavement counselling:

- expressing and regulating the emotions of grief
- cognitive understanding and making meaning
- behavioural adaptation to a changed life.

I have separated these for clarity and simplicity, although in reality they are interconnected, like the way a prism splits apart light into its constituent colours of the rainbow (C. Siederer, personal communication). For example, a client's emotional experience of grief needs to be made sense of so that it doesn't adversely inhibit the social adaptations they make. This work requires both a narrative approach to produce insight and meaning, and a focus on the embodied nature of grief that normalises it and helps with the repetitive bodily and emotional experiences (Zandvoort and Zandvoort 2012). Also, these are not a sequence of steps in grieving; rather, they are interconnected themes that clients need to revisit and work through many times.

This work is significantly influenced by the context of a client's life, attachment style, previous losses and life events, experiences of others' care and support, differences and diversity, and by their family, culture and spirituality or worldview.

These themes are offered to support normal counselling practice and not to replace it. However, this chapter is written for those who are able to address all aspects of substance-related bereavements, such as experienced counsellors, psychotherapists and psychologists. You need to decide whether you are ready for this and have the clinical supervision you need.

Expressing and regulating the emotions of grief

The need for clients to express their grief emotions and the recognition that not doing so prolongs and complicates grieving is well established (Leick and Davidsen-Nielsen 1991; Rando 1993; Rando *et al.* 2014; Worden 2009). However, grieving is an emotionally dysregulating experience that needs to be brought within manageable limits before integration of the loss can occur (Kosminsky and Jordan 2016). This does not mean eliminating emotions; rather, it is developing ways to regulate them so they are felt and expressed, and their unique contribution to grieving made available, in ways that are manageable for a client. In other words, effective grieving reduces pain despite being painful. This involves the skill to work moment by moment with a client's embodied emotional experience and facilitate reflecting upon and making sense of these emotions.

In addition to this section, see page 142 for grounding an overwhelmed client, pages 152–62 for developing clients' support, and later chapters on particular emotional experiences.

Differences in emotional expression

You will need to discuss and then take account of a client's individual experience of grief emotions and how to work with their emotional experience. These can include verbal and non-verbal expression, such as writing a journal, letters to and from a deceased loved one, or poetry, as well as drawing, painting, sculpting and movement. As discussed in Chapter 2, attachment style has a significant influence on emotional expression during bereavement. Also, clients may experience re-stimulated emotions from past losses and traumas.

Regarding gender, differences in emotional expression of grief are probably inherent and much influenced by cultural experience (Parkes 2009). Women tend to be more loss-orientated, such as crying more than men and coping more through sharing and by expressing emotions (Parkes 2009), and often have more distress in the first year of bereavement than men (Parkes and Prigerson 2010). Men tend to be more restoration-orientated, such as adopting problem-solving approaches, are less inclined to ask for help, and can 'avoid or inhibit the natural expression of separation distress and other emotions' (Parkes 2009, p.150). Although this is often due to their socialisation (Worden 2009) and a desire to be strong for their families (Martin and Doka 2011), they can fare worse over the longer term (Parkes and Prigerson 2010). The dual process model suggests that people need to engage with both orientations. Schut *et al.* (1997) found that women can benefit from a gender-opposite, cognitive approach and problem-focused help, whereas men can benefit from emotion-stimulating interventions, described below. These gender differences have been found in substance-related bereavements (Cartwright 2019).

Emotional intelligence

Clients often struggle with painful and difficult grief emotions. They are unaccepting or confused about their emotional experience; apologise for how they feel; fear breaking down, losing control or what their emotions might lead them to do; refer to 'negative' emotions; talk about 'feelings' that are actually cognitions, etc. However, all emotions can be recognised, understood and expressed or managed in ways that serve us. This capacity is often referred to as emotional intelligence, as popularised by Goleman (1996).

An analytical study of the models of emotional intelligence established a common definition of 'the skill with which one perceives, expresses, reasons with and manages their own and others' emotions' (p.72); these skills 'are culturally universal and have comparable functions across cultures', and culture has a role in 'the development, display and interpretation of emotions' (Palmer *et al.* 2007, p.73).

I have found this concept particularly relevant for counselling bereaved clients. Emotional intelligence is integral to mentalising (see page 35) and emotional self-regulation. Both are often necessary for effective grieving, and often need to be developed in people with insecure attachment styles. Also, although emotions such as sadness are inevitable in substance-related bereavements, other common emotions are probably not, such as fear, shame and enduring guilt, which require emotional intelligence to work through. Below are ideas for you to offer clients and encourage them to practise between sessions:

- **Explain emotional intelligence to a client.**

- **Acknowledge their emotional experience as it occurs in the session.**

- **Normalise their emotional experience when appropriate.**

- **Encourage them to sense, express and name their emotions.** This often requires the discomfort of actually experiencing it for long enough to become aware of it. Additionally, encourage awareness of the intensity of the emotion, e.g. anger ranges from mild irritation to rage; and enquire beyond the first emotion as one emotion often occurs with others, e.g. anger with hurt, or despair with anxiety.

- **Develop their ways to regulate emotional experience** (see below) and self-support ideas from page 156. Although they cannot choose their emotional experience, they can over time, with our help and through regular practice, develop their ability to step back from it, reflect and choose how to respond to it.

- **Develop their capacity to accept their emotional experience, non-judgementally**, rather than avoid, deny, denigrate, rationalise away or prematurely try to change it (Pearlman *et al.* 2014); and to understand that all emotions are part of human experience, can be made sense of and can be effectively regulated or expressed.

- **Be curious about their experience and make sense of it.** Although clients can believe 'I am what I feel', emotions are only a part of them. A useful intervention is 'It feels real, and is it true?' This both validates their experience and invites reflection. Each emotion occurs with particular perceptions, tells us useful information, urges us to react in a certain way and communicates to others what is happening for us (Stanton, Dunkley and Melly 2008), e.g. during grieving:

    [S]adness must be accompanied by an awareness of what one has lost, anger needs to be properly and effectively targeted, guilt needs to be evaluated and resolved, and anxiety needs to be identified and managed. (Worden 2009, p.96)

    Then this emotional information is used in reasoning and decision-making.

- **Consider both the present context**, i.e. grieving, **and the influence of past events, and habitual ways of perceiving and regulating emotions**, e.g. attachment style. Consider whether any habitual responses still serve a client now, e.g. whether to act as their emotion urges them to (Stanton *et al.* 2008).

- **Perceive and understand the emotions of others**, by inviting a client to have empathy and mentalise, and, if necessary, adding your thoughts too. Where appropriate, this requires an understanding of substance-using behaviour, possibly including addiction, and any mental health difficulties the deceased had.

Through this kind of work, a client's emotional experience is integrated into the rest of their life narrative.

Related to the capacity of emotional intelligence is the Buddhist idea, used in mindfulness, of the 'second dart': existence inevitably comes with the 'first dart' of emotional discomfort, such as bereavement, but it is often our reactions to these, the 'second dart' we throw at ourselves, that cause most suffering (Hanson and Mendius 2009, p.50). I have found it useful to introduce this idea to clients and work with their 'second darts'.

This work requires a client to 'stand back', to be aware of and to consider their emotional experience with an open mind. One increasingly popular way to do this is through mindfulness, the practice of paying attention to our own experience in a particular way: on purpose, in the present moment and non-judgementally (Kabat-Zinn 1994). You will need to have training in mindfulness and practise it yourself before being ready to teach it to clients.

MINDFULNESS RESOURCES
Headspace phone app from www.headspace.com
Williams, M. and Penman, D. (2011) *Mindfulness: A Practical Guide to Finding Peace in a Frantic World*. London: Piatkus.

Regulating emotions

A particular skill of emotional intelligence, as noted above, is regulating emotional experience, so clients can stay mostly in their window of tolerance (see pages 142–3). It is important to say to clients that this is about keeping their emotional experience manageable and not that they have done or felt something that is wrong.

This is particularly relevant for clients with an insecure attachment style, for traumatised clients (see Chapter 11 for more on regulating trauma symptoms) and for many clients who use substances addictively who have often not yet developed this capacity. For these clients, the aim is to help them develop an acceptable, manageable and effective way to regulate their emotional experience. They can then express their grief emotions in an effective way, without avoiding or being overwhelmed by them, and thereby be able to engage with the cognitive and adaptive aspects of grief. Clients usually appreciate having more control of their emotions.

Typically, this needs you to offer and teach how to do it, a client practising this between sessions and developing their self- and social support, all with the intention of them feeling able to choose to do the painful and difficult work in grieving.

Helping clients regulate their emotions

- **Be guided by a client's emotional experience**, i.e. can they be aware of and experience/express their emotions, self-regulate in ways so they are mostly in their window of tolerance, and flexibly oscillate between loss and restoration?

- **Normalise any habitual difficulty** with over- or under-regulating their emotional experience and in oscillating. However, also explain the need to become aware of and express grief emotions and to do so in a regulated way, and that it is probably necessary to keep their old ways – at least for now.

- **Offer to teach practical strategies for self-regulation** as described below; to explain emotional intelligence, the window of tolerance and the dual process model; and to develop their self- and social support.

- **Recognise that it often takes a lot of practice** for clients to develop emotional self-regulation. Ask them to practise emotional intelligence between sessions.

Often this practical approach is not enough for a client to regulate more effectively. For example, some clients do not just avoid emotional experience, but dismiss it, are untrusting of it or even feel antagonistic towards it, such as 'there's no point crying', 'it's irrational to worry' or 'nice girls don't get angry'. This self-talk and associated attitudes inadvertently create a negative self-evaluation, drain energy and hope, and, rather than promote resilience, reinforce a sense of futility and despair (Kosminsky and Jordan 2016). It can help to make sense of and consider the origin of a client's emotional experiences:

- **Invite a client to consider their emotional experience.** Model an attitude of curiosity and acceptance. Explore their expression of emotions to bring into awareness the associated attitudes, self-talk and behaviour.

- **Track back in time to when this originated** and consider what happened that they needed to be like this. Typically, what was learned was a necessary adaptive response to others, often their caregivers, and was probably the best that could be created in the circumstances – e.g. 'there's no point crying' was a successful childhood defence against caregivers who were indifferent or disapproving of crying; it is now habitual and would evoke childhood shame if not followed, despite no longer being needed. This can be seen as 'resistance as assistance' (Houston 2003, p.23) and needs to be respected but not colluded with.

- **Work with internal conflicts between beliefs and the body.** Clients may have an internal conflict between their mind's beliefs about expressing emotions and their body's actual experience of those emotions, e.g. believing it would be shameful to cry and so inhibiting their body's urge to cry. Consider the origin of their beliefs, as described above, or invite an imaginary dialogue between their mind and body (see two-chair work below).

- **Invite them to feel the necessity of their strategy in the past** to honour it and to develop self-empathy and compassion. Clients often find such insight reassuring and validating of their earlier life decisions.

- **Sometimes the origin is unclear**, e.g. experiences that predate cognitive memory, early formation of attachment style, or have been 'lost' to awareness such as through trauma. Offer general information and invite a client to reflect on what it means:

  'We develop our way to regulate our emotions through life experiences. As infants and children, this is through how our parents responded to us when we were emotional. Later, it can be through difficult and stressful experiences. Either way, we figure out something that works, usually without being aware of that, and keep using it because it *does* work. If you want, I can help you develop new ways of regulating your emotions to help you grieve more effectively.'

- **Consider whether their old strategy serves them now**, with a view to making a more informed choice about how to emotionally self-regulate.

- **Develop new self-talk** that is empathic and compassionate:

  'I learned as a kid that crying didn't work with my mum, because "big boys don't cry", and I recognise that during this bereavement my body needs to cry.'

Down-regulating emotions

In addition to the ideas above, the following ideas are for clients who get emotionally overwhelmed, such as those with an anxious/ambivalent or disorganised attachment style. This can be seen as developing the flexibility to move towards the restoration orientation.

- **Use the 'grounding' ideas** on page 143.

- **Ask a client to slow down** their speech and gestures; suggest they stand up and move around.

- **Develop self-trust in their new capacity to regulate**, e.g. taking a moment after they use a strategy to acknowledge how they feel 'better' than they did, and creating evidence-based self-talk, e.g.

  'I can moderate my distress when I relax my body, prolong my out-breath and focus on something nice.'

- **Take regular breaks** to breathe and self-calm.

▓ Emma

Emma easily became overwhelmed and distressed by crying, deep sadness, anxiety and anger during counselling. Her counsellor proposed that he intervene when this happened to help Emma down-regulate, to which she agreed.

At first, her counsellor would be directive and ask Emma to stop, breathe and 'ground' herself in the room. As Emma learned how to use these strategies, her counsellor changed their response to reflecting back that she was overwhelmed and asking her, 'What would help you right now?' In response, Emma would pause, breathe and turn her attention to the present moment. Later in the work it was enough for her counsellor to just reflect back her becoming overwhelmed, until eventually Emma could regulate independently.

This took Emma a lot of practice, including between sessions when she practised calming breathing, 'grief in a box' (see pages 159–60) and doing Sudoku puzzles to self-regulate her grief.

Up-regulating emotions

In addition to the ideas above, the following are for clients, such as those with an avoidant or disorganised attachment style, who appear not to feel or do not express emotion, despite you imagining they would. Such clients may experience emotions and regulate them by avoiding that experience. This can be seen as developing the flexibility to move towards the loss orientation.

- **Start counselling with engaging a client's intellect** before engaging emotionally:

  When allowed to take their time and draw their own conclusions, avoidant clients will often get to a point where they can let down the defences they have erected against their own emotions, and the help offered by others. (Kosminsky and Jordan 2016, p.140)

- **Enquire how they feel:** 'I'm curious what emotions go with that.'

- **Invite them to imagine someone else** going through the same thing and how they would feel; if they struggle, suggest how you imagine someone would feel.

- **Raise a client's bodily awareness** by inviting them to slow down, give attention to their body and describe what is happening. This can be developed to give a 'voice' to a part of their body where there are sensations to 'hear' what is 'said', then explore what emerges with an open mind and normalise grief emotions. Often old beliefs about emotional expression still inhibit expression (see above).

- **Confront them with their loss** and ask how they feel:

  'This is huge; your loved one has died and isn't coming back. I expect you feel something about that.'

John

John was very angry, but deflected his attention away from that when his counsellor reflected it back. The next time this happened, his counsellor reflected back how John was angry and deflected attention away from it; John paused, looked self-conscious and became defensive. The counsellor responded, 'All of you is welcome here, John, including your anger. I'm curious, not critical, about what happens to you when I comment on your anger. Are you curious about that too?' This developed into considering when this began in John's childhood, when it was necessary for him to be well behaved to avoid punishment from his parents and some teachers. In summarising this work, his counsellor said, 'So not being angry was a clever strategy you figured out as a child. It kept you safe, and now it's safe to be angry here.'

Subsequently, when John became angry, his counsellor invited him to be aware of his body as he spoke and then invited John to consider this bodily experience. John still felt apprehensive and self-conscious about showing anger, but gradually came to trust his counsellor through repeatedly experiencing her acceptance and ability to withstand his anger.

Through this work John began to feel less angry and to feel more guilt and a deeper sadness for his loss. He was moving through his grief and facing the next part of grieving.

Dissociating from emotions

Dissociation is the regulation of overwhelming emotions and bodily sensations by disconnecting or separating from them so they are not experienced. It happens out of awareness and occurs in response to being either above or below the window of tolerance: by disconnecting from emotions by going numb, or from memories by going blank or having amnesia, or from oneself by being an outside observer of oneself, and from the world by experiencing it as unreal. These experiences of dissociating can be unpleasant, disorientating and confusing. Dissociation is more likely to happen to clients who are traumatised, as well as those who have a disorganised attachment style.

In addition to the ideas above, when working with dissociation:

- We often experience dissociation as a client having 'gone away' and no longer being completely present with us.

- Use the 'grounding' ideas on page 143 and give the client time to feel calmer and grounded with you in the safety of the counselling room.

- Honour the usefulness of dissociating. Say that, at least for now, they need to keep this way to regulate the experience and that they could add new ways to cope with you (Rothschild 2017).

- Explore what triggered dissociation, e.g. an emotion, a bodily sensation, a memory, something in the environment, etc.

- Be mindful of their triggers in future and regulate exposure to what is disconnected from, as if turning a tap on and off, and work in little steps. Note, being very tired or depressed needs gently increased stimulation, whereas dissociating from overwhelming trauma symptoms needs reduced stimulation (Rothschild 2017).

- Develop a client's capacity to regulate this experience in other ways.

- See Chapter 11 about trauma.

Mahi

Mahi was traumatised by seeing her son in intensive care and by realising that she could not keep her children completely safe. When recalling these experiences, Mahi would become overwhelmed and retraumatised, and could then unknowingly dissociate.

Her counsellor could observe this happening: Mahi would quickly become very anxious and tense, the colour drained from her face, and her breathing was rapid and shallow. Then she could dissociate by subtly seeming to 'switch off' – for example, she would become very still and either lose eye contact or have a fixed stare. When this first happened, her counsellor would 'ground' her and then explore what had happened and normalise it. What emerged was then used to inform how both of them could intervene to down-regulate her emotional experience (see above) before she would dissociate.

Also, over time both Mahi and her counsellor became familiar with what triggered her trauma and subsequent dissociation, and used this awareness so Mahi could decide how much she would engage with a traumatic memory during a session (see Chapter 11).

Crying

In grief, clients' sadness tells them they have lost a loved one and urges them to slow down and be introspective to help adapt to their loss (Bonanno 2009).

Sadness is often, but not always, accompanied by crying. Crying relieves emotional stress (Worden 2009) and evokes sympathy and support from others, thereby meeting the need for attachment at stressful times (Bonanno 2009).

There are different depths of crying, from shallow 'calling weeping' that attempts to reunite us with someone we are attached to, to deeper 'letting-go weeping' that only comes after finally letting go of a deceased loved one. In 'calling weeping' we just shed tears, it can last for hours and does not lead to longer-lasting relief. In 'letting-go weeping', breathing is slower, we sob and empty our lungs of air, and then need to take a big breath in before emptying again. This affects many more muscles, seems to last for only 10–20 minutes, and is usually followed by a sense of peace through relaxing muscular tension held as a defence against the pain of loss (Leick and Davidsen-Nielsen 1991, pp.10–12).

Seen through the dual process model, 'letting-go weeping' fully embraces the loss, which then enables a subsequent shift to restoration. I have noticed a tendency for anxiously attached clients to use 'calling weeping' over 'letting-go weeping' that suggests a reluctance to let go.

'Letting-go weeping' requires psychological strength to withstand being so distressed. Some clients fear that if they really cry, they will not stop, they will 'go mad' or 'lose control', etc. However, if they could not stop, their body would eventually get tired and stop crying. You could suggest they risk crying with you if that helps them. Normalise crying in grief, and give your client both permission and the choice: 'Crying is a normal part of grieving; you're welcome to cry here, but please don't feel you have to.'

It is unhelpful to imply a client *has* to cry with you, because you could unintentionally shame them. Consider whether they could cry in private if that is more acceptable to them. Also, consider clients' culture; 'crying is a perfect example of how grief takes on dramatically different meanings in diverse cultures' (Bonanno 2009, p.179).

Cognitive understanding and making meaning

The death of a client's loved one results in much that needs to be understood and then given meaning, and creating a coherent narrative of the life of the person who died is a principal task of grieving (Walter 1996). Unfortunately, as this often happens at the same time that their assumptive world (see page 26) has been undermined by the death, they do not have their former coherent and trustworthy worldview to make meaning of their changed lives, and this in turn reduces their capacity to grieve successfully. Some things about the loss may be incomprehensible to a client, whereas others are known to be possible – for example, parents know that their child might die before them, but life is lived assuming that this will not happen. Put another way, the narrative (or 'story') a client has constructed about themselves, their loved one and the world is disrupted, or even shattered. Being so psychologically disorganised feels disorientating and dislocates clients from their world. Potentially, this is perceived as so threatening to a client's psychological self that it is traumatic (Pearlman *et al.* 2014) (see Chapter 11).

Grieving, therefore, needs to involve narrative repair (Neimeyer and Sands 2011). If a client's assumptive world has been significantly damaged, they need to revise or construct believable assumptions before this narrative repair work is practical. Narrative repair happens through clients making meaning of their bereavement and thereby updating and reconstructing their narrative. This is an ongoing process rather than a goal. This helps clients create enough meaning to integrate the death, the consequences of it and all that this means for who they are now and their life going forward. Or at least to find a way to integrate the loss into who they are and find their way live with it (Pearlman *et al.* 2014).

■ Mahi

When Mahi's son Jake unexpectedly died through a drug overdose, she needed to reconstruct key assumptions about her world, including 'I can keep my children safe'; revise her sense of who Jake really was and her relationship with him; understand his death; revise her identity now she was no longer his mother; and find new meaning and purpose for her life.

Studies support the importance of this work for a favourable outcome to bereavement (e.g. Holland *et al.* 2006) – in particular, making sense of the loss, finding something of benefit in the loss and re-forming identity. Unrepaired narratives leave someone stuck between their old world and the new reality of living with what has happened and all its implications, and can lead to difficulties in grieving (Holland *et al.* 2006) (see 'Complexities and difficulties in grieving' in Chapter 1).

Understanding and making meaning is often very difficult in substance-related bereavements, particularly with confusing and complex matters such as the effects of the substance(s) used; substance-using behaviour, especially if addictive; disturbing or unexplained aspects of the death; any co-occurring mental health difficulties; unfinished business from relationship difficulties caused through substance-using behaviour; and unexpectedly severe and prolonged grief (Cartwright 2019). It is important for bereaved people to process these experiences after the death (Cartwright 2019; Templeton and Velleman 2018). This can involve giving up long-held yet also unrealistic, unhealthy or unhelpful parts of their assumptive world – for example, assuming they can control someone else's behaviour.

Public accounts of events, such as at the funeral or inquest and in the media, can have an authority that legitimate or undermine a client's narrative (Walter 2005), and have been found to significantly influence making meaning in substance-related bereavements (Valentine and Templeton 2018). Similarly, socio-political narratives such as stigma also influence making meaning (Guy and Holloway 2007). Making meaning is harder still for clients who are also traumatised (see page 202).

A client's attachment style influences how they make meaning: someone with a secure style may have positive assumptions about others and the authorities, which can leave them less prepared for a sudden and unexpected death, and in turn increases the risk of a shattering of their assumptive world; an anxious ambivalent style can lead to an unhelpful ruminating or preoccupation with the deceased (see page 78); an avoidant style can lead to avoiding or dismissing the need to make meaning; and a disorganised style is often associated with difficultly mentalising and forming a coherent narrative. Also, habitual, attachment-motivated ways of relating will influence making meaning of the relationship with the person who died – for example, deep ambivalence or compulsive caring. As noted above, regulating emotional experience and emotional intelligence are necessary for making meaning.

Facilitating making meaning

The work is to help a client feel unburdened of their past so that they can get on with their life, as far as is possible; to update or reconstruct a good enough, coherent, realistic narrative about what happened; and to discover who they are now and what is meaningful to them going forward. These have to fit with their experience of the loss and the available evidence (which may be incomplete and/or unsatisfactory).

What needs to be understood and given meaning typically emerges through normal counselling practice, where you are guided by a client's needs, wants and interests. This potentially is both loss- and restoration-orientated work.

It is often necessary to explain to clients that, at least in part, their assumptions about life, the meaning they gave it and the purpose it held no longer hold true for them, and that their old identity has been lost. Clients can then be aware of and make sense of their disorientation and dislocation from life.

Making meaning can happen implicitly while doing other work. However, clients can often be confused, misunderstand, assume they cannot make sense of what happened and/or fail to resolve what is unfinished, and they often do not know that counselling can help with these (Cartwright 2019). Therefore, you need to reflect back when this work is necessary and inform them how counselling can help. Also, you need to be clear that there are limits on what is possible, to avoid the 'myth of closure' (Joyce and Sills 2014, p.129), as clients and the people in their lives can expect counselling to provide closure.

Making meaning requires that a client 'moves from a reactive, to a reflective, to a reintegrated stance' (Kosminsky and Jordan 2016, p.156). In practice, this means slowing down, regulating emotions and reflecting with curiosity, combined with emotional awareness and expression when needed. Also, it involves the capacity to mentalise, which you may need to provide by offering your interpretations of the mind of the client and others, as well as inviting a client to experiment with doing this to develop their own capacity. Mentalising may be a necessary part of reducing activation of the attachment system and trauma response (Allen 2013). Additionally, there are often strongly held beliefs that need to be considered or even challenged when making meaning, such as 'I should've been able to stop them using'. Through these, and with your help, a client comes to understand what happened and can then consider what it means to them.

However, some clients may never succeed in fully making sense of what happened, such as never really knowing why a loved one took their own life. This reality needs to be accepted. As there is a limit to what a purely logical approach can provide, consideration of existential themes and of spiritual practices can help (S. Mahajan, personal communication) (see Chapter 17).

This is an intrinsically individual, subjective and ongoing process, and cannot be forced. Meaning changes over time and the implications of a death continue to become apparent over a lifetime. Therefore, a client's truth may not be *the truth* as you see it; what matters is that a client finds enough credible meaning for now, in order to move forward in life. There is a therapeutic balance between your holding, and, when appropriate, presenting, an evidence-based view that counters a client's misperception, and your accepting what they are able to manage at this time and letting go of any need for accuracy. Remember that this work often occurs when a client's world seems unempathic, unsupportive and even stigmatising. For example, a recently bereaved and stigmatised client may need to see the death of their loved one as an accidental overdose rather than the suicide it seems to be. A lack of fit with reality can be returned to later in the work.

It is important to keep a sense of perspective: recognise that the loss is only a part of a client's life; avoid generalising from particular difficult and painful experiences of the loss to the rest of their life; include experiences of other people who were kind or supportive and integrate these into any new narratives and assumptions about the world (especially if they are traumatised and need to re-establish a sense of safety in the world).

Over time, encourage clients to shift from making meaning of the loss to making meaning of their life and the future (see Chapter 17).

Ways of facilitating making meaning

- **Normal counselling practice** of empathic listening, well-timed helpful statements and questions, reflecting back perceptive observations and inviting a client to consider what something means for them. Start where a client is now, and explore their current narratives and assumptive world beliefs that no longer 'work' for them. Consider what that means for them and create new narratives and assumptions. The counselling relationship offers safe opportunities for a client to create and test new assumptions about other people.

- **Offer to educate** about bereavement; substance use, especially if addictive; how relationships are co-created; and any other matters (see page 140). Having this information and considering what it means may be enough for a client to make new meaning, or is at least a necessary first step.

- **Invite them to use their own experiences to empathise** with how, perhaps, the deceased used substances to cope with grief, shame, guilt, trauma, etc.

- **Consider public accounts of events** and their influence on a client's narrative. Validate their experience where appropriate.

- **Support groups** of similarly bereaved people can be another effective way to make meaning (Murphy, Johnson and Lohan 2003). Groups can be helpful for substance-related bereavements (Adfam 2011a; Cartwright 2019).

- **Creative techniques** (Neimeyer 2012). It often helps clients to imagine or experience what needs to be made meaning of, rather than talk about it, e.g. using photos or possessions of the deceased;[1] journal writing; poetry; drawing; painting; sculpture, etc. Always invite a client to reflect after such experiences and consider what it means for them.

- **Create a dialogue between different parts of a client's experience.** A particularly effective creative technique is to 'separate in order to integrate', i.e. separating and differentiating parts of a client's experience to explore them, by 'hearing' from each part, having an imaginary

---

1   Often addicted people sell everything they have of value to buy substances; also, their family often have few, if any, photographs of them in later addiction.

conversation between them, and then considering what emerges to integrate any new insight or awareness (Korb, Gorrell and Van De Riet 1989). This can be between people, e.g. a client and the deceased, or between parts of a client's inner experience, e.g. 'I should have saved them' and '...but I'd tried everything and I was exhausted'. Ways to do this are 'two-chair work'; writing letters to the deceased and writing one back from them; using Russian dolls or objects such as stones, seashells, toy figures, etc. This way of working needs to be understood and takes practice, and is beyond the scope of this book (see further reading suggestions at the end of this chapter).

Such dialogues can be very effective, as, for example, giving counselling greater emotional depth. However, it is not the same as actually speaking to the person who died, so check how a client feels about this.

Psychics and mediums

A contentious and often avoided aspect of bereavement support is clients seeing a psychic or medium to contact their deceased loved one. In the USA, Feigelman et al. (2012) found that of parents whose children died of a drug overdose, 54% contacted psychics, and many found it helpful, were reassured and better able to focus on other important things, such as relationships with other loved ones. In the UK, Ford et al. (2018) found that some people bereaved through substance use reported receiving answers to questions from spiritual practitioners, which brought them relief and some resolution. In contrast, Parkes (2001) found in a study of people bereaved by all deaths that visits to séances or spiritualist churches were generally unsatisfying, a few were frightened and none became regular attendees.[2] Similarly, the experience over 25 years at Lewisham Bereavement Counselling in London is that clients bereaved through all deaths generally found this unhelpful and even disturbing (P. Austin, personal communication).

I imagine this difference in experience reflects the deeply ambivalent relationship, with much unfinished business, that parents so often have with an addicted child. Also, this seems to be attachment behaviour, at least in part, because bereaved parents desperately want to know if their child is okay and where they are. However, it can be a denial of the death (Worden 2009).

This needs to be handled sensitively so that it does not inadvertently induce shame in a client or get between you; worse, a client may keep it secret.

---

2   Parkes has also found that spiritualist churches usually have the odd member whose 'conversion' followed a bereavement (C.M. Parkes, personal communication).

- Suggest that contacting a psychic might be better left until later in bereavement when a client has adjusted enough to form a healthy continuing bond.

- Be alert to vulnerable clients being exploited.

- Offer to explore their needs, hopes and expectations of seeing someone; consider the nature of their relationship with the deceased; and explore what they imagine it will be like if they do not get what they wanted.

- If they go, reflect afterwards whether any 'contact' is supportive or not, and consider together whether this attempt at a continuing bond is healthy and adaptive.

Adapting to a changed life

Through the emotional and cognitive work described above, clients adapt internally to their new world without their loved one, and it becomes increasingly possible to make behavioural adaptations to live in their new world. This is a move from 'hopelessness to purposefulness and from isolation to engagement' (Kosminsky and Jordan 2016, p.109) that happens through restoration-orientated activities, so clients regain a sense of purpose and further integrate the loss into their lives. In addition, clients can benefit from small behavioural adaptations throughout grieving – for example, activities that increase pleasant emotions, having a break from grief or being aware of coping effectively (Pearlman *et al.* 2014).

Adaptation can be difficult and often happens gradually, and it may be a long time before a client is ready to start in earnest. Significant life-changing decisions are generally best left until someone's judgement is not influenced by acute grief (Worden 2009). Unfortunately, some changes need addressing before a client might be ready – for example, what to tell people at work or replacing the emotional support provided by the deceased loved one. This is typically stressful and demanding because it occurs at what is already a very difficult time. Your support will probably be crucial to a client making such changes. It may well be necessary to develop a client's self-support. Additionally, social support helps adaptation, although this may be problematic due to stigma (see page 113). There are limits to this work: a loved one can never be replaced, a parent will never be able to care for their child again, and stigma may inhibit forming new relationships, etc.

Facilitating adaptation work

Behavioural adaptation requires clients to feel the hope that they can rebuild a meaningful life that has purpose, a commitment to fulfil their hope and a belief that they can influence what happens in their life. These characteristics may be part of their assumptive world that no longer holds true and their life may have lost its meaning and purpose.

Another aspect of clients' assumptive world that is important for adaptation is the values by which they live (Pearlman *et al.* 2014). Values include what is of importance, significance and worth to them, as well as their morals and ethics. Values provide meaning, purpose and identity, and guide how they relate to others; they are lived through the direction and goals of life and relationships with others. After the death these values may also no longer hold true, and thereby direction, goals and relationships lose meaning. For example, a bereaved parent's values about caring for their offspring and the self-worth they gain from that are lost through bereavement.

For successful behavioural adaptation to happen, therefore, clients need to have identified old assumptions that have survived the death, updated those that did not survive, and have a sense of hope and capability. Often this meaning-making work requires experimenting with behaviour change to identify and test these new cognitions, so that meaning-making and behavioural adaptation happen in a cycle where each promotes the development of the other. This in turn reconstructs a sense of meaning and purpose in life.

Additionally, adaptation requires clients to *feel* what they want, what matters most now, so that 'when the future is scanned for opportunities to accomplish what is worth accomplishing, purpose is created and motivation and will-power emerge' (van Deurzen 2002, p.155).

Much behavioural adaptation is essentially practical work. Help clients to identify activities, projects, goals, relationships, roles, etc., that they want to experiment with, plan ways to do that, then reflect on the evidence of what happened to raise their awareness of what to take forward and what needs further work. Often this involves many small steps. Celebrate together clients' achievements and successes, and check that these build their sense of hope, efficacy, esteem and control. One example might be identifying a value of maintaining good health that is then lived through the goal of exercising three times a week (Pearlman *et al.* 2014), which a client then affirms for themselves.

◼ John

Early in his grieving, John needed to use his counselling to adapt to how he managed his grief around his manager. With his counsellor he prepared what he felt able to say about Sarah's death and developed the self-support to say it.

He began by telling those colleagues he thought would be sympathetic. As this went okay, he then told other colleagues and finally had the confidence to tell his manager. Most of those he told, including his manager, seemed not to know what to say, and John was relieved that most people avoided raising it, yet also he felt unexpectedly alone and vulnerable in his grief at work.

Many months later John could still feel alone and vulnerable. His counsellor reminded him about telling the people at work, and that despite it being very difficult he had succeeded, so the counsellor asked John if he was interested in engaging with others again. John recognised this need and was deeply reluctant to try. His counsellor acknowledged that and proposed instead that they explore what *was* important to him about engaging with others to see if he could find a way that interested and motivated him. John found pleasure in the intellectual challenge to establish what mattered to him now, and he combined this with the emotional intelligence he had already developed in bereavement counselling to also feel what he wanted.

He decided to join a group for bereaved parents, where he thought that limited and clearly defined engagement would be manageable. Through the group, John realised he could honour Sarah's death by engaging with others; as he said to his counsellor: 'I had to lose Sarah to find other people!' After some months, he volunteered to administer the group's meetings. His counsellor commented that the group members seemed to be benefiting from the care he had not given to Sarah; John agreed, and this gave administering the group additional meaning for him.

Difficulties in adapting

Getting on with their own life can be the most difficult task of grieving for clients (Worden 2009). Watch for clients who avoid behavioural adaptation and, if necessary, explore what stops this. Possible reasons include:

- denial that the person is dead

- needing to work further on loss-orientated activities, e.g. enduring guilt

- fears about forgetting their loved one, of others believing they do not care enough about their loved one, of forming new relationships and being bereaved again, and traumatised clients feeling threat at the prospect of engaging with the world again, etc.

- attachment style, e.g. a client with an anxious ambivalent style clinging on to grief as an unhealthy continuing bond or struggling to imagine making their own way in the world

- lacking the life skills to adapt.

A client's continued suffering is not adaptive, nor is it a healthy continuing bond (see Chapter 17).

FURTHER READING ON BEREAVEMENT COUNSELLING

Kosminsky, P.S. and Jordan, J.R. (2016) *Attachment-Informed Grief Therapy: The Clinician's Guide to Foundations and Applications*. New York, NY: Routledge.

Worden, J.W. (2009) *Grief Counselling and Grief Therapy: A Handbook for the Mental Health Practitioner* (4th edition). Hove: Routledge.

FURTHER READING ON CREATIVE AND EXPERIENTIAL WORKING

Houston, G. (2003) *Brief Gestalt Therapy*. London: SAGE Publications. Pages 63–72, including 'two chair work' on pages 65 and 66.

Joyce, P. and Sills, C. (2014) *Skills in Gestalt Counselling and Psychotherapy* (3rd edition). Chapters 9 and 11. London: SAGE Publications.

Neimeyer, R.A. (ed.) (2012) *Techniques of Grief Therapy: Creative Practices for Counseling the Bereaved*. New York, NY: Routledge.

10

Themes in Bereavement Counselling

The previous chapter considered *what* needs to happen in bereavement counselling. This chapter covers eight themes that describe *how* to counsel a client, considering both general and substance-related characteristics of bereavement. These themes are adapted largely from Kosminsky and Jordan's thematic questions (2016, pp.156–159), Rando's six 'R' processes of mourning (1993) and Worden's four tasks of mourning (2009):

- recognition and acceptance of the death

- how the client is coping and what support they need

- relationship with the person who died

- the death and its aftermath

- what the client has lost

- who the client is now

- a continuing bond

- what a client wants for their future.

Each of these themes combines emotional, cognitive and behavioural parts, as described in Chapter 9. Themes may emerge naturally during counselling, or, as clients often do not know what is possible, you can suggest a theme and say why you believe it needs attention (and, as ever, respect a client's choice).

Themes are returned to many times during bereavement counselling; in any one session there is a unique blend of one or more themes, as needed by a client. Although these are themes and not a sequence of steps, they tend to unfold in roughly this order, with earlier themes being loss-orientated and later themes restoration-orientated. A theme is not a separate piece of work; rather, it is interrelated with and often merges into other themes. As this is complex, it can help to create a spider diagram, or similar visual representation, so that both you and the client can keep track of all its constituent parts and how they interrelate, and to see the whole bereavement. These themes provide an overview of the potential work a client might need to complete (see also page 287).

However, although working through these themes facilitates a client through their grief, they do not imply the right way to grieve; what is important is whether a client's way of grieving is healthily adaptive. Also, these themes are offered to support normal counselling practice and not to replace it. Therefore, as usual, focus on what a client wants; stay with how they are now and resist the temptation to push them forward; accept when they do not want to do all that might be worked on; and, if appropriate, invite them to come back in future.

Clients can continue this work between sessions and I believe this is an important and integral part of bereavement counselling. It helps them practise ideas from their sessions, integrate the work into their lives, develop confidence in their own capacities, and also undertake work that cannot be done in the sessions.

Multiple bereavements

Clients may not have fully grieved for past deaths due to other causes and, sadly, some have experienced more than one substance-related death. This may create bereavement overload, which is potentially traumatic, can elicit survivor guilt and reduces the number of potential people who can provide support (Rando 1993).

Therefore, consider taking a history of all a client's significant experiences of separation, loss and bereavement. Identify those that still feel 'live'. Separate them and work on them one at a time (Leick and Davidsen-Nielsen 1991). Start with the loss that has the fewest complicating factors (Worden 2009). Periodically 'step back' together to identify themes, make connections between losses and consider how those losses affect each other.

Recognition and acceptance of the death

This theme is characterised by loss-orientated activities. When a client has enough support, repeatedly talking about and facing the reality of the loss:

- **Ensure you use words such as 'died' and 'dead'**, and speak of the deceased in the past tense.

- **See the body, attend the funeral, go to the grave, etc.** Offer to explore whether or not a client will see the body (see page 117), and, if relevant, their experience of doing so. Clients can also imagine experiencing these events.

- **Where there are uncertainties about the circumstances of the death**, gather and consider what information and circumstantial evidence is available. Establish what still needs to be known, if and when such information could be available, and how a client might obtain it (Pearlman *et al.* 2014).

- **Unfinished business can block grieving** – see Chapter 12.

- **Explore what it means for a client to recognise the loss**, e.g. a parent no longer having a child to care about, or the end of addictive substance-using behaviour.

- **Consider what life is like without the deceased**, e.g. remember the past and look at photos, or explore a client's hopes and expectations for the future that are no longer possible.

- **Recognise if a client has traumatic bereavement** – see Chapter 11.

As a way to cope with the enormity of the death, a client may not emotionally accept it. Full recognition and acceptance of the permanent and irreversible nature of death happens gradually, with alternation between recognition and disbelief. Further grieving cannot begin in earnest without recognition and acceptance (Worden 2009). If necessary, explore what stops these.

Mahi

When she began counselling, Mahi was traumatised but did not know that she was. Therefore, her counsellor helped her to make sense of that experience and to develop the self-support she needed to withstand re-stimulating her trauma when recalling her son, Jake (see page 210). Once she was confident in her ability to do this, she found out about the condition of Jake's body and, having been reassured, decided to see him. By touching him, she confirmed that he really had died.

Later, her counsellor reflected back how she often said, 'I can't believe it', and spoke about Jake in the present, not the past tense. They explored this; Mahi became aware that the reality of his death had not fully sunk in and she agreed to work on this next.

At first, this involved inviting Mahi to recount what she knew of the circumstances of Jake's death and to piece together what she knew had happened, when it gradually became clear that until the post-mortem and inquest there were key pieces of information she did not yet have. Through considering this many times, the death became more real. This stimulated Mahi's interest in the implications of Jake's death, so she used counselling to explore her lost hopes for Jake's future. By doing so, she began crying and pining for him – she had accepted Jake's death enough to start really grieving.

Ambiguous loss

Occasionally, there is a client who has an ambiguous loss, where the physical presence of their loved one has gone due to their seemingly having died, but as they are unable to verify the death, their loved one is still very much psychologically present (see page 78) – for example, the body being too badly damaged for visual identification. A client's uncertainty may be temporary or permanent. The challenge is for them to learn to live well with this ambiguity, rather than try to resolve what is impossible in order to gain the illusion of certainty and comfort (Boss 2006).

Boss proposes six guidelines, which are not linear and prescriptive, but themes that are returned to many times in a unique way with each client (2006, 2010). These are summarised and adapted below:

1. **Finding meaning.** Help a client to recognise the ambiguity. Acknowledge both sides: the loss and their uncertainty whether the person has died, and how both are valid and inevitable. Consider the implications for a client of each alternative. Recognise the power of attachment and how difficult it is to accept death while there is the possibility a loved one is alive.

2. **Tempering mastery.** Help them not to try to master a situation by going for one or the other side, but rather to develop the capacity to live with ambiguity, uncertainty and not having all the answers, and to learn to hold a paradox: 'Someone we love can be both absent and present at the same time' (Boss 2010, p.141). Explore what promotes a client's resilience to live with ambiguity and what inhibits it, and develop their support, e.g. mindfulness, differentiating between what can and cannot be changed, still having control of what is controllable, such as how to respond to the ambiguity (Boss 2006).

3. **Reconstructing identity.** Identity changes because a loved one is absent. Help them grieve what is lost. In time, offer the idea of expanding their identity in new ways that are consistent with what is not lost.

4. **Normalising ambivalence.** Help them to recognise and accept the normality of their ambivalent response to the situation. Develop compassion and acceptance for their very human struggle. See forgiveness in Chapter 14 and also Chapter 17.

5. **Revising attachment.** Help them to accept the changed relationship and 'celebrate what of that person is still available and grieving the

connections that are no longer possible' (Boss 2010, p.144). Be mindful of the influence of a client's attachment style.

6. **Discovering hope.** To be resilient, a client needs hope. This can come through 'religion, prayer, worship, meditation, nature, exercise, and the arts… [I]n all cases, it is more easily found in the company of others' (p.144). It can also come through recognising that life can continue in a new way.

FURTHER READING
Boss, P. (2006) *Loss, Trauma, and Resilience: Therapeutic Work with Ambiguous Loss.* New York, NY: Norton.

How the client is coping and what support they need
This theme is characterised by loss- and restoration-orientated activities. Explore a client's experience of grief and use what potentially emerges to:

- **Develop their self- and social support as needed** – see page 152. Be mindful of their attachment style and how that influences their use of support.

- **Normalise the emotional experience of grief,** including wanting to avoid it, how successful grieving will alleviate the pain, and that grief can be broken down into manageable steps during counselling.

- **Offer to inform about bereavement** – see Chapters 1, 5 and 6.

- **Consider and work through any shame, stigma and disenfranchised grief,** and the impact on self- and social support. See Chapters 6 and 13.

Dreams frequently parallel the grieving process and often show where a client is stuck (Worden 2009). Return to their experience of grief as it changes and their associated need for support.

Relationship with the person who died
This theme is characterised by loss-orientated activities. A client's relationship with the person who died, the 'back story', is an essential part of making meaning of the death (Holland and Neimeyer 2011) and can be highly emotive work (Rando 1993).

- **Create a coherent, compassionate and accurate narrative of the relationship.** Invite a client to recall as many experiences as possible, e.g. what was valued and appreciated, what was difficult and hurtful, any ambivalence, regrets, what is not known, etc. Work with the associated emotions, e.g. guilt, blame and anger – see Chapter 14. Their narrative needs to be accurate and comprehensive, because anything missing may cause difficulties later in grieving (Pearlman *et al.* 2014), e.g. it is normal to have only an idealised image of the deceased early in grieving. To make meaning their narrative only needs to be good enough. Be mindful of the influence of a client's attachment style.

- **Include the impact of substance-using behaviour and other associated difficulties**, e.g. the impact on a client's physical and mental health.

- **Where appropriate, include the impact of parental substance use** on a client's childhood and personal development, and how that impacts their bereavement.

- **Reconcile family difficulties.** As far as it is possible, offer to work through family relationships strained or broken by the deceased's substance-using behaviour – see Chapters 4 and 6.

- **Work through any unfinished business** from the relationship – see Chapters 6 and 12.

- **Recognise if a client has traumatic bereavement and/or is depressed** by past experiences – see Chapters 11 and 15.

Emma

Emma needed to use her counselling for the loss of Steve. However, her counsellor had asked Emma about her past so knew her father had been addicted to alcohol and that she had helped care for him as a child.

While her counsellor held the focus on bereavement, he used this information to inform the work Emma did – for example, making connections to her past to raise her awareness of her habitual patterns of attachment and caregiving that had inadvertently assisted Steve's drinking.

Towards the end of counselling, Emma's counsellor suggested that she have further help with the relationship with her father when she felt ready.

The death and its aftermath

This theme is characterised by loss-orientated activities. The way the person died, or 'event story', is an essential part of making meaning of the bereavement (Holland and Neimeyer 2011). Often the death is very significant in substance-related bereavements, especially when traumatic and when there are official procedures (see Chapter 6).

- **Create a coherent, compassionate and realistic narrative of the death and its aftermath.** A client needs to make good enough sense of the circumstances of the death itself (including what might remain unanswered, withheld or unknown) and have considered what this means for them. Where the deceased is likely to have been traumatised by the circumstances of their death, clients are typically relieved to know that being traumatised probably spared the deceased unbearable pain and terror (Levine 2008).

- **The funeral and other ceremonies or rituals.** Explore what a client wants from these for themselves and the deceased, and how they might get those. These are rare opportunities to reclaim a sense of control, e.g. deciding how much to say about substance use, or arranging a funeral so that at the end a client leaves the coffin rather than the coffin being removed from them. Afterwards, reflect on their experience, whether it helped and what it means to them. If necessary, suggest they can create their own ceremony or ritual, with your help, that is helpful and meaningful. A second ceremony some time after the funeral can be helpful, e.g. the funeral was too soon after a sudden death, or to mark the passage of time (Parkes *et al.* 2015). See page 90 about memorialising the deceased.

- **Official procedures.** Explore a client's hopes, expectations and concerns about these, and develop their support to cope with these as required. Afterwards, reflect on their experience of these and whether they were helpful and what it means to them.

- **Work through unfinished business** associated with the death and/or its aftermath – see Chapter 12.

- **Recognise if a client has traumatic bereavement** from the death and experiences during the aftermath – see Chapter 11.

What the client has lost

This theme is characterised by loss-orientated activities:

- **The loss of a client's loved one and their old attachment.** Facilitate a client's repeated crying, pining and searching, so they fully experience and make meaning of their attempts to 'reunite' with the deceased (see Chapter 1). Thereby, they more deeply accept the death and relinquish their old attachment (which is not forgotten, and for parents may continue indefinitely). Normalise their pain and any reluctance to go through this, and offer to develop their support. Explore 'What do you miss about them?', celebrate the life and consider lost roles, hopes, dreams and plans for them. Over time, ensure a client grieves for the whole of who the deceased was, including both what was loved and hated. An overly positive view of the deceased may mask anger about them. Propose that they can form a continuing bond.

- **Say goodbye to the deceased**, especially if they did not get to say this before the death, e.g. in counselling, at the funeral, at the graveside, etc.

- **Explore 'Where do you believe your loved one is now?'** and reflect on what it is like for a client to believe that.

- **Consider a client's old assumptive world** about themselves, the way their life works, about others, the world in general and their spirituality/world view (Rando 2014 cited in Pearlman *et al.* 2014, p.217). Potentially, each one can be challenged, changed, invalidated or shattered and needs to be grieved for, including the implications of what these losses mean for their life now. Consider whether lost assumptions will need recreating (see below), e.g. assuming they are basically safe in the world, or needed to be lost, assuming they can control others' behaviour. Listen for a client's explicit and implicit assumptions in what they say, how they think and feel, and what they do. If in doubt, ask them.

- **Consider their old identity.** This is, in part, defined through relationships with others, so when a client's loved one dies, 'we' becomes 'I', and the associated loss of life roles, parts of self and/or meaning and purpose in life, e.g. no longer being a parent. Reflect on how they performed their roles and how they believe others saw them in their roles.

- **Consider secondary losses** that occur as a consequence of the death, e.g. a grandparent needing to care for grandchildren, thereby losing their retirement. Explore what changes a client needs to make now, e.g. develop the ability to do things the deceased did for them. For other adaptations, allow the time needed.

- **The secondary loss of being a carer.** For clients who cared for the deceased, work through any unfinished business associated with caring (see Chapter 12). Normalise any resentment about caring and relief felt for no longer needing to care.

Additionally, where a client cared compulsively,[1] this secondary loss can

---

1   Compulsive caring can often be recognised by someone taking responsibility for what is not their responsibility, intervening when others have not given permission, using caring as a way to feel control in a relationship, and/or a young, unrealistic, grandiose sense of their own ability to care (see page 77).

extend to their identity, self-esteem and meaning and purpose in life. This is because who they are and their sense of agency are tied up with caregiving. In addition to the above, consider what a client wanted for themselves when caring and the origin of that, e.g. the grandiosity and approval a child can feel when caring for their parent, which is then repeated in adult relationships. Encourage a client to give their care to themselves by having self-empathy and compassion for their young self, and help them develop healthier, more realistic ways to care, e.g. supporting others to help themselves.

- **Recognise if a client is traumatised by the loss of their assumptive world and/or is depressed** – see Chapters 11 and 15.

It can help to list a client's losses, take each in turn, express associated emotions, consider the implications of the loss and make meaning of it.

Mahi

Mahi became aware through counselling that she had unknowingly lived by assumptions she learned as a child about being a wife and mother. When Jake died, many of these assumptions were invalidated, which disorientated and frightened her and contributed to her being traumatised. As part of developing her self-support, Mahi's counsellor helped her create self-talk from her 'wise self' when she felt anxious, such as: 'In losing Jake I have also lost what I assumed to be true as his mother. Right now, I'm lost, but my counsellor believes I can construct new assumptions and I trust him enough to be hopeful for that.'

This self-support, plus her counsellor's support, enabled Mahi to consider her old assumptive world, in particular her assumption about being able to protect her children. At her counsellor's invitation, she recalled her own childhood and came to appreciate that parental control is to some extent an illusion, because even when she was very young, sometimes she could resist her parents' demands.

Next, Mahi's counsellor invited her 'wise self' to consider: 'With that in mind, what could you have done to save him?' to which Mahi had the painful realisation that it was not realistic that she could have controlled Jake's life in the way she would have needed to in order to keep him safe. This realisation evoked disorientation, anxiety and deep sadness for this loss.

See the following page for reconstructing this assumption.

Who the client is now

This theme is characterised by restoration-orientated activities. A client needs to 'affirm what continues, and incorporate what is new' (Pearlman *et al.* 2014, p.219).

- **A client's new assumptive world.** Consider what assumptions survived the death that can reassure a client. Revise or construct new assumptions and experiment with them to see if they are valid, until a client's assumptive world fits well enough with their new reality. Consider any new unhelpful assumptions, e.g. 'I deserve to be punished for them dying'. Ideally, new assumptions develop from a client's strengths and encourage moving forward in grieving (Pearlman *et al.* 2014). As assumptions were often formed in childhood and have a simplistic, idealistic or naïve quality to them, invite clients to evoke their adult wisdom for this work – even their healthy cynicism helps sometimes! Consider how their wise self can support their younger self whose world no longer holds true.

- **Reframe secondary losses as needs.** A client's losses can be seen as unmet needs, e.g. the deceased met their needs by driving the car, providing emotional support, was the one who dealt with difficult people or situations, etc. These needs can be met in other ways: a client can meet a need themselves (which may mean developing new skills), find someone else to meet the need, find another way to meet the need, or learn to do without meeting the need. If possible, a client needs to grieve the loss before meeting the associated need in a new way.

- **In loss there is gain.** Sensitively explore 'What won't you miss about your loved one?' and 'What, if anything, have you gained through your loss?', e.g. feeling glad their life is no longer affected by addictive behaviour and relief that the deceased's distress is over. If needed, normalise a client's responses. Often any gain is not of personal benefit (Holland *et al.* 2006). This gain does not balance out the loss; rather, it lies alongside it, because both are true. Also, counselling is an opportunity for personal growth, e.g. clients with an insecure attachment style acquiring earned security (see Chapter 2).

- **The client's new identity.** As far as practical, a client's new identity will not be defined by the loss, grief or the past, but will integrate the loss into being a part of who they are now. They may need to create renewed meaning and purpose in life – see below.

- **Finding a way to live with what has happened,** including the self- and social support to cope with re-stimulated grief, coping with any ongoing stigma and shame, what remains unfinished, and (if relevant) re-stimulated trauma. When recovery from bereavement does not seem possible, consider how to live with loss and grief.

These activities are a process rather than an end point for grieving; they often take years and may never be completed. The timing of this work is important: it is usually appropriate once a client has grieved their losses enough. Before then it can be a way to avoid the pain of the loss by prematurely moving to restoration.

Mahi

Mahi's counsellor proposed they reconstruct her assumption about keeping her children safe and she agreed. He asked her: 'What can you still do to keep your other children safe?' She recognised that she *did* still have influence, if not control, and how important it was for her to use this. Her counsellor proposed that a new assumption might be: 'I really couldn't control my adult son and save him, but I recognise that I still have influence, so will do all I can to keep my other children safe.' Although she found this helpful, she was disappointed by its limits.

Mahi wrote this new assumption in her journal and lived with it for a while before accepting it. She found it was a useful addition to her self-support for her trauma symptoms when she felt panicky at the thought of being unable to save her other children.

A continuing bond

This theme is characterised by restoration-orientated activities. See Chapter 2 for the characteristics of healthy and unhealthy continuing bonds. Clients often find remembering and memorialising a loved one difficult, which complicates any continuing bond – see Chapters 4, 5 and 6.

- **Explain the idea of a continuing bond** and invite a client to consider whether this interests them. If it does, then…

- **Consider the nature of the existing continuing bond or create one.** This needs both to fully acknowledge the loss and be compatible with existing and new relationships. Aspects of a client's relationship to the deceased that were hurtful, frustrating, disappointing, etc., need to be accepted and distanced from, as far as possible, by finding their way to balance remembering and forgetting (Rosenblatt 1993). Remembering positive aspects of the deceased and good times with them helps restoration.

- **Work through any unfinished business** that inhibits forming a satisfactory continuing bond (see Chapter 12).

- **With the client, explore a way to honour the significance of the old attachment**, e.g. 'I will always be your mother'.

- **Explore a way to honour or give meaning to the life of the deceased.** For many bereaved through substance use, it is necessary to honour the memory of the deceased that counters substance use, the death and stigma. Also, to create something good from something so bad, that is significant, meaningful and manageable for a client, e.g. fundraising for a charity associated with the deceased, rituals and ceremonies, taking social action against stigma, etc. Suggest this to a client and help them fulfil their ideas; although be open to this as a way they may be managing guilt (see page 242). See Chapter 17.

- **Conversely, it may be healthy to *not* continue the bond**, e.g. a client whose deceased parent was abusive and unable to meet their childhood needs. A healthier outcome to work towards might be:

  'He will always be my father, but I needed and deserved a better father, so I will let him go and seek others who meet my needs.'

There is much scope for creativity in forming a bond. During this work be aware of what can be continued, what needs to be relinquished, and of a client holding on to grief as an unhealthy way to stay connected.

◼ John

When the counsellor explained bereavement to John early in the work, John dismissed the idea of a continuing bond, so she left it for the time being.

Much later, John spoke about giving Sarah's death meaning by engaging with others in the bereaved parents' group and by his giving the group the care he had not given to Sarah. His counsellor reintroduced the idea of a continuing bond and suggested that one way of viewing these activities was as a continuing bond with Sarah. John could 'see the idea', at which his counsellor asked: 'I'm curious what that's like for you?' John replied: 'It's good...but I'm still sad...and it's about me and not her, and that's not right.' His counsellor offered, 'We could consider what would be right', but John declined.

However, the following session he announced that he had given money to Sarah's favourite charity as a bond that *was* about her.

What a client wants for their future

This theme is characterised by restoration-orientated activities:

- Explore 'What do you want for your future?' and 'What would you want to be doing if you weren't bereaved?' Consider both returning to previous activities and plans and new activities and plans, even if just small steps.

- Explore 'What would your loved one who died want for you now?' However, consider this carefully because it might induce guilt or produce an unhelpful 'reply'.

- Explore 'What gives your life meaning and purpose now?'

- Help a client to act on the outcome of these explorations to create new activities, projects, roles, relationships and identity.

- See Chapter 17.

When to offer this work is significant because it is important that it does not become a way to avoid grieving. However, loss also needs to be balanced with restoration and a client continuing their own life. Watch for clients who have difficulties in grieving and struggle to get on with their life (see 'Complexities and difficulties in grieving' in Chapter 1).

Emma

Emma had real difficulty imagining a future beyond her marriage to Steve. Her counsellor both acknowledged her difficulty and made the connection back to her attachment style and that although Emma's difficulty felt very real, it was not necessarily always true now. Also, he invited her to reflect on what it was like when she did restoration activities, however small, such as buying herself a glossy magazine or having coffee with a mother of her children's friends. Through this, Emma gradually accumulated experiences that indicated that it was possible to occasionally feel happy and content without Steve.

After Emma had worked through her guilt and resentment towards Steve and her father (see pages 252–53), she began speaking about wanting her children to be spared addiction. This also became a way to give Steve's death meaning: 'I still miss him terribly, despite the drinking, and his death is a wake-up call to keep my kids safe.' She stayed in counselling to work through how she could avoid another relationship with a man who would behave like Steve and that she would cling on to.

11

Anxiety, Stress and Traumatic Bereavement

This chapter considers how to work with clients' responses to the various risks and threats that occur in substance-related bereavements. It begins by considering:

- anxiety and stress in bereavement, and associated ideas to support clients.

As some clients will have experienced severe threats and are traumatised, consideration is given to:

- understanding what trauma is and how it happens, and traumatic bereavement

- assessing whether a client is traumatised

- counselling a traumatically bereaved client

- developing a traumatically bereaved client's support to manage their trauma symptoms.

However, the complete treatment of trauma is beyond the scope of this book and further reading is suggested.

Anxiety and stress

Anxiety is a normal response to our anticipating mild to moderate risks; it urges us to be careful and mobilises us to be safe. Therefore, we often seek a 'friend' to help us, typically an attachment figure. Also, we mobilise to help ourselves through the moderate activation of the sympathetic nervous system (SNS), which acts like an accelerator in a car. This then produces the familiar increased heart rate and breathing, feeling sweaty, having worrying thoughts, etc. Once we perceive we are safe, the parasympathetic nervous system (PNS) activates to enable us to relax, rest and recover, like a brake slowing down a car. Where the risk seemingly continues, anxiety builds up and becomes stress, and the PNS does not activate. Choosing to relax often feels counterintuitive, because we are mobilised for action and not rest and recovery (Porges 2011; van der Kolk 2014).

In our evolutionary past, it was important to prioritise short-term threats to life and assume the worst would happen. In our relatively safe modern world, however, this response can be ineffective and an overreaction, and much of what we anxiously anticipate does not actually happen.

Anxiety and stress are common during bereavement:

- Separation anxiety urges someone to reunite with the deceased who they are attached to; that is likely to be more severe for someone with an insecure attachment style characterised by anxiety (see Chapter 2).

- Bereavement challenges someone's assumptive world and thereby potentially their sense of security and safety (see Chapter 1).

- There can be existential anxiety, including someone's realisation of the randomness of life events and awareness of their own mortality (see Chapters 1 and 17).

As discussed in Chapter 6, potential further sources of anxiety for someone bereaved through substance use include:

- disclosing information about substance use and the nature of the death to others, that also may have been withheld in the past

- potential stigmatisation

- the stress of ongoing official procedures and any media intrusion

- where the death was by suicide, anxiety about further suicides and their own suicidal thoughts

- experiencing grief that is unexpectedly severe, complex and long-lasting

- their own use of substances in problematic or addictive ways, and the risks this poses to their life.

Clients who become depressed are often also anxious (Worden 2009) (see Chapter 15), and some clients respond to life events in a habitually anxious way that predates bereavement (see further reading suggestions at the end of this chapter).

Working with anxiety and stress in bereavement

Offer to explain anxiety and stress, both in general and during bereavement, to both normalise it and develop a client's emotional intelligence. Develop a client's support (see Chapter 8). Also, consider the following:

- **Calming the body first.** Calming breathing is particularly effective for activating the PNS (see page 158). Gently stretching tense muscles. Alternatively, discharging their mobilised energy through physical activity may activate their PNS, e.g. a brisk walk or running up and down stairs.

- **Develop supportive self-talk** (see page 156). Specifically, a reassuring 'voice' that identifies with their experience, makes sense of it, affirms their own capabilities and reminds them of the support they have from others, including you.

- **Create visualisations** that are calming and self-supportive, and encourage a sense of capability.

- **Seeking social support from others**, especially attachment figures.

- **Assessing risk**, e.g. asking themselves: 'My anxiety feels real, but is it true I'm at risk right now?'

- **'Doing not stewing.'** Where something can be done about what provokes anxiety, this is often the most effective way to reduce it. Then saying, 'I've done all that I can for now', and calming the body.

- **Consider whether anxiety is suppressed anger** (see page 232).

Traumatic bereavement

Traumatic bereavement happens when the way a loved one dies is so threatening that it traumatises the person who is bereaved. This results in a fusion of trauma and grief responses.

This section explains what trauma is, how it occurs in the context of bereavement and its subsequent impact on grieving. The following sections consider how to assess whether a client is traumatised, how to counsel a traumatically bereaved client, and how to develop their support. For less traumatically bereaved clients, this may be enough to recover from trauma. Integrating this work into the work on bereavement is often enough to enable grieving to happen without it being unduly inhibited by trauma symptoms. This is important, because trauma that happens through being bereaved is *better considered and worked with as the single, inclusive entity of traumatic bereavement*, rather than separately as trauma and bereavement (Pearlman *et al.* 2014; Zandvoort 2012).

This is the minimum you need to be able to do to work safely and effectively with a traumatically bereaved client. These are considered the first phase of any trauma work and are essential for undertaking the next two phases: processing and resolving traumatic memories, and integrating the traumatic experience into a client's life. Where aspects of this work are the same as grief-related work – for example, enduring guilt – this book aids working these through. However, the exclusively trauma-related aspects of these two phases are beyond the scope of this book. It is important to note that no one treatment approach works for all traumatised people nor for all traumas (Rothschild 2017; van der Kolk 2014) (see further reading suggestions at the end of this chapter).

Furthermore, the death may be just one of a series of traumatising events, such as experiencing domestic violence before the death and viewing the body afterwards. Additionally, a client can potentially remain traumatised by childhood events (see page 68). Such trauma work is also beyond the scope of this book, although what is presented below is probably still the necessary first phase of this work.

It is important to decide whether you are capable of working with trauma or need to refer a client to others. Unfortunately, referring on is often problematic. Bereavement counselling services rarely provide trauma work. Typically, accessing effective trauma treatment through the NHS can be very difficult and doctors often only prescribe antidepressants or minor tranquillisers for trauma. Although private counselling may be effective, it is expensive.

What is trauma and how does it happen?

Trauma is the normal survival response that is triggered when someone's ability to respond to a perceived inescapable threat is in some way overwhelmed, which results in re-experiencing the threat, avoidance of re-experiencing it and heightened arousal to protect against further threat (Levine 2008; van der Kolk 2014).

Threats that can traumatise include someone witnessing or imagining (and developing a mental picture of) the horror of a loved one suffering (Pearlman *et al.* 2014) or a sudden unexpected death, especially if also horrific, that threatens someone's psychological self by shattering their assumptive world so that their life is no longer perceived as safe, predictable, fair and benign, and they lose their sense of control and efficacy (Parkes 2009). Other such threats include when someone perceived that their own life was at risk during the same event that killed their loved one (Levine 2008) and the threat of being permanently separated from an attachment figure, or, conversely, the threat of permanent separation from someone for whom someone is an attachment figure (Jordan 2019).

How trauma happens is described next (Levine 2008; Porges 2011; Rothschild 2000, 2017; van der Kolk 2014): when someone perceives an overwhelming threat, it elicits normal, automatic responses from our evolutionary past intended to maximise survival from short-lived threats to life, such as from a predator. Their mind and body mobilise for 'fight, flight or freeze', involving the full activation of the SNS (the body's 'accelerator'). They can experience immense fear or rage, and do everything to survive by dominating or fighting, taking flight and escaping, or freezing like a rabbit in the headlights, hoping not to be noticed and then escaping if the opportunity arises.

If this response is not viable or does not work, particularly if someone perceives being trapped or helpless, their mind and body may then collapse into 'flop' and they immobilise. This involves the excessive activation of the PNS (the body's 'brake'). They surrender, dissociate, have amnesia and become numb to bodily and emotional pain, thereby 'escaping' when no actual escape is possible. This response probably evolved to prevent suffering while being killed.

All of these responses are like a complex reflex, are almost instantaneous and are not within conscious control. If one of the responses is effective, or the threat passes, many people 're-set' to normal over time.

Occasionally, a client will have faced a short-lived threat to their life, such as being in the car crash that killed their loved one who was drink-driving. However, the typical threats clients face, as described above, cannot be resolved by these automatic survival responses as being bereaved is long-lived and not an immediate threat to life. Subsequently, a client's survival responses may continue automatically and inevitably continue to be unsuccessful.

A client remains feeling as if the traumatic event is still happening and is unable to 're-set' to normal, despite knowing rationally that it is over. As they are either over-mobilised or immobilised, or oscillating between the two, they are above or below their window of tolerance (see pages 142–3) and feel profoundly dysregulated. This post-traumatic stress occurs across a spectrum of severity, from temporary to the severe and enduring post-traumatic stress disorder (PTSD). Furthermore, as clients are often unaware of being traumatised, they easily feel overwhelmed, confused and frightened by what is happening to them.

Post-traumatic stress is the result of a fundamental reorganisation of someone's central nervous system following an experience of overwhelming threat, which reorganises self-experience to feeling helpless and the world perceived as dangerous. This happens because parts of the brain that normally form a sequential, factual, autobiographical memory of events tend to be disorganised or go 'offline' during the traumatic event (probably to prioritise action over thinking to maximise survival). What they *do* remember are fragments of emotions, sounds, images, thoughts and bodily sensations. Consequently, traumatic memories lack a coherent narrative, including that the event is over and they survived, and the memory remains frozen in this original form. Therefore, 'traumatised people simultaneously remember too little and too much' (van der Kolk 2014, p.179).

> Consider how you would describe trauma to a client. You might want to create an informal script that summarises this section and then rehearse how you would say it.

The characteristics of traumatic bereavement

Being traumatised inhibits, prolongs and complicates grieving in many ways (Kosminsky and Jordan 2016; Parkes 2009; Pearlman *et al.* 2014): as someone's mind and body are focused on threat, other activities are compromised, including grieving. Being traumatised undermines the ability to remember, think and speak about loss coherently. Often, traumatically bereaved people are preoccupied with whether their loved one suffered, and the associated memories or imagined images are typically intrusive and distressing. Shame and guilt are common, and often associated with trying to attribute responsibility and thereby make sense of what happened, although, typically, someone's actions were not within conscious control during the automatic trauma responses described above (see Chapters 13 and 14). Also, as being traumatised is so distressing, frightening and confusing, there is a natural urge to avoid experiencing it, which in turn both inadvertently inhibits grieving and causes someone to feel disconnected from real life.

Traumatic bereavement typically damages, or even shatters, someone's assumptive world, particularly their sense of safety, trust, intimacy, control, self-esteem, meaning and purpose. This results in an ongoing perception of threat and continued re-traumatisation. They may form new unhelpful assumptions, such as believing they are helpless or need to be overly protective of others. Losing old assumptions and potentially forming unhelpful new ones further reduces their capacity to grieve, and in particular their capacity to meet the overwhelming need to make sense of the death (see Chapters 9 and 10).

Furthermore, traumatic deaths can be completely disorientating, with a sense of life before the death and a completely changed life afterwards. One example of this is the disbelief and tragedy when occasional or first-time drug use is fatal for a young person.

The circumstances of a substance-related death tend to lead to specific characteristics of traumatic bereavement as described next.

Deaths that are sudden and unexpected are harder to grieve for, because they were not anticipated and prepared for, and there was no opportunity to say goodbye. Often the death seems unreal and difficult to comprehend. Also, as the death is experienced as unpredictable and random, this can significantly undermine a person's assumptions about their world being basically predictable, safe and controllable. This easily provokes intense fear of further deaths.

Where someone died in hospital, what happened is significant (Rando 1993). For example, it can be traumatic, disturbing and very distressing to see a loved one who is unrecognisable or to have to make life-changing decisions:

> So we agreed to having the machine turned off. And he died I think it was a day later…it was absolutely shocking – absolutely awful…he didn't slip away peacefully. (Mother) (Templeton and Velleman 2018, p.31)

Deaths that are perceived as preventable, such as the result of drug dealing for financial gain, tend to be more traumatic (Pearlman et al. 2014). People ruminate on what happened, and their trust in others is severely damaged. There is intense anger towards those believed to be involved in, or responsible for, the death; striving for justice takes its toll, often with no legal redress due to a lack of evidence (Templeton et al. 2016). This may include believing that services could have prevented the death:

> So, it just goes to show how the doctors are completely and utterly wrong… I found out that all ambulances in the UK carry a phial of naloxone[1]… [I]f they'd just gone up to him and given him an injection of naloxone…if they'd got to him on time then that would have been fine. (Father) (Templeton et al. 2016, p.7)

Deaths that were probably traumatic for the person who died often involve at least some violence, with their body being damaged – for example, being killed in a car crash while driving intoxicated. Typically, for those bereaved this is also traumatic and provokes horror, violation and a sense of being victimised (Rando 1993). They easily can get stuck in re-enacting their narrative of the death (Rynearson and Salloum 2011). This often involves distressing images, whether real or imagined, of what happened. These may be avoided or become repetitive, overwhelming and unresponsive to treatment (Pearlman et al. 2014). Typically, there is also intense rage, blame, guilt and desire for retaliation.

Where someone was present at the death, it increases their own risk of trauma and prolongs grief and depression, especially if they believe they were responsible in some way or could have prevented it (Kristensen et al. 2012). Examples include someone using the same drugs that killed the person who died or having tried to resuscitate them.

---

1 Naloxone is a medication that reverses an opioid overdose.

It is even more traumatic when there was intention to harm, such as murder or suicide (Perlman *et al.* 2014). In addition to the characteristics above, a person's assumptive world is often shattered and they lose their sense of being safe, and in control and having trust in others. All civilised norms are violated; they may perceive being confronted by evil and have an exaggerated sense of powerlessness, helplessness, humiliation and loss of self-respect (Janoff-Bulman 1988). Furthermore, they can feel betrayed and alienated (Riches and Dawson 1998). Such bereavements are likely to be very long-lasting and complicated, and they pose a risk to mental health, such as depression. Deaths through murder typically have even greater horror, rage and vengefulness that easily frightens a bereaved person (Pearlman *et al.* 2014).

Post-traumatic growth

Some clients have psychological or spiritual growth as a result of working through their trauma, especially where their assumptive world was challenged (Tedeschi and Calhoun 2008). Three themes are a changed identity, such as an increased sense of personal strength and resilience; changed relationships, such as feeling greater love and compassion for others; and a changed assumptive world, such as deepened spirituality or a new purpose in life (Jordan 2019). However, any growth is often dwarfed by the negative consequences of the trauma (Lehman, Wortman and Williams 1987; Pearlman *et al.* 2014). Do not expect this growth and any gain needs to be balanced by acknowledging what has been lost.

Assessing whether a client is traumatised

Assessing whether a client is traumatised can be difficult. As described above, it is not the event that traumatises but someone's perception of it. Their memory of the traumatising event is typically fragmented and distressing to recall, and is therefore avoided. People often do not know they are traumatised. Also, some symptoms of trauma and grief are seemingly inseparable (Jordan 2019; Pearlman *et al.* 2014). Therefore, assessment usually requires a combination of the ideas presented below, an open mind and a willingness to discuss this with a client before hypothesising whether they are traumatised:

- A client's subjective experience is of primary importance. Explore how easily they are retraumatised, their symptoms and how they cope with these, including any risks, e.g. substance use or self-injury. Explore their meaning of these experiences, e.g. believing they are 'going mad'.

- Invite them to be aware of their bodily and emotional experience while they recount a brief summary of what happened (see safe working below). Then explore and consider what they experienced (see signs and symptoms next).

- Be aware of a client moving out of their window of tolerance (see below).

- Consider your own responses to a client's 'story', e.g. it sounds traumatic, as well as your own bodily and emotional responses.

A client may have a fragile, even shattered sense of themselves after being traumatically bereaved, so offer any hypothesis of trauma tentatively and do so in such a way that they can reject it. Usually, it helps to explain trauma, including the window of tolerance, normalising the trauma response and how it evolved to protect us, and how you imagine trauma relates to them. Use the guidance for educating and interpreting on pages 140–2.

Previous traumatic experiences, particularly in childhood, increase the risk of trauma in adulthood (van der Kolk 2014). Attachment styles affect how someone regulates their bodily and emotional experience (see Chapter 9). Also, a disorganised attachment style tends to leave someone less able to cope with traumatic bereavement in adulthood (Parkes 2009).

The signs and symptoms of trauma

The following signs and symptoms of trauma may occur (Levine 2008; Rothschild 2000, 2017; van der Kolk 2014). Note that they may not be caused by trauma; some are inseparable from grief. They may be continual, intermittent or absent, and over time they may vary, become more complex and be less obviously connected to the traumatising event.

Clients tend to go outside of their window of tolerance when their trauma is re-stimulated and do so in particular ways that you can observe and sense:[2]

- above their window: rapid heart rate and breathing, sweating, panic, anxiety, tensed muscles, hyper-vigilance (being on guard), exaggerated startle and emotional responses, etc.

- below their window: very slow heart rate and breathing, immobility, collapse, utter helplessness, etc.

- have dissociated (see pages 171–2): numb, seemingly 'switched off' or 'gone away', eyes closed or fixed stare, amnesia about death, denial of reality, lack of emotions, etc.

---

2   For a comprehensive easy-to-use table of what to look for, see Rothschild (2017) or www.somatictraumatherapy.com

Other symptoms include:

- intrusive images, flashbacks and/or nightmares, and associated bodily and emotional responses

- disturbed sleep, feeling stressed, having difficulty concentrating

- mood swings, e.g. rage, crying, shame

- avoidance of people, places, activities, etc., associated with traumatic event

- withdrawal from others; inability to love, nurture or bond

- self-criticism; shame and/or guilt about actions or inaction during traumatic event

- impaired judgement, inability to manage boundaries, difficulty making decisions

- compulsion to repeat actions associated with traumatic event

- difficulty making connection between the 'there and then' traumatic event and their 'here and now' emotions, bodily reactions and thoughts; having a negative interpretation of this, e.g. 'going mad' or being fundamentally damaged

- excessive substance use, eating, self-injury, etc

- loss of worldview and spirituality

- alternation between periods of overactivity and exhaustion.

Counselling a traumatically bereaved client

There are several important aspects to counselling a client with traumatic bereavement.

Unlike other counselling, letting a client talk and express how they feel may be unhelpful as they can easily become retraumatised during counselling. In addition to the ways that trauma negatively affects grieving described above, this is needlessly distressing and risks entrenching any avoidance.

Where a client feels under continued threat following the shattering of their assumptive world, revising and reconstructing this is typically a priority. Where the traumatising threat continues in more tangible ways, such as ongoing domestic abuse, focus on support and safeguarding until they are safe enough for other work.

A safe and effective way of counselling

First, create a safe and effective way of counselling, where generally, a client stays within their window of tolerance. This will help them to keep 'online' the thinking parts of the brain that tend to go 'offline' when traumatised, including, importantly, the capacity for self-awareness (van der Kolk 2014). Only when a client's feelings and thoughts can occur simultaneously, when a client's trauma symptoms are regulated so they feel tolerable and their responses are appropriate in a given situation, is counselling for bereavement safe, manageable and effective. This effectively parallels and can be inseparable from the regulation of grief emotions (see Chapter 9). How to create this is described next.

Working with trauma needs a safe, trusting and dependable counselling relationship and usual good practice, such as letting a client lead the session, working at their pace, checking whether the work is manageable for them, etc. Additionally, it requires knowing trauma theory and using that to inform how you counsel. Furthermore, it requires the skills to track a client's bodily and emotional experience moment by moment and to recognise trauma symptoms.

Sometimes you will need to intervene and be directive, and ask to teach key skills to a client. This needs balancing with a client still feeling a sense of control (as people often lose this when traumatised) as well as respecting client autonomy. If you sense or imagine a client might be traumatised, intervene and explain:

> 'Sometimes people can be so shocked by the death that they continue to experience distressing symptoms long after the death occurred. I imagine this might have happened to you. If it has, there may be times I'll need to interrupt and ask you to do certain things, such as pause and switch your attention, so that your counselling feels manageable and stays effective… I'm interested how that would be for you.'

The first time a client speaks about what you observe, sense or imagine will be traumatic, ask them to pause. Then say that you only need them to give you a couple of bullet points about what happened and ask that they pay attention to their emotional and bodily experience when doing so. As they speak, notice whether they seemingly stay within their window of tolerance. This reduces the risk of re-traumatisation, demonstrates from the start that you will helpfully intervene, and provides useful evidence for assessment.

You will need to recognise when a client is outside their window of tolerance and know how to 'ground' them so they can come back inside (see pages 142–3 and assessment above). Also, you need to know how to work with dissociation (see page 171).

As ever, respect when a client wants to stop, as trauma work is challenging and demanding. This could be an opportunity to practise self-support ideas (see following page).

Two skills a traumatised client needs to develop

Over time, a client needs to develop self-awareness of their trauma symptoms and the ability to return inside their window of tolerance. This requires developing dual awareness and the ability to 'ground' themselves (Rothschild 2000, 2017).

Dual awareness is being able to alternate between experiencing trauma symptoms *and* observing those symptoms[3] – that is, keeping self-awareness 'online'. To start with, you will probably need to observe for a client and reflect back that what happened 'there and then' is seemingly affecting them 'here and now'.

When a client becomes retraumatised and moves out of their window of tolerance, they need to come back into their window. They can do this by learning to self-ground by deliberately switching their awareness away from experiencing trauma and towards engaging their sensory experience in the 'here and now', such as noticing and sensing the counselling room and their bodily contact with their chair, and recognising that the traumatic event is not happening any more and that they are safe now. They will probably also benefit from using a breathing technique and going to their safe-enough place for a while (see below).

Teach both these skills and encourage a client to practise them until they can reliably, thoroughly and confidently use them when needed. Begin developing these skills when they are not experiencing trauma symptoms, so they can experience what to do before needing to use them.

Once a client is aware of being retraumatised and able to regulate their symptoms, other aspects of bereavement work typically become more manageable, as do the further phases of trauma work. However, both you and your client will need to continually monitor the client's trauma symptoms and intervene as necessary.

Developing a traumatised client's support

The following ideas can develop a client's self-support to regulate and reduce their emotional and bodily experience of trauma. This reinforces the safety and effectiveness of counselling, and, critically, helps clients begin to recreate a sense of safety, stability and control in their lives.

As described above, explain trauma and develop a client's dual awareness and their ability to self-ground. Also, when relevant, explain the damage to their assumptive world (see above).

---

3   As dual awareness involves *feeling* symptoms, it is different from the type of dissociation where a client *disconnects* from their bodily and emotional experience, and perceives being an outside observer of themselves.

Explore the self-support a client already has, particularly what helps them ground in the 'here and now' and to have a break from trauma. Honour the usefulness of these; consider how effective they are – and any unintended consequences of using them. Also, select and offer ideas you consider appropriate for a client, and encourage them to practise these between sessions:

- **Breathing practices** (see pages 158–9).

- **The safe-enough place.** This is somewhere a client can imagine being in, preferably somewhere real, that *feels* safe and calming when recalled. Invite them to 'go there' when they need a break from trauma (Rothschild 2000).

- **Use the ways to engage with restoration orientation** on page 161 to have a break from trauma, in particular those that promote calm and secure bodily sensations.

- **Encourage self-talk** that checks whether they are still threatened, e.g. 'I'm feeling scared and do I need to be, or is it just my trauma?' Encourage the client to see symptoms for what they are, e.g. 'This is just a memory with feelings.' Confirm that the traumatic event and any suffering are now over, e.g. 'It's over, I survived' or 'It's over, my daughter can't be harmed anymore.'

- **Visualisations.** For clients who are troubled by distressing images of the deceased, whether real or imagined, offer to create a guided visualisation that uses a more tolerable image, e.g. the deceased in heaven, paradise or similar place (Jordan 2012).

- **Remove triggers in everyday life**, as far as possible, that re-stimulate trauma until a client is better able to cope (Rothschild 2000).

- **Revise or reconstruct the damaged parts of their assumptive world** (see Chapters 9 and 10). The next idea may help with this…

- **Reflect back evidence that counters a client's traumatic memory**, e.g. acts of kindness and care from others during and after the traumatising event, or aspects of them that are still intact, of value and give life meaning and purpose, etc.

- **Create an ending to the trauma narrative** by giving attention to life events following the traumatic event that demonstrate it is over, they survived and their life went on (Rothschild 2000, 2017).

- **Shame and guilt** are often felt for actions or inaction during a traumatic event. As discussed above, these were not within a client's conscious control (see Chapters 13 and 14).

- **Social support.** It often helps clients to explain trauma to others and discuss how those others can support them, e.g. recognise symptoms and say when they see them.

Mahi

When Mahi saw Jake in intensive care, he was unconscious, initially unrecognisable to her and connected to many machines. As she watched him dying, she felt utterly helpless and powerless at not being able to protect her son. She had little memory of what happened next, although later she was overwhelmed by intense fear for the safety of her two other children; she slept badly and had nightmares about Jake in intensive care.

At the start of her first counselling session, Mahi launched into recounting Jake's death and her counsellor noticed she quickly became very anxious and tense, the colour drained from her face and her breathing became rapid and shallow. He asked her to pause, apologised for interrupting and said she had done nothing wrong. He then said he sensed she felt very distressed, and that although counselling could be difficult and painful, it was important it also felt manageable. He asked that they leave Jake's death for now and focus on developing ways of coping with how she was feeling. This came as a relief to Mahi as she generally avoided her grief because of how she felt when she experienced it. As a part of this work, she realised that a dry mouth and fast breathing were useful clues that she was becoming distressed, and she learned how to use calming breathing and switch her attention to counting while doing so, thereby calming herself. The next two sessions continued developing her self-support.

Following Mahi's success at this, her counsellor proposed that she experiment with saying a couple of sentences about Jake's death, while both Mahi and the counsellor also paid attention to her bodily and emotional experience. Mahi agreed and experienced the same response as she had in the first session. They both reflected on what happened, and Mahi said she feared she was 'going mad and couldn't ever be right again'. Her counsellor said that he imagined she was traumatised by seeing her son die and how that shattered parts of her assumptive world, such as assuming that she could always protect her children. Then he explained trauma by using Mahi's personal experience to illustrate the idea. Although Mahi thought it 'helps to know what's wrong', she was frightened by the idea, so the rest of the session was used to further explain and normalise trauma, including explaining the window of tolerance. Mahi's counsellor gave her a handout on trauma and asked her to live with the idea until the next session. Mahi's understanding of trauma and why it occurs deepened, and this in turn helped her to accept she was traumatised.

In the next session, her counsellor asked that Mahi develop dual awareness, self-grounding and further self-support. Mahi liked the idea of being able to regain some control. They began practising dual awareness and self-grounding while she spoke about her garden (her counsellor used her garden as it was the only part of her life that felt unaffected by Jake's death). This developed into speaking briefly about Jake's death and self-grounding as soon as she experienced symptoms, and in time letting her symptoms build a little more before self-grounding, and so on. Mahi continued practising this between sessions whenever her symptoms occurred.

Other work Mahi found helpful was discussing trauma with her husband, Jag, who read the handout Mahi had been given, and they both agreed how he could better support her. Also, to support herself when waking in the night after continued nightmares about Jake's death, Mahi used a postcard of an ornamental garden to keep by her bed. Mahi and her counsellor created supportive statements she could read at night and wrote them on the back of the postcard:

> 'I'm feeling anxious, sweating and breathing fast because I'm remembering Jake's death *and* look around, I'm in the bedroom now and not in the hospital anymore.[4] Jake cannot be harmed now and is at one with God and the universe. Calming breath and count. Imagine my garden.'

This work gave Mahi the ability and confidence to manage her trauma symptoms, and thereby enable work on other aspects of her bereavement. However, both she and her counsellor continued to be mindful of her symptoms and would pause the work when necessary to manage these.

FURTHER READING ON ANXIETY
Joyce, P. and Sills, C. (2014) *Skills in Gestalt Counselling and Psychotherapy* (3rd edition). Chapter 19. London: SAGE Publications.

FURTHER READING ON TRAUMATIC BEREAVEMENT
Pearlman, L.A., Wortman, C.B., Feuer, C.A., Farber, C.H. and Rando, T.A. (2014) *Treating Traumatic Bereavement: A Practitioner's Guide*. New York, NY: Guilford Press.

FURTHER READING ON TRAUMA TREATMENT
Joyce, P. and Sills, C. (2014) *Skills in Gestalt Counselling and Psychotherapy* (3rd edition). Chapters 20 and 21. London: SAGE Publications.

---

4   Adapted from Rothschild 2000.

Rothschild, B. (2000) *The Body Remembers: The Psychophysiology of Trauma and Trauma Treatment*. New York, NY: Norton.

Rothschild, B. (2017) *The Body Remembers Volume 2: Revolutionizing Trauma Treatment*. New York, NY: Norton.

FURTHER READING ON WORKING WITH CHILDHOOD TRAUMA

Fisher, J. (2017) *Healing the Fragmented Selves of Trauma Survivors*. New York, NY: Routledge.

12

Unfinished Business

As discussed in Chapter 6, unfinished business[1] is a key characteristic of many substance-related bereavements. It tends to keep clients stuck in loss orientation and complicates any continuing bond, and thereby inhibits grieving. Therefore, as it is important to work through unfinished business as far as is possible, this chapter considers how to do that. Potential unfinished business can happen in the following ways:

- from the impact of substance-using behaviour *before* the death, described in Chapter 4 and from page 103, e.g. suffering domestic abuse or being unable to stop someone's substance use

- when what happened before the death only becomes apparent *after* the death, described on page 107, e.g. not knowing that someone's substance use was problematic

- as a result of the death and its aftermath, described from page 107, e.g. some circumstances of the death remain unknown or an unsatisfactory outcome to an inquest

- when there is deep ambivalence about the person who died that remains unresolved, described on page 107, which can also complicate working through other unfinished business, e.g. feeling both love *and* hate for the deceased, that in turn complicates working through domestic abuse from them.

Look for these situations, events and issues that a client keeps returning to and that still have emotional energy. Additionally, you may need to enquire about what still feels unfinished or unresolved, because some clients will not open up about these as they do not want to damage the reputation of the person who died, or because of their own guilt or shame about what happened.

---

1   Unfinished business refers to difficult situations and events that have not had a satisfactory resolution.

Working through unfinished business

The goal of this work is to facilitate a client to find the support, emotional expression and enough resolution to allow them to get on with their lives as far as is possible (Joyce and Sills 2014).

- **A client can still look at and explore their half of the relationship with a loved one**, despite the death, and you can be a witness to and validate that.

- **Offer to psychoeducate a client** if necessary, to help inform working through unfinished business: about addictive substance use and associated behaviour (see Chapters 3 and 4); how relationships are co-created and what a client is, and is not, responsible for (see pages 65–6); the substance(s) the deceased used and its potential role in the death; any other co-occurring difficulties. This often leads to a need to...

- **Consider and revise their assumptive world** in order to work through unfinished business, e.g. letting go of the assumption they can make others do what they want.

- **Work through, as far as possible, any ambivalence about the deceased.** Recognise a client's ambivalence, encourage expression of all associated emotions, and make sense of the ambivalence. Consider how substance use (and any other difficulties) contribute to ambivalence. Consider how ambivalence may complicate other unfinished business. Encourage remembering and discovering positive aspects of the deceased and good times spent with them (which in turn helps restoration). During this work stay mindful of the whole of who the deceased was, as well as of a client's attachment style and any habitual ambivalence.

- **Use creative techniques**, such as 'two-chair work'. Where the deceased used substances addictively, it is important to 'hear' from both their addicted part and the other part of them that was not addicted. This helps a client to appreciate the impact addiction had on their loved one and reduces the risk of a client feeling coerced or controlled by them again.

- **Explore the layers of meaning beneath what is unfinished** to uncover what may be beyond a client's awareness (J. Kuykendall, personal communication.), e.g.:

A parent's fixation about why the deceased drank and then drove their car, which led to their death.

↓

Difficulty accepting that the deceased could be so irresponsible and reckless.

↓

Feeling guilty that their offspring behaved that way.

↓

Ultimately discovering doubts about their parenting and difficulty accepting they could not control their offspring.

- **Express and/or work though associated emotions**, e.g. blame and guilt.

- **Consider the intentions of those involved** as well as their actions.

- **Consider possible positive outcomes**, e.g. the outcome of this work has something positive for a client, such as compassion and forgiveness for themselves and/or the deceased; or some sense of gain from the loss, or a way to honour the life of the deceased:

  'Your suffering helped me to see that I want to live in a way where I don't cause further suffering.'

- **Consider forgiveness** (see pages 248–50).

- **Consider involving other surviving family members**, e.g. other family members who are also struggling with the same unfinished business. Family therapy or a mediation service could be helpful.

Ending the work

Unfinished business is likely to be worked with many times. If a client's energy has finally diminished (at least for now), consider the outcome – for example, what it means to them and how it fits into their overall narrative of the life and death of the person who died.

If completion or resolution has not happened, the next step is working towards acceptance of that. Consider asking, 'What would your loved one want for you now?' and reflect on their answer, remaining alert to potential guilt in a client. If necessary, consider what stops their acceptance of what is unfinished and potentially, how that might serve them. However, remember some things are very difficult to accept, such as a loved one murdered by the people to whom they owed money for drugs.

A client may need to periodically revisit their unfinished business and it may never feel completely 'finished'. Whether completion or resolution is achieved or not, at some point they need to integrate the experience and face the future.

Clients' unfinished business can live on in other ways to those covered above: as trauma from events in the relationship, the death and/or its aftermath; as an unhealthy continuing bond; as enduring guilt, blame and anger; and as depression, which may predate the death (see relevant chapters).

◼ Emma

Emma was preoccupied by her inability to stop Steve drinking and used her counselling to speak about this. The worse he had treated her, the more she tried to get it right for him; she felt guilty for failing to stop his drinking, and felt angry at Steve for drinking and occasionally being aggressive towards her. However, as this did not seem to be enough to process this unfinished business, her counsellor reflected this back to her and outlined further work, to which Emma agreed.

First, her counsellor explained how relationships are co-created and illustrated this by using his own relationship with Emma. Also, he explained about addictive substance use in general terms and invited Emma to consider whether that applied to Steve; she said it did.

They then considered Emma's deep ambivalence about Steve. What emerged was how inevitable this was given both that she loved him and he was the father of her children *and* that he was addicted to alcohol and his associated behaviour. They identified how this template for ambivalent relationships had developed through her childhood relationship with her father who also had used alcohol addictively.

Next, Emma's counsellor asked: 'What would successfully stopping Steve drinking have needed to be like and how would that have affected your relationship with him?' This brought into Emma's awareness how she would have had to have constantly been with Steve to monitor his behaviour and how he would probably have become more aggressive. This would have been unrealistic and eventually have been unbearable for both of them. Her counsellor suggested that Emma 'ask' the addicted part of Steve if that was true, which she did, and Steve 'confirmed' her thoughts. This dialogue developed into 'hearing' a conversation between the addicted part of Steve and the rest of him. Emma began to see just how stuck Steve had been in his addiction and that his compulsion to drink overrode anything she and others did. In summarising this dialogue, her counsellor said: 'It sounds as though Steve was effectively saying to you, "I won't let you help me and I won't help myself"; does that fit for you?' This realisation was helpful for Emma, and also provoked her despair, anxiety and anguish.

Her counsellor saw the need to place Emma's reaction in a wider context. Together, they explored again the connection to her father's drinking. From this, it emerged that as a child, she had a deep reluctance to recognise that caring for her father was not enough to keep him safe, and that not trying would have provoked despair and anxiety that she would lose him and could not cope. Emma made the connection to Steve for herself and also saw how ambivalent she was about her father.

Using this insight, Emma's counsellor invited her to disidentify with her young, compulsively caring part and evoke the wise adult part of herself. Emma saw how hard it is for one person to make another do something they do not want to, however caring they may be. From this, Emma and her counsellor created a statement for Emma to experiment saying to see how that felt: 'I can't make someone else do something if they don't want to; I do have influence, which may or may not work; with Steve it did not.' After this, they reflected on the experiment, Emma could see the statement was true and she found that anxiety-provoking. Therefore, her counselling focused next on developing the adult part of her to soothe the anxiety of her young part. Over time, this belief became part of her new assumptive world.

John

John was fixated with knowing why his daughter Sarah had died and whether she had suffered, but was frustrated at being unable to get the answers he needed while waiting for the post-mortem report. At his counsellor's suggestion, they pieced together what little he *did* know. After this, his counsellor proposed: 'Anyone finds it difficult not to know what is so important to them. However, you could view this as: what you know is that you don't completely know how Sarah died.' John considered this and found it helped, but only while he waited for more information.

His counsellor proposed (and John readily accepted) that he find out about heroin overdoses. The following session, he reported his immense relief at knowing Sarah's death was 'probably like falling asleep' while feeling the desired effects of heroin, so she had probably not suffered as he had feared.

During this work, his counsellor also raised how else John might be grieving, to which he replied: 'Nothing else matters, everything else is on hold until I find out.' The counsellor saw the need to wait and supported John in his frustration about not knowing.

When the post-mortem report came, John was distressed by its formal biological approach and was frustrated that it only confirmed what was suspected: that Sarah died of a heroin overdose. He needed to express his deep resentment and anguish at still not knowing.

Four months later, John attended the inquest. He got some answers that helped, but not enough, and also found out there had been an unexpectedly pure batch of heroin, resulting in several people overdosing. His counselling focused on continuing to piece together a narrative about how Sarah died, including what was not known. Over time all sources of further information had been exhausted. His counsellor offered John: 'I don't want to take away responsibility from the person who prepared and sold Sarah heroin and also, from Sarah's point of view, sometimes things happen by chance or misfortune. Rather than "Why?", is it a case of "Why not?"?' John quickly dismissed this, so his counsellor said: 'As you know, you don't have to accept what I say, and you hardly gave yourself time to consider that.' John thought again and said it did help on an intellectual level but felt unsatisfactory because he quite reasonably wanted to know why his daughter had died. His counsellor agreed.

Following this, they considered what it would be like if he never fully knew. John replied: 'Frustrating, disappointing and very unsatisfactory.' His counsellor acknowledged this, then asked: 'What will support you while feeling that?' John did not know, so she suggested: 'Consider whether you can live with uncertainty and not battle to know why.' This interested John, so it became the focus of counselling and developed into his finding empathy and compassion for his not fully knowing and the injustice he had suffered, and towards finding some acceptance that the world is not fair. As John put it: 'Sometimes bad things happen to good people,' later adding: 'And I choose not to add to the injustice in the world in how I live my life.' This gave him a welcome sense of some autonomy and control, as well as honouring Sarah's death. However, this work also evoked despair in John, which both was difficult and, as his counsellor remarked, allowed the psychological space to reflect and come to terms more deeply with the circumstances of the death than when he had been angry.

FURTHER READING

Joyce, P. and Sills, C. (2014) *Skills in Gestalt Counselling and Psychotherapy* (3rd edition). Chapters 9 and 11. London: Sage.

Neimeyer, R.A. (ed.) (2012) *Techniques of Grief Therapy: Creative Practices for Counseling the Bereaved*. New York, NY: Routledge.

13

Shame and Stigma

Shame is an emotion commonly found in substance-related bereavements; it often predates the death and is a key emotion in stigma. The chapter covers:

- Defining shame and guilt, how they differ and considerations for working with these similar emotions.

- An explanation of shame and stigma in substance-related bereavements.

- The implications for counselling clients who feel shame.

- Ideas for working with shame and stigma.

Through working with shame, you can help a client engage more deeply with you and benefit more from counselling, and enable them to better self-support and to reach out more to others for support.

Shame and guilt: Similar yet different emotions

Both shame and guilt are social emotions that have the potential to help people navigate relationships with others. Guilt is about *what you have done* and shame, at worst, is about *who you are* – for example, 'I feel guilty for not stopping my son's drug use' and 'I feel ashamed for being a bad parent'. However, both can occur in unhelpful ways during bereavement, and this tends to keep clients in loss orientation.

Considerations for working with shame and guilt

These are complex emotions and many clients benefit from developing their emotional intelligence about them.

Clients are usually only too aware of feeling guilty, but are often not aware of feeling shame, even though they still react to how shame urges them to behave. As neither emotion seems to diminish for being felt and expressed, unlike sadness or anger, clients typically just try to avoid or put up with them. It is therefore important that you offer to work through their shame and guilt.

If they agree, recognise that they probably have limited understanding of how they have come to feel shame and guilt. A useful rule of thumb is that both shame and guilt feel very real, but the reasons for feeling them are often not true. To work successfully with both, therefore, you need to appreciate that particular perceptions, beliefs and constructs of thinking go with feeling each one. This entails working with a client's cognitions, and requires an understanding of addiction and how relationships often get distorted by substance use (see Chapters 3 and 4). Also, it entails exploring socially constructed beliefs (such as stigma and morals), while being mindful of clients' culture and any faith. Interestingly, Piers and Singer (1972) propose that cultures can be either shame- or guilt-orientated. The work is about making sense of these emotions and managing them so they diminish, rather than being able to eliminate them.

Your support during shame and guilt work is vital, in particular having a genuinely non-judgemental attitude towards who they believe they are and what they believe they have done.

Clients can get trapped in 'shame–guilt binds' (Yontef 1993, p.498), where they believe 'I'm damned if I do and damned if I don't' – for example, feeling guilty that they could not stop their loved one's substance use and feeling shame if they did not keep trying to stop it.

Both guilt and shame may effectively paralyse a client, making it hard for them to access their anger, self-forgiveness, empathy for others, etc. Therefore, these emotions probably need to be worked through first. Shame can obscure guilt, as it is difficult to successfully consider whether you really are responsible for doing a 'bad' thing if you see your whole being as 'bad', so work through shame before guilt. Also, guilt may turn to shame over time – for example, from 'I did something bad' to 'I am bad'. Severe shame or guilt can lead to depression (see Chapter 15) and potentially lead a client to become suicidal.

Traumatised clients often feel shame and guilt for their actions or inaction during traumatising events. Therefore, understanding trauma and that 'flight, fight, freeze and flop' responses are not within conscious control is necessary (see Chapter 11).

Underlying shame and guilt associated with bereavement may be habitual shame and guilt that originate in childhood. These may be substance-related, such as parental addictive use, and/or due to other childhood experiences. Additionally, people with insecure attachment styles, especially disorganised, can be more prone to shame. It is therefore necessary to check with a client whether feeling these emotions predates their bereavement and, if it does, their childhood shame or guilt will probably need attention first. The subject of shame, guilt and blame originating in childhood is covered only briefly as it is beyond the scope of this book (see the further reading suggestions at the end of this chapter).

Understanding shame and stigma in substance-related bereavements

An explanation of shame

People experience shame as an excruciating self-consciousness (where they believe they are unacceptable, defective or inferior) that encompasses their whole being and urges them to withdraw from others.

People have shame to help regulate their social interactions with others (Lee and Wheeler 1996; Schore 2012). Shame is created through these relationships and lies at one end of a polarity that has support at the other (Lee and Wheeler 1996). Therefore, when a person expresses a need, want or aspect of who they are, and others are supportive of that, they come to believe that these are acceptable. Conversely, where a person experiences a lack of support from others for their need, want or aspect of who they are, they may then feel shame as mild self-consciousness or embarrassment, and then may inhibit themselves from expressing it in future (much as you might stifle a yawn while working with a client!). Importantly, this negative response from others is experienced as temporary and appropriate, so that the relationship survives largely unaltered and has the possibility of forgiveness.

The support of others enables a person to take a risk; a lack of others' support inhibits them. This is how they learn how to navigate social interactions with others. Part of how this works is being unaware of feeling shame, yet still experiencing self-consciousness, an urge to conform and inhibit or withdraw. Shame is therefore 'the price of the fit between self and other' (Lee and Wheeler 1996, p.9) that maintains relationships, particularly with attachment figures. However, as substance-related stigma is typically continual and holds no possibility of forgiveness, the associated shame is unhealthy.

Unhealthy shame originating in childhood

This process of socialising can produce unhealthy shame when an infant experiences their caregiver as ignoring, hostile or rejecting, especially when this is repeated (Schore 2012). Then, as an adult, someone is vulnerable to experiencing unhealthy shame about a need, want or aspect of themselves when it is not supported by others. This aspect of them is then forever associated with feeling excruciating, enduring shame, both when they are by themselves and particularly with others. It becomes unacceptable, secret or even 'lost'. One way of avoiding feeling this shame is to habitually blame others.

Stigma and substance use

Various theoretical reasons exist to explain why substance-related deaths are stigmatised. A theme throughout these is society stigmatising subgroups by making them the 'other' and disreputable, rather than 'us' and respectable, thereby keeping the 'other' away or down from 'us' (Walter and Ford 2018, p.67).

For much of society, substance use and its related deaths are unacceptable and threatening, and challenge cultural norms; stigma tries to keep people like 'us' (see page 113). This is based on assumptions, such as substance-related conditions being self-inflicted (so could easily be stopped) and those who use as faulty, disgusting, not contributing to society, criminal or dangerous; their families as complicit or dysfunctional; and 'being seen and treated as part of an underclass characterised by fecklessness, immorality and ignorance' (Templeton *et al.* 2018a, p.134). In shame-orientated societies a loss of control is seen as shameful (Yontef 1993) and addictive substance use is characterised by an inability to control use. Also, studies have found that even social and healthcare professionals, who would be expected to be better informed, have negative attitudes towards people with substance-related conditions, especially illegal drug use (Crisp *et al.* 2000; Room *et al.* 2001; van Boekel *et al.* 2013).

There is a hierarchy to stigma, with heroin, intravenous drug use and the associated stereotypes at the bottom (Walter and Ford 2018). Additionally, bereaved people from BAME groups can experience more stigma about substance use (Cartwright 2019), implying that stigma and racial discrimination intersect.

However, as described in Chapters 3 and 4, the reality of substance use is very different to the assumptions that create this stigma, and therefore any associated shame is arguably unwarranted.

How clients can feel shame

Research demonstrates that stigma can be internalised as shame 'even in the absence of hostile treatment by others' (Walker 2014, p.68), by unquestioningly 'swallowing whole' society's beliefs about substance use. Even if someone *does* question and disagrees, it still takes courage to risk being different. Therefore, stigmatised people often protect themselves from stigma and shame by assuming others will judge them and acting defensively (including towards their counsellor), regardless of the presence or absence of stigma (Yontef 1993). This shame often predates bereavement and may occur in many ways:

- feeling stigmatised by a loved one's substance use and possibly also their criminal behaviour, mental health difficulties, suicide, etc; also feeling stigmatised by 'family shame' where there is intergenerational addictive substance use

- being ashamed for perceived failings as a parent, partner or other person who cared for a loved one who used substances

- being ashamed of how a loved one treated them, such as being a victim of domestic abuse

- being manipulated by a loved one into feeling shame, where the motive was the coercion and control of them to assist substance use

- feeling ashamed of their own substance use, particularly if it is addictive

- the expression of certain grief emotions being considered unacceptable and thereby shameful, e.g. 'It isn't manly to cry.'

Implications for bereavement counselling

Shame adds insult to injury during bereavement by adding a difficulty that is probably unwarranted and that keeps clients in loss orientation and complicates any continuing bond.

Clients may well be unaware of feeling shame, but still experience excruciating self-consciousness and a powerful urge to inhibit themselves or withdraw from you, thereby being unable to receive your support at the very time they need it. Ironically, their withdrawal leads them 'away from the cure, which is loving encounter' (Yontef 1993, p.504). Therefore, see pages 128–30 for ideas to avoid stigmatising and disenfranchising your clients. Also, embracing your own shame will better equip you to tolerate and work with clients' shame.

When a client experiences shame, it is an ideal opportunity to work with it.

Ideas for working with shame

As explained above, what is shameful is learned through the rupture of relationships with others. Fortunately, the opposite is true because shame 'can only be deconstructed and constructed differently within a relationship' (Lee and Wheeler 1996, p.17). It is probably unrealistic for a client to cease to feel shame; rather, the work is on reducing it and changing their relationship with it. This happens both implicitly through experiencing your support and acceptance, which contradicts past experiences, and explicitly through the following interventions. A few carefully selected ideas that emerge from your work are often better than doing it all. Additionally, given the relational nature of shame, it may be more effective to work on this in family therapy or a family support group, if all parties agree.

Recognising when a client feels shame

You need to be tuned in to a client's shame because they may be unaware of feeling it and, if they are, may well not tell you. You can observe, sense and be told about:

- **Behaviour and body language.** Covering their face, head down, eyes down, looking away or darting eyes; difficulty speaking and finding what is shameful almost incommunicable; and sinking back and making themselves smaller. Saying sorry, being self-critical and wanting forgiveness. Avoiding shame triggers, such as words, topics, events and possibly not coming back to counselling.

- **Bodily sensations and emotions.** Shyness, embarrassment, humiliation or disgrace. Isolation, disconnectedness or self-monitoring. Pain in the pit of the stomach and the sensation of choking or suffocating. Bodily arousal, faster pulse, interrupted breathing, blushing and feeling hot; conversely, going numb and feeling almost paralysed. Also, longing for connection; for the unacceptable to be acceptable.

- **Cognitions.** Believing they are intrinsically unacceptable, unlovable, defective, less than others, not good enough and that 'I can't be me and belong with you'. Also going blank.

- **Defences against experiencing shame.** Strategies include 'deflection, rage, contempt, control, striving for perfection, striving for power, transfer of blame through projection, internal withdrawal, humour and denial' (Lee and Wheeler 1996, p.6).

  Also self-righteousness or grandiosity. Shamelessness can be a defence against severe guilt, by projecting that guilt on to others (McGregor Hepburn 2012) – for example a client revelling in their family's notoriety and perhaps their counsellor feeling the guilt that is projected.

How to relate to a client who is ashamed

When you pick up on a client's shame, 'the overall task is to re-establish both internal and environmental relational safety and support that has been lost' (Joyce and Sills 2014, p.89). Shame thrives in an atmosphere of secrecy, judgement and silence. It reduces in an atmosphere of support, acceptance and empathy. Therefore, at first just 'be' with them (without 'doing' anything yet):

- **Reflect back that they feel ashamed** (see pages 140–42 about interpreting) as it often takes your naming it for a client to become aware of feeling shame. However, this risks further shame, because it can be shameful just to feel shame (Yontef 1993). Therefore...

- **At the same time, get 'alongside' them.** It can be very powerful to make 'an empathic statement that shares the experience rather than stands back from it' (Joyce and Sills 2014, p.90), e.g. 'I know how excruciating I find feeling ashamed.'

- **Consider using it as an opportunity to work with shame.** If you do and they agree, reflect back their courage to engage with such difficult work. Then...

- **Accept their perception at the start.** Neither agree with it nor say they have nothing to be ashamed about, as this risks deepening the emotional distance between you.

- **Normalise and explain shame** – see above. Explain that shame is only a part of who they are, and that shame 'can be tolerated, accepted and shared with another human being' like any other emotion (Joyce and Sills 2014, p.91).

- **Establish a link between the present and the past**, e.g. a client's vulnerability to unhealthy shame from their childhood and/or recent events:

  'If I had been treated like that by my colleagues, I too would be feeling ashamed telling others what happened to my loved one.'

- **Honour the usefulness of any defences** against shame, and consider together how effective they are.

- **Hear and validate their longing.** Sometimes it comes out as a reproach or criticism, e.g.:

  Client: 'They never listen to me.'

  Counsellor: 'How would you like to be listened to, and who would you want to hear you?'

  Sometimes their longing is hidden under self-sufficiency, e.g.:

  Counsellor: 'I hear how well you can look after yourself and wonder what it might mean to you to be supported by me?'

- **Consider how you might inadvertently shame them** and be willing to take responsibility for your part if you do.

Healing shame lies in your relating to them where they experience 'Now I can be me *and* I can belong'. As what is shameful is now in the open, further work becomes possible.

Building clients' self-support

Offer what you imagine is helpful and work together on what appeals to them. Suggest they develop these with you when they feel shame and then practise between sessions. It usually helps a client to develop and then be able to evoke a wise part of themselves, uncontaminated by shame, that can use the ideas below to support the rest of themselves when feeling shame. Changing chair and body posture often helps when developing this wise part. While to start with this is usually just a cognitive experience, with practice this wise part can also be felt. Encourage the client to do the following:

- **Develop supportive 'self-talk'**: a compassionate and empathic attitude or 'voice' towards themselves that sees shame for what it is. If that is too difficult, propose they hear you or someone else they trust.

- **Know their triggers to shame.** Then, with 'steady breathing, bring attention back to body sensation and find a way to be mindful, letting contact with their body be a grounding support' (Joyce and Sills 2014, p.93). See calming breathing on pages 158–9.

- **Support through the body**: being aware of both the bodily experience of shame and the opposite bodily experience of feeling accepted, supported and relaxed, then experimenting with how to move towards the latter when ashamed (Yontef 1993).

- **Re-own projections of stigma from others** (see page 113) by assessing whether they do actually stigmatise.

- **Feel resentment** towards those who do stigmatise. Potentially, they can use this angry energy to respond assertively to stigma.

- **'Feel the fear and do it anyway'** (Jeffers 2007). The fear of shame can inhibit having social support. However, clients can still seek social support, despite feeling fearful, if they have enough self-support to risk feeling shame with others.

- **Reduce shame** by doing/talking about what is shameful, over and over again, with supportive people, e.g. join with similarly bereaved people. At one DrugFAM annual 'Bereaved by Addiction' conference an attendee said: 'It is one of the few days in the year when I feel "normal" and able to just be me as I am now.'

- **Find pride** in themselves and in their loved one who died.

- **Consider what helped them before.**

Working with shame beliefs and associated thinking

Shame involves believing we are defective or inferior, so challenging those beliefs can help:

- **Explore shame beliefs.** A client's self-talk is a place to start. This detective work can be assisted by using a set of Russian dolls (or similar) to get to the shameful secret:

  The largest doll says: 'I could have stopped my son using drugs.'

  ↓

  The doll inside says: 'No, I *should* have stopped my son using drugs.'

  ↓

  The doll inside that says: 'I'm his mother and any good mother would have done that.'

  ↓

  And the next says: 'I was a bad mother.'

  Once nothing new emerges, the belief is effectively described by that last statement. This raises awareness and assists the next steps...

- **Consider the shame belief.** Is it warranted or unwarranted and only shameful because some other people say so? As what is shameful is often impossible to change – a client will always be related to the deceased who used substances – question the ideal that is implicit in the belief, e.g. invite them to imagine their idealised self and describe them and then explore their response to this image (Yontef 1993).

- **Create new thinking.** Make a statement that describes their new, believable thinking, e.g.:

  'I find it hard to accept that I couldn't save my son. I am realising how powerless anyone is over someone else's addiction. I still got some things right as his mum.'

- **Practise becoming aware of habitual shame beliefs.** When this becomes 'sharp and current', people often gain control of them (Yontef 1993, p.518).

However, changing deeply ingrained shame beliefs is often not enough (Lee and Wheeler 1996). This work needs much deliberate repetition of evoking new beliefs when the old beliefs are triggered. As new beliefs gain vitality, old beliefs gradually lose credibility, even if they often never quite go. Often counselling starts this process and clients need to continue it independently.

Coerced shame

Consider together whether a client was coerced into feeling shame by their loved one (see Chapter 4). It can be useful to ask, 'Whom did it serve that you felt ashamed?' or 'What were the consequences of your feeling ashamed?' Stay open-minded about where this exploration goes, while also being open to shame being the result of coercion. Real life examples include:

- Threats to tell a client's work colleagues 'that I'm a fucking junky and think how ashamed you'd feel then? So just give me the money.'

- 'If you don't give me a tenner, I'll go robbing and it'll be your fault I go to prison, and what will your family say then?'

- As well as a partner saying, 'Looking like that, you'd never get anyone else.'

This work requires understanding of both addictive behaviour and how relationships are co-created. You may need to educate a client about these (see Chapters 3 and 4). If relevant, once they see they have been coerced, they may feel ashamed about that, too. Often later they feel resentment; this is healthy anger and needs encouraging and expressing (see Chapter 14). It is important not to inadvertently imply that their loved one was 'bad' and therefore shameful. As ever, an understanding of addiction helps to see that anyone could behave badly if addicted, and that anyone is more than their addiction.

Reveal or conceal?

It is important that clients feel in control wherever possible over whether to reveal or conceal in order to protect themselves from potential stigma (Chaudoir and Fisher 2010), after they have not had control over substance use and the death. This dilemma may have begun long before the death.

- **Consider what a client wants to reveal and what to conceal** that feels manageable at that time. Consider what revealing or concealing would mean for them, for the public memory of their loved one, and any potential consequences for them and for other people. Also, concealing includes avoiding stigmatising people.

SHAME AND STIGMA   229

- **Being 'economical with the truth'** can help some clients find a form of words that feels manageable for the present, e.g. 'He died in an accident and it's too painful to talk about.'

- **Develop support to reveal**, including what they fear happening and rehearsing how to respond, e.g. imagining being told, 'I can't believe you'd let your son become like that', a client could rehearse 'I don't see it that way; from what I've learned about addiction, my son was ill, so it's very hurtful when you say that.'

- **Explore revealing as a longer-term process**, e.g.

  'My son died in a road accident.'

  ↓

  'My son had been drinking when he died in the road accident.'

  ↓

  'My son had a drink problem and that's why he had been drinking when he died.'

  ↓

  'My son had a long-term dependency on alcohol.'

- **Revealing what happened to challenge stigma** or depicting the deceased as more than a 'user' is important for some clients (see page 90 and page 114).

Emma

Emma felt ashamed for being a bad wife and through being stigmatised by her family and her neighbour's children (who called Steve 'the piss-head'). Emma needed to develop her self-support to withstand feeling shame, particularly imagining 'hearing' her counsellor's 'voice' between sessions saying, 'This is the feeling of shame; it will pass and it doesn't define who you are.'

Also, Emma considered how stigmatising her network of people were. With much support from her counsellor she began to feel resentful and through this felt more esteem. Later in the work she explored how Steve had manipulated her fear of shame to assist his drinking. She felt resentful again and, with her counsellor's help, decided to use that angry energy creatively by resolving not to be manipulated again.

Mahi

Mahi felt ashamed that her family was associated with drug use and sex outside of marriage as a result of Jake's death, both of which contradicted her Sikh faith. Counselling was the first time she had told anyone outside her immediate family about this and she felt shame but also relief when her counsellor took it calmly and non-judgementally, and said how difficult he found talking to others about what was shameful to him. It took her counsellor to suggest that she consider this situation and how she might cope with it. As part of this work, Mahi considered what to reveal and to whom, within the limitations of knowing that the death would eventually become public knowledge once the inquest was held.

Also, Mahi needed to consider her inner tension between her Sikh beliefs and knowing her son was involved in chemsex, which resulted in her shame. This included the painful realisations that children grow up and do things their parents do not like, and that her Sikh beliefs had deepened the emotional divide between the two of them, which in turn had inadvertently led to her having less influence over Jake's safety.

Over time she used counselling to develop the self-support she needed to risk revealing a bit more about Jake's death to her wider family, friends and colleagues. Sometimes she was surprised by the support she received from others, and this helped her to own the stigma she was projecting on to them. Also, with her counsellor's support, Mahi considered what she was proud of as a mother and about her son, to go part of the way to balancing out her shame. This helped Mahi to develop a part of herself that did not feel shame, which in turn she used to support the shamed part of herself.

FURTHER READING ON SHAME THAT ORIGINATES IN CHILDHOOD

Kaufman, G. (1989) *Shame: The Power of Caring.* Rochester, VT: Schenkman.

Lee, R.G. and Wheeler, G. (eds) (1996) *The Voice of Shame.* San Francisco, CA: Jossey-Bass, for the Gestalt Institute of Cleveland.

14

Anger, Blame and Guilt

Anger, blame and particularly guilt are characteristics of substance-related bereavements (Cartwright 2019). Clients can experience blame and guilt in several different ways, some of which they may not be able to make sense of. This can be confusing for counsellors, when these emotions are seemingly unwarranted. These emotions tend to keep clients in loss orientation and often occur as part of unfinished business (see Chapter 12). When not worked through, they can lead to enduring bitterness or guilt that can come to define a client's identity and worldview. Additionally, anger and guilt occur more frequently when someone's relationship with the deceased was ambivalent and/or the attachment was insecure (Parkes 2009). This chapter offers ways to make sense of these emotions, and gives ideas for working with them:

- anger in substance-related bereavements
- blame and guilt in substance-related bereavements
- blame and guilt that are warranted
- blame and guilt that are seemingly unwarranted
- parent and other attachment figure guilt
- forgiveness
- common difficulties with blame and guilt and ideas to help
- living with residual anger, blame and guilt.

For the difference between guilt and shame, and general considerations for working with guilt, see Chapter 13.

Anger in substance-related bereavements

Although anger at its best tells a person that something is wrong and provides them with the energy to put it right, it is also potentially unhelpful and even destructive.

Clients can be surprised by the intensity of their anger, be afraid of it and mistakenly believe anger and love are mutually exclusive (Leick and Davidsen-Nielsen 1991). However, much anger in bereavement can be seen as normal attachment responses: protest at being separated from a loved one who died, and irritability and bitterness about how unsafe and insecure the world has become. It is as if somehow anger could prevent the death or reunite with a loved one (Leick and Davidsen-Nielsen 1991). Other anger may be associated with a difficulty in accepting reality, as well as blaming those perceived to be responsible (including self-blame and guilt), covered below.

Anger is a common emotion in substance-related bereavements (Cartwright 2019) – for example, towards the person who died for 'loving drugs more than me', for 'everything you put me through', being so reckless, taking their own life, etc. Although this anger often predates the death, it may have been masked or supressed by anxiety or fear and only come into awareness or be expressed afterwards when it finally seems safe to feel it. It can also come with guilt.

As Stedeford (1994) explains, clients' unexpressed anger can become persistent moodiness, criticism, headaches, fatigue and bitterness; that can then manifest as disproportionate anger at others who do not deserve it. Holding on to anger about something that cannot or will not change continues unrealistic expectations and may become bitterness or depression (see also Chapter 15 of this book). Denied anger can be deflected on to others who are not responsible, or at themselves as guilt that may become depression. Suppressed anger can lead to tiredness, depression and physical illness. Anger occasionally leads to regressing by acting it out, as if being a rebellious child again. As discussed earlier in this book, enduring anger can lead to difficulties in grieving (see 'Complexities and difficulties in grieving' in Chapter 1).

Additionally, out of awareness, anger may be a defence against feeling other emotions such as sadness, pain, fear, guilt or shame. Anger can be preferable to feeling powerlessness and despair. Beneath feeling anger is usually hurt.

Ideas for working with anger

- **Unacknowledged anger at the deceased.** Look for non-verbal clues and reflect them back to a client, e.g. tone of voice, bodily gestures and facial expressions. Alternatively, rather than asking directly, it often helps to ask, 'What don't you miss about them?' to get to unacknowledged anger (Leick and Davidsen-Nielsen 1991).

- **Offer to inform about anger** and normalise its part in attachment and love: to be angry is to care; someone has to matter.

- **Consider if they can use this energy creatively** to put right what has gone wrong, either literally or metaphorically, e.g. through fantasised scenarios.

- **Where only anger is felt towards the deceased,** explore how a client might stop themselves feeling other emotions. Develop their support where their anger is a defence against other emotions. Also invite them to mentalise about the deceased, to enable them potentially to find deeper understanding and acceptance (tell a client that understanding is not sympathy, making excuses or denying what happened).

- **Where anger is seemingly misdirected, impotent, unreasoned or unreasonable,** it can help to reframe this as a distorted expression of something valid, e.g. an attempt to reunite or to put something right that had gone wrong. Challenge unrealistic assumptions, e.g. expecting substance treatment services to make someone stop using. Invite a client to mentalise about others to see the intention behind the behaviour – was it really so bad? It is important not to deny their anger and to acknowledge that it needs to be expressed (see below).

- **Where the anger is at God,** accepting this anger and working it through can give a client 'a better-defined attitude to their faith, the meaning of existence and to their own death' (Leick and Davidsen-Nielsen 1991, p.48). This may also evoke guilt for feeling that anger. (See Chapter 17.)

- **Where enduring anger has become bitterness,** if in doubt, ask a client if they are bitter; often they will agree if they are and appreciate that finally they are understood; explain how both sadness and anger are in bitterness and then separate out both emotions, e.g. by writing letters for both emotions to the person who died (Leick and Davidsen-Nielsen 1991).

A client will probably still feel angry, especially if they are not able to put right what has gone wrong. Therefore, it needs to be expressed – but not to the point of distress – and to express it until the energy fades (at least for now). Rationalising anger away, such as 'There's no point to being angry', tends not to work; what does work is being actively angry, in an effective and safe way:

- **Angrily repeating a phrase, ranting or even shouting** (where it will not alarm others) at the source of their anger, perhaps while also visualising or looking at a photo of the source.

- **Doing an activity** in conjunction with recalling what they are angry about, e.g. walking briskly, digging the garden, working out at the gym, hitting pillows, ripping up newspapers, making a Plasticine® model and destroying it, etc.

- **They can write a letter** to the source of their anger to express it and then potentially reading it to you.

- **Transforming anger's energy into something constructive** – see Chapter 17. This can be an opportunity for personal development, e.g. an unassertive client who tolerated unreasonable substance-using behaviour reconnecting to an angry energy that they can use finally to assert themselves. However, a client needs to know that initially their new behaviour may accidentally go too far and be aggressive (Leick and Davidsen-Nielsen 1991).

- **Calming breathing.** This is probably best done after expressing anger (see pages 158–9).

Expressing anger may need 'permission' from you. It often helps if you 'join in' by having a slight edge to your voice and raising the volume, validating their experience. Alternatively, clients can express it with others or in private. Many clients, often women, can be self-conscious or fearful of expressing anger. It is no coincidence that it is often anxious clients that 'don't get angry' because it feels so risky, so say that it is safe to express it with you. Expression of anger often gives rise to a pleasant feeling of tiredness and release of tension (Leick and Davidsen-Nielsen 1991). Once they feel less angry, invite them to feel any hurt beneath their anger.

Any residual anger usually needs acceptance of what cannot be changed, although anger about old wounds is 'sticky' (Kosminsky and Jordan 2016, p.147). Acceptance does not mean having to like what happened; it can still be unacceptable and unjust – and accepting this is part of accepting. Consider forgiveness (see below). It is important to keep a balance between what they are angry about and what they miss about their loved one.

Blame and guilt in substance-related bereavements

Blame can be seen as a form of anger arising from someone's perception that *others* are responsible for wrongdoing. Often this is felt with the intention of punishing others so they feel guilt, thereby discharging some pain and discomfort. Linked to blame is wanting revenge, typically as an attempt to reclaim power, restore pride and find justice. As revenge is unacceptable in Western culture, it may be denied, yet then expressed in subtle ways – for example, as blame, cynicism, bitterness, paranoia about future injustices, turning revenge against the self, moral superiority, or withholding self from others (Fuchs 1999).

With guilt, someone perceives that *they* are responsible for wrongdoing and so blames themselves. Through taking responsibility and feeling remorse, they say sorry, make amends for what they did and want to be different in future, thereby repairing what they did wrong, which in turn helps others to trust them again (including maintaining attachments). This requires someone to have assimilated useful social rules, be aware of breaking them and have understanding of the impact on those they wronged. Typically, these social rules come from moral, family, cultural and religious beliefs that are learned as a child. In healthy guilt, these are realistic, reasonable, proportionate and socially useful, and they are in harmony with someone's basic needs and desires. Healthy guilt is a temporary sense of responsibility, in which there is regret and remorse about causing harm to others, and forgiveness is possible, and it thereby promotes personal growth (Yontef 1993). However, not all guilty feelings are actually guilt. Some are regret or a fear of persecution for getting something wrong (Yontef 1993), while others are more obscure, as discussed below.

Therefore, both blame and guilt occur as a result of a cognitive construct through which the reality of what happened is perceived (Paul 2006) – that is, someone needs to believe what happened was wrong, allocate responsibility for it and believe that a reprimand is due. Like shame, these potentially useful social emotions may occur in unwarranted ways when someone's cognitive construct is distorted or unhealthy. For example, guilt is unwarranted if a client believed the emotional blackmail of their addicted loved one who said they were to blame for their substance use. Therefore, recognising and working with these cognitive constructs is an important part of counselling clients who feel blame and guilt.

As discussed in Chapter 6, blame and guilt are common characteristics of grief associated with unfinished business from both before the death and the death itself – for example, guilt for not stopping a loved one's substance use, preventing the death or perceived failings as a parent (Cartwright 2019; Feigelman *et al.* 2012). These self-accusations of wrongdoing are often unwarranted, lower self-esteem and inadvertently add insult to injury during bereavement. However, for some, their guilt is warranted; for example, supplying someone with the drugs that killed them can result in guilt, which may lead to suicide attempts (Templeton *et al.* 2018a). Other clients genuinely do not feel guilty or have already worked through their guilt.

Potentially, there are several ways clients can experience blame and guilt: when these emotions are warranted; when they seem unwarranted; and guilt felt by parents and other attachment figures that may be warranted or unwarranted. However, first it is helpful to look at general considerations.

General considerations for working with blame and guilt

Much of this work is about making meaning of blame or guilt, because of the cognitive constructs that lead to feeling them. However, blame and guilt are often not open to logical argument, objectively looking at reality; nor are assurances of forgiveness by others or by God (Paul 2006). A different, more complex approach is required:

- **Engage a client's interest**: 'Isn't it interesting that your guilt isn't open to logic. I'm sure there must be a good reason for it and I wonder if you share my interest in that?'

- **Track back to when they started feeling blame or guilt.** What appears to be guilt about bereavement may be guilt from their relationship with the deceased (see below) and/or habitual guilt formed in childhood.

- **Explore a client's cognitive construct that results in blame or guilt.** Establish what a client feels blame or guilt about, and where responsibility actually lies for what happened, as these emotions tend to occur through accusations rather than consideration of the facts. Establish how their cognitive construct explains to *them* how blame or guilt are apportioned. This often needs to include considering their moral, family, cultural and, if relevant, religious beliefs. However…

- **Ruminating on blame and guilt are typically unhelpful** – see page 259.

- **A client may experience these emotions in more than one way**, as well as switch between ways. Each way requires a particular kind of work, as described below.

- **Offer to educate** as necessary (see page 140), e.g. how relationships are co-created and where responsibility actually lies for what happens (see pages 65–7); addiction and how it is often unrealistic to expect someone who is addicted to take full responsibility for their behaviour and how few, if any, of the reasons for addiction are the responsibility of a client (see Chapter 3); and the innate urge to protect and care in attachment figures that leads to guilt when they perceive they failed (see page 76–7). These all help challenge inaccurate perceptions of blame and guilt.

- **This work often requires moving from criticism to curiosity** and mobilising the capacities to mentalise and have emotional intelligence. You may need to model these and initially provide these for a client.

- **Offer a client your interpretation** for the more complex forms of blame and guilt, as it is unrealistic to expect them to know about these possibilities (see pages 140–42).

- **Blame or guilt challenges a client's assumptive world.** Blame may manifest as wanting to humiliate, take revenge and even harm those held responsible. This can easily be an unfamiliar, distressing and potentially insoluble urge for a client to deal with, which challenges their assumptions about who they are. Also, blame may challenge their assumptions about others, e.g. loss of confidence in services that seemingly failed in their responsibilities. Similarly, guilt may challenge their assumptions about themselves, e.g. 'I thought I was good person; how could I have done that?' Update and reconstruct their assumptive world as necessary (see page 26).

- **Consider proposing a client forgive themselves and/or others.** Usually this needs to happen towards the end of the work (see below).

It helps to explain to a client that this work often takes time. It may be necessary to experiment with different ideas to find the true meaning of their blame and guilt, and there may be more than one way they experience these emotions. Interventions often need repeating. Furthermore, the work may end with them still feeling some blame or guilt.

Habitual blame and guilt originating in childhood

Typically, habitual blame and guilt that formed in a client's childhood needs to be worked with first. These are only covered briefly below, as they are beyond the scope of this book (see the further reading suggestions at the end of this chapter).

- Habitual blame may be a defence against feeling shame (see page 221 and page 224).

- Habitual guilt can form when a child creates fixed cognitive constructs through unhealthy family dynamics. This guilt elicits self-persecution rather than the personal growth of healthy guilt (McGregor Hepburn 2012; Yontef 1993), e.g. a child who is regularly and unreasonably criticised by their parent adapts by criticising themselves into behaving as their parent wants, and thereby maintain the attachment. Although this is an attempt to pre-empt and protect against further parental criticism, inadvertently the child takes too much responsibility and habitually feels unwarranted guilt.

- Habitual guilt or resentment can form when a child repeatedly experiences that being different from their parent is unwelcome in some way. They adapt by losing their differentness and merging with the parent, so that the distinction between self and others becomes blurred (thereby inadvertently lose awareness of their own needs, wants and desires).

Then, when differences, disagreement or separateness happen in a relationship, the child can either feel guilty for upsetting the balance or resentment at the other person for doing so; both strategies aim to restore mergence in the relationship (Perls, Hefferline and Goodman 1972). This 'clinging on' can be seen as attachment behaviour and is probably most likely in those with an anxious ambivalent style.

Particular considerations for working with guilt during bereavement

Clients can have difficulty saying what they feel guilty about, particularly if they also feel ashamed, so you probably need to work through shame first (see Chapter 13). It is important to acknowledge the reality of a client's guilt. Resist the urge to say they have nothing to feel guilty for because this denies how they *do* feel. It probably will not change how they feel and it makes it difficult for them to raise it with you again. Conversely, avoid inadvertently appearing to agree they *are* guilty:

> 'I appreciate that you feel guilty. However, I'm open-minded about what actually happened and suggest we explore your guilt.'

As guilt typically increases if someone perceives others are blaming them, be non-judgemental and use 'responsibility' rather than 'blame' or 'fault'. Be aware of counter-transference that urges you to be 'prosecutor' or 'defence' for a guilty client – for example, as if you are either their critical parent or their forgiving parent – or of counselling becoming a confessional where you become their 'priest'. Your support is important, as being guilty can be a lonely experience.

As with working on shame, it helps if a client can develop the ability to disidentify with their guilt (it may help to change chair and body posture). Then evoke their curiosity, empathy, capacity to mentalise and compassion for their inevitable human failings that may give rise to their guilt. The work involves hearing from both the dis-identified part and the guilty part. It is not that one is right and cancels out the other that is wrong. It typically helps to name these parts, such as 'the adult reasoning part of you' and 'the guilty part of you'. Although, to start with, dis-identifying is usually just a cognitive experience for clients, with practice it can also be felt. If this is too difficult, see if they can 'hear' what you would say alongside their guilt.

Blame and guilt that are warranted
Blame
Clients' blaming of others can be warranted – for example, blaming other family members who responded unhelpfully to substance use; blaming a dead parent

who used substances addictively might be someone's way of continuing to protect their 'child self' against that parent's neglect (Kosminsky and Jordan 2016); the shortcomings of services, such as the high risk of overdose when leaving or transferring between treatment providers (Bogdanowicz *et al.* 2018; Walter *et al.* 2017). Furthermore, deaths among people with long-term heroin use have in part been due to UK government policy (Royal Society for Public Health 2016) and reductions in funding that have compromised treatment services (ACMD 2016). In the United States of America, top executives have been successfully prosecuted for conspiring to increase sales of the highly potent opioid Subsys, by bribing doctors to prescribe it and misleading insurers about patients' need for the drug (New York Times 2019) (see Chapter 5).

In addition to the ideas for working with anger above, also consider the following:

- **Encourage using this energy** to put right what has gone wrong or to complain (Leick and Davidsen-Nielsen 1991). However, it is important that the blame is proportionate and not also serving another purpose (see below).

- **In the case of a client wanting revenge**, normalise wanting revenge, while being clear that you do not support them taking revenge. Find ways for a client to safely and effectively express this anger, probably many times. Consider creative uses of this energy, e.g. fantasising about taking revenge or campaigning for change. Consider the potential consequences of holding on to revenge, such as inhibiting grieving, preventing them from fulfilling their potential, and keeping them from being in contact with themselves and others; as Gandhi said, an eye for eye only leaves the whole world blind (Fuchs 1999). Occasionally, revenge can become a duty to the deceased that may also be an unhealthy continuing bond. Alternatively, choosing to live well may be the best revenge and is probably a more constructive approach, i.e. 'I won't let you ruin my life.'

- **Reconstruct their assumptive world.** A client's sense of injustice about the death may be both warranted *and* an unsatisfying realisation that others, such as services and government, did not perform as assumed. Losing such assumptions is a significant secondary loss and needs to be grieved for, including reconstructing new assumptions about others (see Chapter 1).

- **Consider whether blame may be misplaced,** disproportionately allocated or the result of misunderstanding others' intentions, or whether it might serve a purpose (see below). Only offer this after you have acknowledged their blame and when they are less angry and ready to consider.

Guilt

Clients can feel healthy guilt, as described above, for their part in something. Ideas to consider:

- **Propose to a client that they work through their guilt** – i.e. say sorry, feel remorse, make amends for their actions and commit to behave differently in future. This could be to someone they hurt who is alive, or to the deceased, e.g. speaking to them in an empty chair, writing them a letter, saying it at the graveside or to their ashes, etc. It is important that you witness their apology and remorse, so that they still have the experience of being heard and acknowledged – even if not by the deceased. This can be developed into a 'dialogue' (see pages 177–8). Where the deceased was addicted, it could be useful to 'hear' two answers: one from the addicted part of them and another from the rest of them. This may help a client deepen their understanding of how addiction changed the deceased.

- **Consider what a client could do to make amends** that is proportionate, e.g. donating to a charity or volunteering their time. Suggest they 'consult' the deceased to 'hear' what they would want. Also, invite them to consider what they can learn for the future to avoid doing something similar again. This usually involves making sense of why they behaved as they did (see forgiveness, below).

- **A client may need to tell others**, who may not have been involved, that they are sorry, feel remorse, have made amends and commit to being different.

- **The client could 'ask' the deceased if there is anything *they* feel guilty about** and want to apologise for. As and when necessary, develop this into a 'dialogue'.

- **Propose this is the best anyone can do** and consider forgiveness (see below).

During the above work ensure you only work with what a client *is* responsible for and recognise where others *also* had a part in what happened.

Blame and guilt that are seemingly unwarranted

The key idea is that what seems unwarranted to others feels very real to a client, and that their thinking that results in feeling these emotions is not true.

Blame and guilt that result from unrealistic expectations

A client may have unrealistic expectations of themselves or others that result in feeling guilt or blame – for example, blaming a substance treatment service for not stopping their loved one's addictive substance use. These expectations often arise from misunderstanding substance use, especially when addictive, and how relationships are co-created.

Also, blame and guilt often occur in bereavement for something that happened or was neglected around the time of the death that may have prevented it, often characterised by clients saying 'If only...' These perceptions of responsibility often seem unrealistic, yet are typically attachment-motivated attempts (usually made out of a client's awareness) to somehow prevent what happened and thereby reunite with a loved one. Ideas to consider include:

- **These ways of feeling blame or guilt may naturally pass** as acceptance of the death deepens.

- **They often mitigate through 'reality testing'** – by exploring the evidence of what actually happened, a client may come to realise that they could not realistically have changed things (Worden 2009, p.20).

- **Offer the interpretation that they are trying to reunite.** If this fits for them, normalise it and facilitate their accepting the reality of the death (see page 24 and page 184).

- **Reconstructing their assumptive world.** See above for warranted blame.

Guilt for feeling relief that a loved one has died

Anyone can feel relief when a loved one dies and is no longer suffering, or because the source of stress in their life has gone. Also, they may feel guilty for feeling relieved, often because they do not recognise the difference between a difficult situation finishing and the life of a loved one ending. Occasionally, however, a client may feel guilty for wanting their loved one's death:

> A very few interviewees, all mothers, admitted that things had been so bad that they had contemplated leaving their son to die, with one believing that it would be better if they or their child were dead, and another querying having her son at all. (Templeton *et al.* 2018a, p.118)

See forgiveness, below.

Suicide deaths

Guilt is common in people bereaved by suicide, particularly for not preventing the death (see page 74 and page 110). Ideas to help include:

- **Normalise blame and especially guilt in suicide deaths.**

- **Offer to educate about suicide and, if relevant, also addiction and/or depression** (see Chapters 3, 4, 6 and 15). This informs the work to…

- **Make sense of the deceased's potential frame of mind** and the wider context of their life. Speculate about their possible motives, e.g. to end their misery, to punish others. Consider how their motives may have been distorted by addiction, depression or other mental health difficulties. This kind of exploration helps to answer *why* the deceased ended their life. Wanting to know why is a key characteristic of grieving a suicide death – not least because clients often want to establish that they were not responsible.

- **Consider whether a client's guilt is warranted or unwarranted** by exploring what happened and then working as described above and below as necessary, e.g. guilt serves the purpose of explaining what seems to be an inexplicable death.

- **Support turning guilt to resentment.** Later in the work, a client may be able to turn their accusatory energy from guilt to resentment about the deceased killing themselves (see coerced guilt below). Before this is realistic, they will need to have worked on their guilt.

Blame and guilt that serve a purpose

There are other, more complex ways in which blame and guilt may occur. Clients may persist in feeling blame and/or guilt despite it seemingly being unwarranted, such as guilt for something they actually had little or no control over, or even where they were a victim. These emotions can serve a purpose by 'functioning as a barrier to more difficult feelings'; this is beyond a client's awareness, and indicates other issues that need attention (Paul 2006, p.51). Offering them this interpretation is usually necessary as most clients have no idea that blame and guilt can occur in these ways.

For clients who were affected by substance use prior to the death (especially addictive use), such forms of blame and guilt often predate the death and may have been a barrier to overwhelming confusion, worry, powerlessness and ambiguous loss (see Chapter 4). These clients then start bereavement already feeling blame and/or guilt, and are likely to continue feeling them for similar purposes.

As long as blame or guilt serves this purpose, a client has no incentive to let it go, or to forgive or be forgiven. Therefore, it is essential to establish the purpose, such as by exploring what they imagine would happen if they no longer felt blame or guilt. For example, asking 'What would it mean to you if it wasn't your responsibility?' may reveal fears about losing a continuing bond to a loved one or being powerless to stop another loved one from dying.

Next are ways that blame and guilt may serve a purpose and ideas for working with them:

- **Blame or guilt help a client to make sense of a situation.** Where reality does not seem to have an explanation, blaming others or themselves finally provides one (Paul 2006), e.g. 'It's the drug dealer's fault my son got addicted.' Also, 'survivor guilt' often occurs for this reason, e.g. a client feeling guilty when they used the same substance as their friend who died. As counselling 'helps to find explanations, provides all necessary information and untiringly discusses the how, the what and the wherefore', a client can develop a new, accurate narrative (Paul 2006, p.52). This often requires first learning about substance-using behaviour and how relationships are co-created.

- **Guilt provides a sense of personal power** (Paul 2006). By blaming themselves for what happened, a client can feel powerful in a situation of overwhelming powerlessness and fear, e.g. 'I caused their drug use.' Letting themselves feel powerless might mean that they could not stop others from dying. This may be worse than the reality of confronting the limit of their power (Kosminsky 2019), or conversely, may prevent 'giving way to the depression that would arise if they admitted their own helplessness' (Parkes and Prigerson 2010, p.87). Consider practical ways a client can develop other strategies to feel autonomy and a capacity to act, while developing the self-support to accept the limit of their influence on others and recognise the existential reality that 'ultimately, matters of life and death are beyond human control' (Paul 2006, p.52).

- **Blame or guilt avoid what is overwhelming**, for example:

  - A client taking responsibility and feeling guilty can be a way to avoid overwhelming emotion, e.g. in a suicide death believing 'It was my fault they took their own life', which serves the purpose of '...therefore they didn't reject me'.

  - A client taking responsibility and feeling guilt can be holding in, and even turning against themselves, resentment that is too challenging to express to a loved one (Yontef 1993), e.g. feeling guilty protects a victim of domestic abuse against feeling their resentment and thereby risking a confrontation, which became habitual before the death and continues into bereavement (see also rumination in Chapter 15).

- Projecting blame on to others avoids taking responsibility and feeling overwhelming guilt (or shame – see Chapter 13). Occasionally, this manifests as long-term campaigns for justice for the deceased that are neither a healthy continuing bond nor a creative way of giving the death meaning that they may appear to be (see Chapter 17).

- Blame and guilt may provide a client with the illusion that aspects of their assumptive world have not been lost, e.g. as if 'I caused the death, so the world is still predictable and I do still have control', as an attempt to maintain a sense of predictability and control.

Develop a client's support so they feel able to engage with what they fear and then work through what emerges using the ideas in this chapter.

- **Blame and guilt are an unhealthy continuing bond.** Blaming others can be a way to maintain an idealised view of the deceased, or make them special and worth the attention that they might not otherwise receive (Paul 2006). Alternatively, in blaming the deceased – e.g. 'You destroyed my life' – or by blaming themselves – e.g. 'It's my fault you died' – they form 'a very stable and time-resistant' emotional bond (Paul 2006, p.51). Explore the function of such bonds and develop alternative healthier bonds (see Chapter 2).

Coerced guilt

As discussed in Chapter 4, as people affected by problematic or addictive substance use are often coerced or manipulated into feeling guilt, they can inadvertently assist that use. This co-created, distorted and fixed dynamic in their relationship often continues after the death, by habitually taking responsibility for the behaviour of their deceased loved one. Therefore, although their guilt feels real, it is not actually true. Parents, particularly mothers, seem vulnerable to coerced guilt, because it often manipulates their innate attachment urge to protect and care.

The key idea is that persecutory energy is directed inwards as self-blame and guilt, rather than outwards as resentment to the person who is actually responsible (Yontef 1996). Although resentment is usually an unwelcome emotion, it is a more accurate and healthy response than guilt. Ideas for working with coerced guilt:

- **Establish what a client feels guilty for and where the responsibility actually lies,** and educate them as needed. It can help to propose that if they could not control what they feel guilty about, then it is not their responsibility. Consider whether the deceased's coercion was deliberate and intentional or happened inadvertently. Also invite them to consider how many, if any, of the reasons for addiction (see Chapter 3) were within their control. This work is often slow as a client gradually reconstructs their assumptions about and narrative of what happened and how the deceased treated them.

- **Help a client to become aware of their resentment.** A place to start is asking them, 'If you weren't feeling guilty, how else might you feel?' If this is unsuccessful, you could invite them to imagine someone else who had been coerced into assisting substance use and imagine how they would feel. Additionally, invite them to notice their bodily experience as they recall being manipulated, to linger with and develop this experience, and then consider what they are feeling. Normalise any resentment.

- **Invite a client to express their resentment** once they can feel it; see ideas for expressing anger above. This may be difficult and a client might need your permission to feel resentful of the deceased. If they inhibit their resentment to protect the deceased's reputation, propose that they can both love someone *and* be angry with them, and that the deceased is more than some of their behaviour. Also, an understanding of addiction helps to see how anyone would probably behave badly if addicted. Although it may have been risky to express resentment while the deceased was alive, consider saying that it is safe to do so now. This is especially important with a client who is traumatised by substance-using behaviour.

- **Resentment can be seen as telling someone what they want.** Encourage a client to say what they want, even if it is unobtainable now, e.g. 'Stop drinking and being so nasty when you're drunk!' Be a witness to this. Suggest they develop this into a 'dialogue' with the deceased.

Parent and other attachment figure guilt

As discussed in Chapter 6, bereaved parents seem particularly vulnerable to guilt. Also, a parent can take responsibility for the shortcomings of the other parent. Others who were attachment figures and cared for their loved one who died (such as partners, siblings and adult children who cared for a parent) often feel similarly guilty.

Miles and Demi found that bereaved parents feel guilty in five ways (1991–1992):

1. Causal guilt for the death, whether that be real or perceived. Also, parents may feel guilty for the inherited genetic aspect of addiction.

2. Cultural guilt due to social expectations that parents will keep their children safe, even when their offspring are adult.

3. Moral guilt where the death happened because of their perceived moral failings. Parents of offspring who use substances can feel this guilt acutely, believing use resulted from their poor parenting.

4. Survival guilt for outliving their child.

5. Recovery guilt for getting on with and enjoying their life after the death, because they believe it dishonours the memory of their offspring or this forms an unhealthy continuing bond.

These ways are exacerbated where a parent has their own history of problematic or addictive substance use. However, often parental and carer guilt is unwarranted.

Parents can really struggle to accept that they could not make their adult child do what they wanted, such as stop using drugs. This is often based on having been able to control them while they were growing up. However, this control is to some extent an illusion, as even when very young a child is both able to resist a parent's demands and influence the parent's behaviour – for example, the formation of attachment (see Chapter 2). Eventually, children grow up and become independent, at least in terms of autonomous thoughts and actions, and sometimes do things their parent wishes they would not, such as driving too fast, marrying the 'wrong' person or using substances.

Ideas to consider for bereaved parents, that can be adapted for others, include:

- **Invite a client to explore warranted guilt for things they are responsible for** – see above.

- **Offer to educate about attachment**, how the associated innate urge to protect and care has not evolved to cope with addiction, and therefore how easily this comes with guilt when protecting and caring were unsuccessful.

- **Offer to educate about where responsibility lies in a relationship.** In particular, whatever shortcomings a client may have had, their adult child is always responsible for their behaviour, including substance use. It can help to invite the client to experiment with saying 'If I can't control it, it's not my responsibility' to experience how that is. Similarly, consider the responsibility of the other parent.

- **Invite a client to consider their own childhood process of individuating** from their parents and how they could resist what their parents said.

- Encourage a client to experiment with saying 'I did the best I could with what I had, with what I knew then, while they were growing up.' Then consider together how it is to say that and, if needs be, explore what makes this difficult to accept. This enables unrealistic beliefs and expectations to emerge or can identify genuine shortcomings that they feel guilty about.

- Hear from the parent part of a client who believes they 'failed' to provide attachment, as this typically stays activated long after the death of a child. Then invite them to disidentify with this part and evoke their adult part, and from that part find self-empathy and compassion for their struggle to parent, being thwarted in their efforts to protect and care, and for being a bereaved parent.

- Suggest the client to experiment with 'handing back' responsibility to others, e.g. saying to the deceased 'I didn't put drugs in your body; you did that, so it's your responsibility.' As ever, there is no correct outcome, although a client could well feel relief and/or resentment, so you may decide to explore how they stop themselves feeling these expected responses. See above for working with resentment.

- Consider the family, cultural, social and media pressures on being a parent and how they inevitably failed to live up those – as all parents do. Guilt seems to be an intrinsic and inevitable part of being a parent, whether an adult child uses substances or not. Invite and encourage their resentment towards a world that expects so much of parents, often fails to adequately support them with their offspring's substance use, and then judges or stigmatises them when they fail.

- Guilt about the genetic legacy for addiction. It is important for a client to recognise that genes *may* provide a predisposition *and* there need to be environmental factors for addiction to happen (see Chapter 3). Consider whether addiction was their intention for their child when starting a family and whether they are being 'wise with hindsight'.

- Recovery guilt. Invite them to describe all the things they got right as a parent and the price they paid for doing that. Consider saying they have earned the right to a life beyond grief for all the grieving they have done (Leick and Davidsen-Nielsen 1991). Ask what the deceased would want for them now.

Forgiveness

Real forgiveness is an emotive and difficult process. To forgive, a client needs to genuinely understand the person who is responsible (be that themselves or someone else), so they can let go of past injuries, the need to punish and any pay-offs, such as the power that comes from being right, and then feel able to pardon. This is 'accepting something just the way it is, accepting the person as they are, without having to fight, be a victim, or need it to be different. That's where the healing is' (Fuchs 1999, p.245).

This enables a client to find peace within themselves. Also, it is focusing on now and the future. The nature of forgiveness strays into the existential and spiritual (see also Chapter 17).

Therefore, forgiveness is not a one-off rosy event where a client says 'I forgive' and then no longer feels blame or guilt. It is not a power play where a client feels morally superior (Fuchs 1999). Nor is forgiveness a duty; it cannot be forced and it is not the premature forgiveness some people give because they believe, or are told, it is the right thing to do – for example, being obliged to forgive by a religious faith. Forgiving does not mean condoning, denying or forgetting, and it does not replace justice – it complements it.

Forgiveness may only be partial and is not always possible. Clients can recognise the need to forgive *and* find it difficult to do. It is difficult for clients whose revenge patterns work well, such as the power of being the victim or having the moral high ground. Also, it is difficult to choose between being right and living with the burden of the past, or being happy and giving up being right (Fuchs 1999).

How forgiveness happens

To forgive, a client needs to understand why they, or someone else, did what they are responsible for. This involves mentalising to recognise the inevitable human limitations or failings that led to what happened. This can be distasteful, unpleasant and difficult where it is beyond their own experience (such as being addicted). This may challenge their assumptive world about how they or others should or should not behave, and adjusting to this reality can in itself be a significant part of grieving. For example, a parent who chose to put their needs before those of their addicted offspring who died has to challenge their belief that 'I should always put my children first'.

A client needs to identify with these limitations or failings in themselves, then be willing to find compassion for those inevitable human limitations or failings, in themselves or others, which in turn allows healing (Fuchs 1999). It may help for them to read first-hand accounts by someone who has done what they find hard to identify with. Identifying with inevitable human limitations and failings does not imply that a client would have acted in the same way as the person they blame; it just enables them to see the potential people have to act that way. It helps to go a step further: once they can own this potential, they can become aware of what stops them acting that way, and that in turn gives them further understanding of how that was probably missing in the person they blame.

Forgiving others

Forgiving someone else is easier when they acknowledge responsibility, apologise, convey empathy for the impact they have had and show remorse – that is, work through their healthy guilt (see above). Where this has not happened because the person has died, propose that a client 'ask' them for these and develop a 'dialogue' between them. However, needing these in order to forgive ties a client to those who hurt them, as they cannot forgive without them. Consider what might have stopped the person who died from doing these, to gain understanding of them, which in turn might enable a client to forgive them. Consider how a client might be able to relinquish these prerequisites and whether they might be able to forgive without them.

For forgiveness to happen, a client will need also to give up any pay-offs for holding on to blame. Forgiving holds within it the possibility of a painful lesson about life: 'an awakening to consciousness, an initiation into our own inner strength, wisdom and maturity' and more sober, less naïve trust of other people and organisations (Fuchs 1999, p.244).

Asking for forgiveness from others

Where relevant, suggest that a client 'ask' their deceased loved one for forgiveness. This can be developed into a 'dialogue' between them. Often a client imagines that forgiveness *is* given (where the deceased was addicted, at least by the part of them that was not addicted). If it is, ask a client, 'What would they want for you now?'

However, if forgiveness is *not* 'given', this is obviously very difficult for a client and likely to induce further guilt and potentially shame. Invite a client to consider what stops the deceased forgiving; this may require you to share your interpretation to help them make sense of this. If forgiveness seems to be withheld unreasonably, probably you need to say it would be normal for anyone to feel resentment about that, as well as probably guilt (see above).

A client forgiving themselves

Regardless of whether forgiveness was given or not, a good outcome for this work is when a client can have compassion for their inevitable human failings, forgive themselves as far as they are able to, and do so while not denying their responsibility. Often clients were doing the best they could with what they knew at that time. Propose they experiment with saying this to themselves to experience what it is like.

It may be easier for them to have compassion and forgiveness for someone else in the same situation as themselves. Describe someone *like* them and ask whether they can feel compassion and forgiveness for that person. If they can, explore what is different between the imagined person and themselves.

How far can a client forgive?

Forgiving is a psychologically sophisticated position to arrive at and often takes much repetition. It is probably unrealistic for some clients, such as expecting a parent to forgive the person who murdered their offspring over a drug debt. It can be difficult to forgive where it is unknown how far an addicted loved one was able to take responsibility for their behaviour. Also, forgiveness is difficult for clients who struggle to mentalise and/or to forgive themselves because of habitual childhood guilt.

Where forgiving is difficult, consider whether it is helpful or not for a client to explore how they stop themselves doing so. If forgiveness does not happen, it is important that this is not seen as a failure by a client, and that their choice is respected.

Perhaps the end of the process looks something like:

'What happened was not all down to me *and* I had my part in it too. I genuinely feel compassion for my own limitations as a person and can make sense of why I behaved as I did. I have learned from that. I also have the right to a life beyond this and I choose not to let what happened define who I am now.'

Or at least an acknowledgement of partial forgiveness, where perhaps just the wise part of a client can forgive:

'Today I choose to forgive you for ending your life. This helps me to find empathy for why you did that *and* another part of me doesn't have empathy for you. This helps me manage my anger so it doesn't become enduring bitterness.'

Suggest they create a ritual to hold on to their work to forgive (see also page 292):

'I take with me the good, I own my part in both the good and the bad, and I leave behind the bad.'

Common difficulties with blame and guilt and ideas to help

Difficulties may arise when a client struggles to mentalise effectively, in particular:

- **A client does not consider the intention behind a particular action** and whether they or others did something deliberately or not. Where behaviour was not intentional, was unavoidable or done for a greater good, 'it is appropriate to feel regret without guilt. Distinguishing true guilt from fear of punishment and regret often brings relief' (Yontef 1996, p.366).

- **The client takes all the responsibility** and does not recognise that others also had a part in what happened, e.g. a client having responsibility for giving a friend the drugs that killed them *and* that friend being responsible for taking those drugs. Therefore, usually it helps to see how relationships are co-created and thereby separate out where responsibility lies. Consider suggesting they write three columns: one for their behaviour, one for the deceased's behaviour and another for what they created together. This can be a profoundly different way of seeing relationships for someone affected by long-term addictive behaviour. As it takes them time to make sense of relationships this way, you will probably need to keep highlighting this.

- **The client has difficulty knowing how far an addicted loved one was able to take responsibility for their behaviour,** given they were in such an altered state. It is not for you to determine this; rather, the work is in supporting a client to become better informed about addiction, apply that to the deceased and consider how far they perceive the deceased was able to take responsibility.

- **The client is 'wise with hindsight'** and feels guilty for something they did not understand when it occurred. Pointing this out can be enough. When it is not, be curious about what keeps the guilt going and develop self-empathy and compassion.

- **The client has deeply held beliefs** that override everything else such as:

  'Being a parent is a lifetime's responsibility, but when their addiction was too much, I put myself first and withdrew from them, and now they're dead. I feel so guilty I didn't fulfil my responsibilities.'

  Consider such beliefs to see where they come from and why they are so important. Sometimes their original purpose is no longer relevant, e.g. as a child they had to follow particular moral values in order to be acceptable to their parents and thereby maintain attachment; or the beliefs may have been formed through emotional blackmail to assist substance use; or, if they are still relevant, the belief may be a fine aspiration that is also unrealistic.

Additionally, enduring blame and particularly guilt can lead to difficulties in grieving (see 'Complexities and difficulties in grieving' in Chapter 1) and/or depression (see Chapter 15).

Living with residual anger, blame and guilt

Clients can continue to feel these emotions despite having worked on them in counselling. Parents in particular can continue to feel guilty. It is important to acknowledge that some things cannot be made up for and that forgiveness can be very difficult. Perhaps a client's enduring guilt serves as a reminder of something important for their future. Consider how they can find at least some compassion, acceptance and forgiveness to help them live with what happened, so they can be in restoration orientation more often. It can help to give the death meaning by creating something good from something so bad (see Chapter 17).

Ultimately, there comes a point where they need to decide to shift the emphasis from the past and associated recriminations to getting on with the rest of their life.

◼ Emma

Emma felt guilty about her husband Steve's alcohol use and for his subsequent death, as well as for staying with him despite knowing the impact his behaviour had on their children. As part of the initial exploration of her guilt, her counsellor enquired what would happen if she did not feel guilty, to which Emma replied, 'Then he really would be gone.' He offered her the interpretation that at least some of the guilt was a way to cling on to Steve and thereby continue her bond with him. Emma agreed. However, her counsellor was mindful that the work had just begun and of Emma's anxious ambivalent attachment style, and therefore chose not to challenge this until later.

Further exploration revealed that Emma had felt guilty since childhood. Her counsellor considered this was important to focus on next, so asked for and got her agreement to this. It emerged that her father manipulated her into assisting his drinking by telling her how special she was when she did as he asked and blaming her when she did not. It was very painful for Emma to acknowledge that her father had manipulated her in this way and that perhaps she had not really been that special to him. As part of broader work to develop her support, Emma began referring to 'Little Emma who's guilty' as a way to disidentify with this part of herself and to evoke her 'wise adult part' to parent that part as she did her own children. This, plus her counsellor's support, enabled her to start work on bereavement guilt.

Emma had already learned about addiction and how relationships are co-created. She realised she had repeated with Steve the same relationship pattern she had with her father. With her counsellor, she explored the fixed dynamics of their marriage and established what each of them was responsible for. During this work Emma still felt guilty and needed her counsellor's support to help her take care of 'Little Emma' and evoke her 'wise adult self'. Emma was initially disorientated and anxious as she realised just how different her marriage was from what she had assumed.

Emma also realised that sometimes Steve had known what he was doing was wrong and probably could have stopped himself, and at other times probably could not. Her counsellor asked how she felt about that; Emma replied she did not feel anything, so he invited her to pay attention to her body as she thought about how sometimes he had known what he was doing. Gradually, she became aware of feeling resentful towards Steve. This was developed into writing a letter to him. Emma read this out many times in counselling, each time letting herself feel a bit more anger *and* feel how it was safe to do so now.

At her counsellor's suggestion, Emma 'handed back' responsibility to Steve for what was his responsibility, which she had carried throughout their marriage. Then she did the same for her father. This ended with Emma feeling partially able to forgive Steve and her father, and considering healthier ways to have continuing bonds.

Following this, Emma used counselling to look at her own responsibility in the marriage – in particular, how 'Steve was spoilt as a child and then I let him get away with everything' and the impact that had on their children. This entailed re-working through how she had repeated a relationship pattern, her attachment style and the associated urge to compulsively care as a way to cling on to others. This helped Emma to find some compassion and forgiveness for herself, despite still feeling guilty. Emma supported herself with this guilt in various ways: by saying to herself, 'I can see now that I didn't make Steve drink nor cause his death, and I unintentionally had an unhelpful influence on him'; by using this new insight to avoid repeating what happened and protect her children, and thereby making amends to her children; finally, by researching age-appropriate information for her children about addiction and committing to explaining her part in what happened when they were old enough.

John

John was very angry with whoever had prepared and supplied the heroin that resulted in his daughter Sarah overdosing. His counselling focused on expressing and validating this anger, through having imaginary conversations with the person who dealt the heroin.

John's counsellor noticed that he remained fixated on knowing exactly why Sarah had died and his associated anger and blame. She enquired: 'I'm curious what might lie beneath your understandable emotions and wanting to know why. Are you curious too?' They explored the layers of meaning and came to realise that if John had someone else to blame, he would feel less guilty for not supporting Sarah and for leaving this to his ex-wife, Anne.

Further exploration looked at what happened to cause John to behave in these ways. What emerged was that he protected himself from the pain of being unable to save Sarah, as well as how he had also been selfish. Beneath these motives was John's avoidant attachment style and how he withdrew too easily and was too independent. Also, counselling focused on John saying sorry to Sarah, how deeply he regretted his shortcomings as a father and the pain he had caused Sarah and her mother. It was important to John that his counsellor had seen how much he meant this and they both acknowledged the sadness in Sarah not hearing it. John also made amends by donating money every month to Sarah's favourite charity and by learning from his experiences.

Also, John used counselling to prepare to meet Anne and say sorry, to share his remorse for the impact of his behaviour on her and to offer to pay for the funeral as a gesture towards making amends. John found their meeting very difficult because Anne remained angry with him. With his counsellor's support, John saw that although he was responsible for his past behaviour, he was not responsible for her response to him and that he had fulfilled what he saw as his responsibility to her by apologising and paying for the funeral.

Following this, his counsellor proposed that they consider Sarah's part in what happened. This established that she was responsible for using drugs and that she was aware of the overdose risk. His counsellor asked: 'How is it to know that?' John replied: 'I want to blame her.' Therefore, the work focused on expressing that blame. This facilitated being able to then feel his hurt and to accept that she had a share of the responsibility for her death.

John's counselling also considered his difficult realisation that he felt a lot of hatred for the person who dealt the heroin. He said, 'This isn't me', to which his counsellor replied, 'No, not in the past, but it is now and it challenges who you assume you are.' She proposed that John consider how any parent would feel towards someone who dealt the heroin that killed their child and John began to find compassion for himself.

Later, they considered whether John could forgive people. He needed an understanding of addiction to make sense of Sarah's behaviour, then he easily felt much love, compassion and forgiveness for her. Forgiving himself was harder. It helped him to disidentify with being a guilty father, understand his thwarted attachment urge to care for Sarah and to say: 'How does any parent know what to do for the best when their child is addicted? I did the best I could with what I knew then.'

John was not interested in forgiving whoever had dealt the heroin. His counsellor said she thought forgiveness would be very difficult for any parent and that forgiveness was his to give, or not, as he decided. Also, she said she feared him becoming bitter, to which John replied he did not feel he had a choice. Therefore, they created a statement: 'I still blame them, but I choose to see that most people are not like them and I'm not going to let them stop me having as good a life as I can.' John also developed putting his blame into his grief box (see pages 159–60) until he chose to express it by letting himself rant until his anger was discharged.

FURTHER READING ON GUILT THAT ORIGINATES IN CHILDHOOD
May, R. (1983) *The Discovery of Being.* Chapter 7. New York: Norton.
McGregor Hepburn, J. (2012) 'A problem of guilt: An exploration of feelings of guilt as an obstacle to psychic change.' *British Journal of Psychotherapy 28*, 2, 188–200.
Yontef, G. (1993) *Awareness, Dialogue and Process: Essays on Gestalt Therapy.* Chapter 15. Highland, NY: Gestalt Journal Press.

15

Depression

This chapter considers how to work with mild temporary depression in the context of substance-related bereavement by:

- considering the depressive response to bereavement
- assessing whether a client is depressed and the associated risks
- working with a client's depressive response.

Working with other causes of depression is beyond the scope of this book and further reading is suggested. Also, moderate to severely depressed clients need medical help and supervision in addition to any support you are providing (see assessing risk below).

The depressive response to bereavement

Depression can be understood as a 'depressive response' to 'life circumstances that seem unmanageable or overwhelming', by withdrawing, isolating and shutting down, with a sense of hopelessness and a diminished capacity to function effectively (Joyce and Sills 2014, pp.206, 203). It is as if someone decides, out of their awareness, 'This is awful and I can't get out of it, so best to just shut down.' Understanding mild depression as a response to adverse life circumstances views it as a part of grieving and one that counselling can help with, although see below about habitual depression.

Feeling depressed during bereavement is a common and usually transient experience for many bereaved people. This can be seen as a 'depressive adjustment' (Roubal 2007, p.38); a relatively mild, temporary state someone goes through, that is 'an economy of effort and a conservation of resources...[that] enables a person to stop, consider the changed situation and make a decision on alternative strategies...and prevents activity that would be wasted' (Roubal 2007, p.38).

It follows that someone can have a depressive adjustment in response to a loved one's death –for example, the normal withdrawing into deep sadness, despair and hopelessness at fully realising a loved one is not coming back. This adjustment protects them from other demands that they may not have the self-support to cope with at the moment, and it enables deeper introspection. In turn, this leads to the only realistic option, greater acceptance of the death, and thereby deeper adjustment to the loss (Roubal 2007).

However, depression during bereavement can have many causes (Parkes and Prigerson 2010). In substance-related bereavements, this includes clients who were affected by addictive substance-using behaviour before the death, who responded to those adverse circumstances by becoming depressed (Orford *et al.* 2013) and similarly for those who experienced ambiguous loss before the death (Boss 2000) (see Chapter 4). These clients start bereavement already being depressed. Following the death, some characteristics of bereavement increase the risk of a depressive response, such as being traumatically bereaved, enduring guilt and damage to the assumptive world and of meaning and purpose in life (see relevant chapters). Also, some clients may be depressed in response to financial, housing or other practical problems that have arisen as a result of substance-using behaviour and/or the death. For these clients, resolving these problems is likely to be the most effective way to reduce their depression.

Furthermore, bereavement may trigger a client's depressive response that is habitual depression, which predates the death and does not serve them in adapting to their loss (Parkes 2009). This is likely to happen through an interaction of a client's genetic predisposition, adverse childhood experiences and as a response to this difficult life event, and is more likely to become moderate to severe depression (Roubal 2007).

Although this is beyond the scope of this book, typically a client's original depressive adjustment, often made in childhood, *was* a necessary response to an overwhelming and unmanageable situation. This then becomes a habitual, fixed depressive response to subsequent difficult life circumstances, including bereavement, which is made out of awareness and is usually unhelpful (Roubal 2007). This is characterised by unquestioned negative self-beliefs and the holding-in of energy that someone often turns against themselves as self-accusation and guilt. In turn, this becomes an unintended, self-reinforcing cycle of perceived helplessness and despair about difficult life circumstances, often with self-criticism, not trying to influence those circumstances, therefore continuing to feel hopelessness and despair, and so on (Joyce and Sills 2014). This phenomenon has been referred to as learned helplessness (Seligman 1975).

People with an insecure attachment style can be at more risk of a depressive response during bereavement: those with a fearful avoidant style are very susceptible to depression when losing someone who they *did* risk forming an attachment to (Worden 2009). Similarly, being dependent on the person who died, as in those with an anxious/ambivalent style, has a higher risk of depression during bereavement (Johnson, Zhang and Prigerson 2008). Also, people with a disorganised attachment style tend to turn in on themselves as a way of coping during bereavement and are then vulnerable to becoming depressed (Parkes 2009).

Rumination

Rumination is a familiar characteristic of a depressive response that, typically, does not help adjustment to the loss and can become unhelpfully habitual. This persistent and repetitive dwelling on aspects of grief tends to be passive and cyclic, and prolongs grief and the associated emotions such as blame and guilt.

Sometimes rumination is someone's attempt to make meaning, although research suggests they are less likely to find it than others who do not ruminate (Worden 2009).

Ruminating on guilt may serve a purpose for a client, such as continuing their bond with a loved one. Alternatively, ruminating on guilt can provide a client with a sense of personal power through their believing that they are responsible for what is seemingly not their responsibility (Paul 2006) (see pages 242–4).

Alternatively, ruminating can be a client's way of holding energy in, rather than expressing it. Where they lived with addictive substance use, this might have begun before the death. This holding-in serves a purpose for a client – 'biting one's lip may be more functional than saying something biting' (Yontef 1993, p.137). A client's ruminating may not be just holding their energy in, but 'doing to the self what one wants to do to someone else' (p.137) – for example, turning accusations inward as guilt serves the purpose of avoiding overwhelming anger at the person who died (see page 243).

However, rumination during bereavement can lead to enduring depression and drive away other people who might provide support. It might inadvertently exclude good memories of a loved one and inhibit forming a healthy continuing bond (Kosminsky 2019). Also, people with an anxious/ambivalent attachment style may be particularly likely to ruminate during bereavement (Worden 2009).

> Consider how you would describe the depressive response to a client. You might want to create an informal 'script' that summarises this section and then rehearse how you would say it.

Assessing whether a client is depressed

Many of the characteristics of a depressive response are also found in grief, and some mildly depressed people do not outwardly show signs of depression and may even seem to be happy. Therefore, assessing whether a client is depressed can be difficult.

A depressive response has some or all of the following characteristics (Joyce and Sills 2014; Lemma 1996; Parkes 2004):

- general appearance of head down, poor eye contact, withdrawn, deflated posture, moving slowly

- persistent low mood, diminished ability to think or concentrate, indecisiveness, marked loss of interest or pleasure in almost all activities

- bodily symptoms, including a loss of appetite and weight, too much or too little sleep, loss of energy and fatigue

- feelings of worthlessness, seemingly unwarranted guilt, recurrent thoughts of death or suicide

- alternatively, being anxiously depressed, including agitation, distress, crying, terrible sadness, possible panic and occasional anger (see anxiety in Chapter 11)

- either way, perceiving this experience as being the whole of who they are and having difficulty experiencing other ways of being.

Consider the differences between a significant depressive response and grief (Table 15.1).

Table 15.1 The differences between a significant depressive response and grief

Significant depressive response	Grief
Persistent sadness and thoughts are almost constantly negative, for most of the day and nearly every day.	Painful feelings come in waves and are associated with thoughts or reminders of deceased, often intermixed with positive memories of deceased.
Persistent depressed mood. Pervasive unhappiness and misery.	May feel empty. Pain of grief may be accompanied by positive emotions and humour.
General feelings of worthlessness, self-loathing and pessimistic rumination.	Self-esteem usually preserved. Self-criticism typically limited to perceived failings in relationship with deceased.
Thoughts about death and dying focused on ending own life because of feelings of worthlessness, undeserving of life, unable to cope with depression, etc.	Any thoughts about death or dying are focused on deceased and possibly about 'joining' deceased.

Adapted from Lemma 1996; Parkes 2004; Worden 2009.

Ask a client: 'Has there been any time in the last two weeks that you have not felt deeply unhappy?' If the answer is 'no', then they are likely to be depressed (Parkes 2004). Consider using regularly a subjective range-scale of one to ten, so a client can quantify how depressed they feel and you can keep track of the severity (Houston 2003).

Gauge the severity of depression (National Institute for Health and Care Excellence 2018):

- **Mild depression** is when a person has a small number of symptoms that have a limited effect on their daily life.

- **Moderate depression** is when a person has more symptoms that can make their daily life much more difficult than usual.

- **Severe depression** is when a person has many symptoms that can make their daily life extremely difficult.

Additionally, it is important to establish whether a client has experienced being this way before the death to help establish whether it seems to be a temporary state, a habitual trait or both.

You may well need to offer a client the interpretation that they are depressed and explain what that is. Be mindful that a depressed client might find it difficult to disagree with your ideas and/or have a negative response to them, such as feeling guilty for being depressed (see pages 140–2 on educating and interpreting).

Assessing risk

Although suicidal thoughts during bereavement are more often expressed than acted upon (Parkes and Prigerson 2010), a history of previous suicide attempts and/or depression is more likely to lead someone to self-injury and suicide (Harding 2014). Furthermore, heavy use of substances can intensify depression (Worden 2009) and excessive alcohol use increases the risk of suicide for bereaved people (Parkes and Prigerson 2010) (see Chapter 16 and page 74 for the three-way relationship between addiction, depression and suicide).

Obviously, take any risk seriously and safeguard a client as usual, which includes being honest with yourself when a client is not responding to your interventions and referring them to their doctor. When a client is suicidal and/or moderately to severely depressed (especially when this is habitual), you need to insist that they are referred to their doctor (who may also refer to a psychiatrist and other NHS services), so that any significant risk is under medical supervision. Joint working is helpful in these circumstances, such as sharing information (which requires a protocol covering confidentiality, etc.), and other practitioners may want to confer with you.

Antidepressants

Antidepressants can often lower the level of a client's symptoms of depression to one where bereavement counselling becomes possible, and may help them through great suffering and reduce their risk of suicide (C.M. Parkes, personal communication).

Antidepressants 'rarely relieve normal grief symptoms, and they could pave the way for an abnormal grief response, though this has yet to be proved through controlled studies' (Worden 2009, p.108), and 'the general consensus among psychiatrists today is that antidepressants should only be used after bereavement if there is clear evidence of major depression', when studies have shown they can be helpful (Parkes 2009, p.254).

Antidepressant use has been linked with suicidal thoughts and behaviour, particularly in children, young adults and people with a history of suicidal behaviour; therefore, it is important that clients are informed about this and are monitored for suicidal behaviour, self-injury or hostility, particularly at the beginning of treatment or if the dose is changed (Joint Formulary Committee (JFC) 2017). Some side effects of antidepressants may be unhelpfully similar to symptoms of both grief and depression. Side effects include anxiety, agitation, dry mouth, sleep disturbances, abnormal dreams, confusion, drowsiness, fatigue, poor concentration, chest pain, etc. (JFC 2017). Additionally, alcohol use can increase the side effects of some antidepressants, such as drowsiness, dizziness and co-ordination problems (National Health Service 2019). Potentially, some of these characteristics of antidepressant use may influence a client's capacity to engage in counselling.

Working with a client's depressive response

It is necessary to start by considering with a client whether their depressive response seems to be a mild temporary depressive adjustment that, while miserable, is still helping them to adjust to their loss, or is an enduring, fixed, probably habitual response that does not serve them. In particular, consider what a client is responding to in a depressive way and whether this response serves them, and explore exactly how they are inadvertently depressing themselves in order to establish their thoughts, emotions, bodily responses and ways of relating to others that you might work with.

Include considering whether you are of more support accompanying a client in their depression and waiting, or offering them ways to shift their experience out of depression. Either way, develop a client's support (see below). Working with a fixed, habitual depressive response is beyond the scope of this book (see the further reading suggestions at the end of this chapter), and, when moderate to severe, will require medical help and supervision, potentially including a psychiatrist.

Such an exploration may well identify that other aspects of grieving have become stuck and need work. Potential causes of a client's depressive response include trauma, unfinished business, shame and stigma, anger, blame and especially guilt, a damaged assumptive world and/or a loss of meaning and purpose in their life, as well as increased substance use, especially of alcohol (see relevant chapters). For example, depression often improves when post-traumatic stress disorder is treated (Parkes and Prigerson 2010).

Developing support

Feeling depressed can drive others away, potentially including you, through being miserable, unresponsive and self-absorbed. Therefore, your support becomes very important. This needs to blend your explicit acknowledgement of their present reality, holding the hope of change in the future, as well as not giving up in response to their hopelessness. Stay curious about their depressive response and encourage their curiosity too. In addition to the support ideas in Chapter 8, consider offering the following.

Ways to lift a client's energy and mood

When trying these ideas, some clients might need to 'fake it to make it', or at least use them knowing they prevent them feeling even worse.

- **Taking moderate exercise every day**, e.g. a 20-minute walk (Mammen and Faulkner 2013).

- **Undertaking small tasks and completing them**, to increase their sense of achievement and control (Joyce and Sills 2014). Recalling times when they were effective.

- **Writing a daily journal** to express thoughts and feelings (Krpan *et al.* 2013), including gratitude for what happens, however small, and lingering on feeling grateful (Emmons 2007).

- **Acting as if 'better'** can be helpful for mild depression, even if they do not feel like it, and expecting their mood to improve gradually (T. Gorski, personal communication).

- **Altering posture.** Invite a client to experiment with changing their posture and reflecting on how that feels.

- **Invigorating breathing** – see page 158.

- **Developing social support**, including contact with others, however minimal, e.g. saying hello to familiar people (Steger and Kashdan 2009).

- **Consider a medical referral for antidepressants and other help** – see above and Chapter 16.

Developing self-awareness to disidentify with a depressive response

A client needs to develop the self-awareness to disidentify with their depressive response and see it for what it is, and thereby not be consumed by it. Such mindful self-awareness is a significant part of coming out of depression (Burns 2000; Joyce and Sills 2014) and is like having dual awareness of trauma symptoms (see page 208). Therefore:

- **Invite a client to separate out their self-awareness and give it a 'voice'.** It can help a client to change chair or stand up. If this is difficult, propose that they have not completely given up as they have come to counselling, and ask to hear from the part of them that hopes to gain something by being with you.

With your support, a client can develop this capacity (Burns 2000; Joyce and Sills 2014; Roubal 2007):

- **The self-aware part can support the depressed part** through evoking their curiosity, self-empathy, capacity to mentalise and self-compassion about the depressed part, e.g. having compassion for being depressed, or recognising that being depressed feels real and as if it is their whole being, *and* is not true, as the rest of them is still there (even if they cannot experience that at the moment).

- **The self-aware part identifies and disproves beliefs** that are negative, self-limiting and/or unhelpfully overgeneralised, and needlessly keep their depressive response going, e.g. disproving evidence from their narrative about the life and death of the deceased, or evidence from behavioural experiments undertaken to test whether they *can* influence their life circumstances now, such as being able to lift their energy and mood (described above).

- **The self-aware part holds this self-knowledge** about how the depressed part may be narrow, rigid and inaccurate in its response to life circumstances.

Mindfulness and journal writing can support a client to do this work.

Working with a depressive adjustment to bereavement

The work is not to 'try to prevent, interfere with or avoid' (Roubal 2007, p.40) a client making their adjustment. Indeed, generating a positive outlook is probably unhelpful, even harmful, as a client may not have the self-support to cope with other demands at the moment (Roubal 2007). Therefore, explore what a client is responding to and consider its meaning to them. If necessary, explore how they may have got stuck in working towards acceptance of the reality of the death, as well as working with any existential themes (see Chapter 17). Also, be with them and help them develop their support, to allow the time needed for this adjustment to happen. For example:

> 'I imagine that you are now able to fully face the loss of your son and are depressed about how hopeless that seems to be. Therefore, I suggest we consider what support you need around you and from there wait until something shifts inside you. Also, I imagine a day will come when it does feel different and that may not make any sense to you right now.'

However, helpful introspection may become unhelpful rumination.

Working with rumination

As described above, ruminating can have various purposes, which probably inhibit healthy adjustment to loss. Therefore, begin by exploring what a client hopes to get from ruminating and/or the purpose it serves that they may not be aware of. This may involve you offering your interpretation (see pages 140–2). Next, work through as far as possible:

- **Ruminating to make meaning.** Encourage a client to actively work through what they are passively and cyclically ruminating about. Rumination is often characterised by dwelling on *why* they or others did or did not do something, and being unable to find the answer. Often it helps to explore *what* happened and *how* it happened, as these are easier questions to answer. If necessary, offer to educate a client about something they do not understand, until potentially meaning is finally made. When this process is unsuccessful, a client faces the unsatisfying choice of either continuing to ruminate unsuccessfully or accepting what remains unknown. Acknowledge and normalise how unsatisfying it is not to know what is important to us, and, if necessary, explore how they stop themselves accepting their reality.

- **Ruminating on blame or guilt that serves a purpose** for a client, such as continuing a bond (see Chapter 14).

- **Ruminating as holding in energy.** Invite a client to become aware of what is held in their body. Invite them to become aware of their thoughts and beliefs that make this holding-in necessary. Consider the consequences of, and any fears about, expressing what is held in, both in the past and as they continue to do so now. Develop the support they may need to express this energy. Create ways to experiment with expressing what has been held in, e.g. with your support in a session or at the graveside (also see Chapter 14 for expressing anger and resentment).

Stay open to the possibility of rumination being symptomatic of an unhelpful, fixed, often habitual depressive response. Rumination can be difficult to treat, so for clients who do not respond to your help, see assessing risk above.

▌ John

John's counsellor noticed that he seemed withdrawn, was not holding eye contact and seemed deflated. Also, he had cancelled the previous session. She commented on this, saying she was curious about what was happening for him and adding that he was not in trouble. John said he did not know and apologised 'for letting down yet another person'. Together they explored his experience and it emerged that once he felt less blame towards his daughter Sarah, he had become aware of just how awful and hopeless Sarah's life was at the end, the deep despair and sadness he now felt about that, and how selfish he had been and that now it was too late for him to change that. His counsellor proposed that some of the blame he had felt towards Sarah had protected him against his despair about the reality of the end of her life, and now that he had worked through much of that blame, he was responding to the end of Sarah's life in a depressive way. John agreed. Also, they established that he had not felt this kind of depression before.

John used his counselling to go over the awfulness of the end of Sarah's life many times. While he did this, his counsellor considered there was nothing more she could do other than provide the space for this and the validation of this awful reality. She shared this with John and they agreed that it seemed a necessary, and also very difficult, part of grieving. John felt a little relief when his counsellor added that she was committed to being with him through this difficult time.

Throughout John's depressive response, his counsellor checked each session how depressed he felt on a scale of one to ten, so she could keep track of how severe it was and whether a medical referral was indicated. Also, they would consider how he could support himself and through this established that it helped to write in his journal and walk part of the way to work, even when he had no motivation or energy to do so. Unfortunately, he did not feel able to discuss how he felt with colleagues, but sometimes work was a useful distraction from how he felt.

However, over time it became clear that John was ruminating about Sarah between sessions. At his counsellor's suggestion, they explored this, and John became aware that through ruminating he could feel closer to Sarah and this was unlike the end of her life when he had little contact with her. His counsellor asked, 'I'm interested in what you imagine would happen if you stopped ruminating?' John replied, 'I wouldn't be so close to her...and I'd feel guilty again.' This led to further work on his guilt and forgiving himself, and also to creating other less depressing ways to continue his bond with Sarah (see Chapter 2).

After two months, John's mood began to lift. When discussing Sarah, he started to add, 'I so wish it had been different for her, but that *isn't* what happened.' As this acceptance grew, John felt less need to dwell on the end of Sarah's life. He found it helpful when his counsellor proposed that although he could not forget the final years of her addiction and his absence from her life, that he need not reduce his memory of her life to that period.

FURTHER READING

Burns, D.D. (2000) *Feeling Good: The New Mood Therapy*. New York, NY: HarperCollins.
Joyce, P. and Sills, C. (2014) *Skills in Gestalt Counselling and Psychotherapy* (3rd edition). Chapter 19. London: Sage.

16

Counselling Clients Who Use Medication, Alcohol or Drugs

Increased substance use is common in bereaved people (Worden 2009), including, ironically, those bereaved through a substance-related death. This chapter considers:

- medication, alcohol and drug use by bereaved people

- practical ideas for working with a client's substance use where it is not addictive, and where those working with the client are inexperienced in this area

- bereavement counselling for clients who use substances non-addictively

- the importance of joint working.

The treatment of addictive substance use is beyond the scope of this book; however, if you work in this field, the following sections, written in collaboration with Rual Gibson, cover:

- bereavement counselling for clients who use substances addictively

- supporting substance use treatment staff bereaved through the loss of a client

- substance use treatment services and the bereaved family of a client who died.

Medication and substance use by bereaved people
Why substance use might increase
For many clients, bereavement can become very distressing and painful, and even feel the closest to madness they will ever get. Unsurprisingly, they can

want this to stop, and, for some, medication, alcohol and drugs are a way to do that. This is using substances to change the way they feel, think or behave (see Chapter 3). Put another way, taking something is an attempt to temporarily move from loss to restoration orientation.

Typical experiences someone might want to change include the pain of grieving itself, feeling depressed and anxious, and disturbed sleep, insomnia and tiredness during the day. These often happen together, heightening someone's urge to escape how they feel – for example, the despair and hopelessness felt when depressed often provokes anxiety about feeling so trapped. However, prolonged or excessive substance use is generally unsupportive of the grieving process because it can prolong numbing and increase anxiety, and risks causing addiction (Parkes and Prigerson 2010).

Clients who were affected by their loved one's problematic or addictive substance-using behaviour before the death may have already increased their substance use before the death (Orford *et al.* 2013).

Recall your own bereavements and other difficult times. Reflect on how you coped and whether your substance use temporarily increased.

Is it a trait or a state?

It can be difficult for clients to separate what is grieving from a pre-existing mental health difficulty. Depression, anxiety and poor or disturbed sleep often occur as temporary states during bereavement. However, these may have been experienced by people whose lives were affected by substance use before the death, where they were a repeating or continuous experience (Orford *et al.* 2013). Also, bereavement can provoke past mental health difficulties (Parkes and Prigerson 2010) and these can be both a trait *and* a state during bereavement. Therefore, you need to check with a client when these difficulties began.

The substances bereaved people may use

As it is impractical to cover every medication or substance that a client might use, this section offers general information and a way to think about clients' use.

Clients often see their doctor first. Unfortunately, 'many still use medication as their first option despite its limited value to bereaved people' (Parkes and Prigerson 2010, p.247) and despite the NICE guidance (National Institute for Health and Clinical Excellence 2018) that medication should not be the first treatment for depression, anxiety and sleep difficulties. Clients may not know that medication, such as sedatives, only alleviates symptoms and does not treat the underlying causes. However, medication, such as antidepressants, can often stabilise a client's mood enough for them to make use of bereavement counselling.

Others may 'self-medicate' (see page 53) with alcohol, tobacco, cannabis and so on. It is important to recognise that the 'heavy use of drugs or alcohol can intensify the experience of grief and depression and impair the bereavement process' (Worden 2009, p.103). Indeed, excessive alcohol or drug use can be a clear sign that someone's bereavement has become problematic; excessive alcohol use increases their risk of suicide, and they may be in need of specialist help (Parkes and Prigerson 2010). Those clients who have a disorganised attachment style are at increased risk of problematic use, and although those who are avoidant are at no greater risk than others, they do seem more likely to use alcohol following a traumatic loss (Parkes 2009).

There are several aspects of medication and substance use that are potentially significant for counselling clients: the intended effect and how well it produces that effect; the side effects, some of which can be unhelpfully similar to some characteristics of grieving and which clients might mistakenly attribute to grieving; the risk of addiction; the interaction between different medications or substances being used; and the influence all of these may have on grieving and bereavement counselling. For an example, see antidepressant use on page 262.

Client's beliefs about their mental health and expectations of medication or substance use are potentially influenced by their values, life experience, cultural background and religious faith. This may be very different from your perspective and from the psychotherapeutic approach of this book.

You need to be mindful of all of this, be willing to raise the subject of substance use and explore what is significant.

How to work with a client's non-addictive substance use

The following ideas are for clients who are not addicted to the medication or substances they use to cope with grief. Working with substance use can provoke anxiety in counsellors if it is unfamiliar; however, normal counselling practice combined with these ideas is often enough.

Counselling dynamics created by substance use

Hammersley (2013) describes the potentially significant interplay between a client, their medication, their doctor and you. A client has expectations of taking medication and possibly also about how they see it affecting counselling, such as attributing any lift in mood to the medication rather than counselling. Also, you need to be aware of your expectations of how their medication might influence your work. Despite the shared goal of helping, potentially a client can get differing or conflicting views from you and their doctor because of the different conceptual frameworks and methods of treatment. Therefore, you need to be aware of the potential undermining influence of the doctor (albeit unintentional).

Furthermore, counselling dynamics may occur through drug and alcohol use. Examples include a client using the demands of counselling to justify increased use after sessions, or a counsellor's attitudes about medication and substance use being non-verbally communicated to a client.

Ethical boundaries

Below are suggested ethical boundaries for your consideration:

- **Stay within your work role** and avoid the impression that you provide the kind of help and information that a doctor, nurse or drug or alcohol worker would (unless you are trained to do so and it is within your work role). If someone asks you to go beyond your work role, refer them on (see below). Talk about substances as an equal, not as an expert, and be explicit, e.g. 'I'm not medically trained so it's not appropriate for me to comment on your medication.' Also offer your ideas in a general, non-personal and neutral way, e.g. 'There is some research questioning the efficacy of antidepressants and you may want to look at that' rather than 'Having read about the research I believe the use of antidepressants is questionable'.

- **See psychoeducation** – pages 140–2.

- **Keep people safe.** There are potential risks through using substances. Treat any safeguarding concerns about a client and the people in their life in the usual way.

- **UK law.** People have the legal right to make an informed choice whether to accept or reject treatment and to change their mind.[1] The law does not require you to break confidentiality if someone discloses that they are using illegal drugs (known as 'possession'). However, you would need to consider informing the police if they were giving or selling illegal drugs to others (known as 'supply'). For legal advice about drug use, contact Release.[2]

---

1   This does not apply to someone who has been sectioned under the 1973 Mental Health Act, who can be given treatment without their consent.

2   See www.release.org.uk/helpline

How to work with substance use

The general idea is to encourage a client's autonomy about their substance use, while also inviting them to be informed and consider their choice. Ideas to consider include:

- **Use normal counselling practice** including the use of empathy and being non-judgemental and authentic. Be neutral about the outcome, unless there are safeguarding concerns.

- **Be willing to discuss a client's substance use.** When you sense there is enough trust, ask about this. It often seems appropriate as part of a wider exploration about how they are coping with bereavement. Most people tend to under-report their use and may be selective about any illegal drug use, so consider exploring beyond their initial response, including any use before the bereavement. Reflect together how substance use, bereavement and counselling affect each other, and be informed about the potential effects of a substance on bereavement and counselling. Be attuned to potential shame about substance use and the risk a client withdraws. For this reason…

- **Normalise** their use without inadvertently colluding with it:

  'Many bereaved people increase their alcohol use and I recognise drinking is your way to get a break from how you feel. We can consider other ways to get a break if you want to.'

  Consider adding that their difficulties may well pass in time; they are getting through their bereavement, and you are there to help them.

- **Trait or state?** Ascertain whether the difficulty for which they are using a substance predates the bereavement. If it does, consider whether you can help or need to refer on.

- **Offer general factual information** about how counselling addresses underlying causes and offers behavioural and psychological ways to alleviate symptoms, even though they might feel more pain, especially at first. Although substances may alleviate symptoms, they do not address underlying causes. The evaluation of what this means is the client's responsibility and you can enquire about that.

- **Help them make an informed choice about substance use.** Encourage them to get the information they need to inform their choice, such as discussing medication with their doctor and the information sources on page 139. Offer to review this information together to help them make an informed choice, by considering their expectations of using and exploring the advantages and disadvantages. Consider whether they are able to choose for themselves and, if necessary, say 'no' to their doctor; or whether they use medication 'because the doctor put me on them', in which case acknowledge their difficulty in asserting themselves, ask what they want to do about it and offer to develop their support, e.g. see the doctor with someone who can advocate on their behalf. Respect their choice, unless you have safeguarding concerns.

- **Recognise 'resistance as assistance'** (Houston 2003), i.e. a client uses substances to resist feeling difficult and painful emotions and this assists them to cope. Clients are often surprised by this approach and expect us to disapprove (often projecting their own disapproval on to us), so this recognition supports them to be more honest about using. Offer to explore their resistance, while not inadvertently colluding with their use, suggest they give their 'resistance' a voice, e.g. 'What do you imagine would happen if you stopped using?', and explore how their use may both serve them and have drawbacks. Then they can make a more informed choice about continued use.

- **Offer that they develop their support** so they are less reliant on substances from (see from page 152).

- **Ask that they reduce or not use before counselling** if it adversely affects counselling.

- **Offer a client sources of support for their family**, e.g. how family members can support a loved one who uses substances problematically.

When to refer to specialist help

There is no clear limit on when a client's substance use is too much. It can be difficult to differentiate between use to alleviate grief, use that has become problematic and use that is a pre-existing problem (Ross 1996). Therefore, you need to make therapeutic judgements about whether to temporarily suspend counselling and/or to refer on. A useful rule of thumb is that a client needs to have enough control of their use to be stable enough to relate to you and make use of counselling. Useful questions to help you assess this include:

- 'Do they have enough control of their use to still make use of counselling?'

- 'Can they relate to me in the sessions?'

- 'Is bereavement counselling increasing their use to an unhelpful level?'

- 'Is their use significantly unhealthy or problematic for them or other people?'

- 'Am I experienced enough to work with this level of use? And would I still be if it increased?'

Refer them to their doctor about medication and mental health difficulties. Local government websites list substance use treatment services in their area. See joint working below.

Emma

Early in counselling, Emma spoke about her increased alcohol use when her counsellor proposed exploring how she was coping with her grief. Emma was initially embarrassed as her husband Steve had died through alcohol use, so under-reported her use for coping with anxiety and deep sadness. She felt less embarrassed when her counsellor acknowledged the value of it 'giving her a break' and normalised her increased use in the context of bereavement. This helped Emma to explore further: she became aware that in the past her use increased at stressful times in life and then reduced afterwards, and that this time it had increased more than before. Also, her counsellor explained that as alcohol lowers inhibitions, some people feel and express emotions *more* than when sober, that this effect may be unexpected and unwelcome, leading them to greater alcohol use to dull how they feel; and that there can be an increased risk of alcohol dependency during bereavement. He then invited Emma to consider what that meant for her.

With all this in mind, Emma agreed when her counsellor asked that they regularly review how she coped, including her alcohol use, and use what emerged to inform them in how she could develop her support to cope with how she felt.

In subsequent explorations Emma was able to be more honest about her drinking, which in turn raised her awareness of her need to better regulate her emotional experience. Although Emma continued to drink more alcohol than before her husband's death, through this work she retained control of it and developed other ways to cope.

Bereavement counselling for clients who use substances in a non-addictive way

A substance-using client can often still benefit from bereavement counselling. There is a therapeutic balance to strike between accepting ongoing use and recognising when counselling is no longer effective (and temporarily suspending counselling). This entails continually noticing how they relate to you and use counselling, sharing these observations with them in a non-judgemental way, and then discussing what, if any, work is possible at that time.

Often you will need to build their support and only work with the cognitive aspects of bereavement (see below). This paves the way for future work when they are better able to engage with their emotional and bodily experience.

- **Develop a client's emotional support to cope without substances**, in particular, self-support strategies that promote a client's ability to regulate their emotional experience (see from page 156 and from page 167).

- **Psychoeducation.** Offer to inform about bereavement (see Chapters 1 and 2). Include introducing and normalising the likely emotional and bodily experiences they could expect.

- **Cognitive work on bereavement.** Consider together those aspects of your client's bereavement that can be worked with in a way that they experience as largely cognitive and thereby probably emotionally manageable. Create a hierarchy of tasks that subjectively ranks how emotionally difficult they expect things to be. Remind them they will always have the right to choose what to do and to stop at any time. Potential work includes developing awareness of the cognitive aspects of their grief; making sense of what the death means to them; working on the cognitive aspects of their unfinished business (see Chapter 12); working through the cognitive aspects of emotions, such as guilt and shame (see page 227 and Chapter 14); and developing life skills for any tasks that were performed for them by the person who died. Restoration-orientated work is often less emotional, and therefore more manageable, than loss-orientated work.

As part of this work you need to say, at an appropriate time, something like:

'I consider you've done some good work on how you think about your loss. This is you grieving and moving through your bereavement. One way you might take grieving further is really letting yourself feel the emotions, and further counselling could help you with that.'

Joint working

Section by Rual Gibson and Peter Cartwright

At its best, joint working ensures the comprehensive, effective and safe support of clients who use substances, and usually helps those supporting them to be more effective. However, although we all know we need to do it, it does not always happen!

In our experience, it is often only substance use treatment services that are willing to work with clients who use substances, especially if they are addicted. Typically, other services can justify refusing due to a lack of specialist training or poor experiences of substance-using clients (such as regularly missing sessions); probably, fear of the unknown, stigma and stereotyping can play a part too. Therefore, it is often necessary for a substance use treatment service to help someone stabilise their use before others are willing to start their work. An additional difficulty is doctors prescribing antidepressants and even highly addictive medications such as benzodiazepines to bereaved people who are using other substances problematically. This is despite more doctors being aware of the potential risks (although the use of supervised medication for such clients can be beneficial).

Potentially, these working practices are unethical, hinder a client's recovery from substance use and delay help for their bereavement. These can be avoided by effective joint working, particularly between substance use treatment services, bereavement services and, where necessary, a client's doctor and any others providing medical help and supervision. The detailed consideration of joint working is beyond the scope of this book, so the following are specific considerations for such clients:

- See key message 5 of the guidance at: www.bath.ac.uk/publications/ bereaved-through-substance-use/attachments/bereaved-through-substance-use.pdf

- When referring a client, make it clear to them that it is because *you* do not have particular training or that this need is beyond *your* role, so you do not inadvertently imply the shortcoming is in *them*.

- Ensure effective communication between services about medication and/or substance use, and associated protocols.

Bereavement counselling for clients who use substances addictively

Section by Rual Gibson and Peter Cartwright

In our experience, someone who uses substances addictively is no different from anyone else when they are bereaved. Therefore, the content of this book is as valid and relevant for supporting them as anyone else. What *is* different is how they typically use substances to cope with their experience of grief, as also found by others (Masferrer *et al.* 2015; Templeton *et al.* 2018a), and how that affects grieving, such as 'regret, sadness or guilt that their own problems with substances prevented them from offering support to others, including to the person who subsequently died or to other close relatives after the death' (Templeton *et al.* 2018a, p.129).

Also, these clients may be particularly vulnerable to complicated grief symptoms (Masferrer 2017) (see 'Complexities and difficulties in grieving' in Chapter 1). This section assumes you have the training and experience to work with clients who use substances addictively.

A client is not usually stable enough for bereavement counselling if they are still dependent on a substance, are unable to engage relationally with you, and/ or they are recently bereaved and their use has increased to cope with their grief. A weekly bereavement counselling session is typically insufficient support for someone to stabilise themselves. However, we believe that some bereavement counselling work becomes possible when they *have* stabilised their substance use (by either controlling it through prescribed medication or gradually reducing their use, such as only drinking in the evenings), and it is often hugely beneficial for a client to know they have bereavement counselling, as also found by Templeton *et al.* (2018a). By the 'maintenance' stage (see page 60) bereavement counselling should be possible; it then often forms part of a larger piece of work to address issues that could contribute to continued using or the risk of relapse. Therefore, what 'stage of change' a client is at hugely influences both what is possible in bereavement counselling and how someone actually experiences their grief.

We have found that the death of a close friend or acquaintance who used substances can be a catalyst for clients to change their substance-using behaviour, as also found by Templeton *et al.* (2018a). This 'wake-up call' comes through the existential recognition of their own mortality. However, we have also noticed that many clients have not learned how to regulate their emotional experience, so the prospect of choosing to engage with their grief is daunting. This typically creates a paradox, where someone uses to cope with grief and this prolongs bereavement, leading to continued use in order to cope. Furthermore, bereavement can be problematic for these people. Parkes found people 'who had always been heavy drinkers had developed alcoholic psychosis after the death of a close family member… [B]ereavement…had been the "last straw"' (Parkes and Prigerson 2010, p.26).

Quite often, other bereavements emerge after a client has started bereavement counselling that they were not aware of before, such as 'My brother died when I was seven, but I've dealt with that' or 'My mum left us when I was 11, but dad was brilliant. I hope for my mum's sake I never bump into her, though.' There can be many previous losses, including deaths of friends and acquaintances through substance use and suicide; the loss of a child through miscarriage or by social services and subsequent adoption; rejection and separation from partners and family; childhood losses of family members, such as through divorce; and grieving the loss of using a substance and the associated way of life.

Supporting these clients usually involves a holistic approach that goes beyond bereavement counselling, including, in some instances, help to meet their basic needs such as housing, food and clothing. It may entail encouraging them to engage with and use social support, such as Mark in the vignette below believing it was other people that got him through. This often happens through participation in group work for their treatment where, despite the focus on substance use, being with and talking to others facilitates grieving and helps to build the emotional resilience to cope without the use of substances. Consider, however, the impact of their bereavement on other service users.

How to work with a bereaved client who is in recovery

The general idea is to facilitate a client to start grieving in a manageable way that moves out of the paradox described above and protects their recovery.

- **Consider what 'stage of change' a client is at** and be realistic about what is currently possible for them (see pages 59–61).

- **Explain the effect of the substance(s) they use** and how it affects both the counselling relationship and their capacity to make use of counselling. This may include explaining that a reduction in use is necessary for counselling to be effective.

- **Consider asking them to reduce or not use before a session.** Exactly how this would happen needs to be negotiated between you both and has to take account of how long a particular substance is likely to affect them. Someone with heavier use may not be able to use counselling, particularly if they are physically dependent on a substance (when a detox would be recommended).

- **Monitor whether they have enough control of their use** to be stable enough to relate to you and make use of counselling, and encourage them to be an active part of this monitoring. It is useful to ask yourself whether they are in such an altered state that they cannot benefit from your support. Be mindful of addictive behaviour and be willing to raise denial, being secretive and only attending in order to be compliant with treatment. This is not always a problem and can often be worked with once a trusting counselling relationship has been established. However, recognise that bereavement counselling does invite these clients to experience the grief they feel urged to avoid and probably do not yet have the capacity to emotionally self-regulate. Be mindful of this vulnerability and balance it with not inadvertently colluding with any chaos in their life associated with addictive behaviour. This needs congruency and acceptance by both of you.

- **Consider temporarily suspending bereavement counselling** until they are able to make use of it again. This stop–start approach is familiar in other aspects of treatment for problematic substance use.

- **Disentangle what is substance use and what is bereavement**, as far as possible, and how these affect each other. Substance use increases because of bereavement, and bereavement can be masked and prolonged by substance use.

- **Consider trauma**, particularly if they were with the person when they died (see Chapter 11).

- **Invite them to consider what the death through substance use means** for their own substance use.

- **Consider using the ideas presented above** for supporting people who use substances in a non-addictive way.

- **Identify past losses and traumas** that may need to be worked through, in addition to the substance-related death, and consider together how to work with them.

- **Offer a client sources of support for their family**, e.g. how family can support a loved one who is in recovery and how to cope with the impact of substance-using behaviour.

Mark

Mark came into the service with his partner of 15 years because his drinking had escalated over the years to the point where he was now drinking daily from lunchtime onwards and by the time he went to bed he was 'comatosed'. Mark's partner was an existing client who had recently completed a residential detox and had persuaded Mark to engage in treatment. Mark explained that his drinking had got problematic since he had been laid off from work – a job he loved. He missed his work colleagues, he missed feeling useful and he missed having a routine and 'something to get out of bed for in the morning'. Mark was already grieving this part of his life.

With the help of his partner and the service, he was able to reduce his drinking enough to access counselling through our service. Mark was able to engage in counselling fully and reported saying that he was coming to terms with being laid off, and gradually his drinking reduced from daily to several times per week.

During the latter part of his counselling (about session 8) his wife started drinking again despite the known risk (her liver was damaged beyond repair and she was advised that 'one more drink could kill you'). One night she was suddenly taken ill, rushed to hospital and died. Mark was understandably distraught and his drinking immediately went up to and exceeded the levels he first presented with. On top of this, the council were demanding he leave his flat and move to somewhere smaller because he was unable to pay the 'bedroom tax'.

Mark became increasingly problematic to our service, resulting in suicide attempts and threats, messages left on the answer machine overnight, and appointments made and then broken. He became well known to the local emergency services, who became reluctant to respond to his calls for help. This all happened over approximately one year.

Mark slowly started to come into our service more regularly, usually in the morning before drinking. Gradually, he started to open up to staff and volunteers, and although he was offered an in-patient detox, he refused because of his cats at home. During this time, Mark had an accident and ended up in hospital, where he was detoxed. Through education and knowing he had someone to talk to, Mark was able to concentrate on his alcohol problem and started to work towards staying sober. Although counselling was offered, he and I decided that he would be better off spending a little longer in learning skills to remain abstinent. This he did and eventually he was able to engage in counselling, where much of the work was grieving for his wife. Mark remains abstinent to this day, he works part-time, he has moved to a manageable property and has a good relationship with his children.

In Mark's own words of this period of time, he said that what kept him going was knowing that there was someone on the end of the phone and knowing that we were there as a service for him. While he was unable to engage in formal counselling and sometimes unable to engage in a coherent conversation, there was a relational element there – other humans – which he claims at some level he engaged with. However, what is clear is that real healing or mourning for his loss could not take place until the alcohol was completely removed.

(Names and identifying features have been changed to preserve confidentiality.)

Supporting people bereaved through the loss of a client who used substances

Section by Rual Gibson and Peter Cartwright

Sadly, the loss of a client is often a reality for those who provide treatment to people who use substances. For example, the national investigation into Scottish drug-related deaths in 2003 found that 78% of people who died had been in contact with services during the six months before their death and more than 50% were still in contact with at least one agency at the time of death (Zador *et al.* 2005). This suggests that many staff are potentially bereaved (although this is another under-researched aspect of substance-related bereavements).

The first quantitative study, conducted by Mcauley and Forsyth (2011), looked at the experiences of 65 self-selecting staff working in drug treatment services who had experienced a drug-related death as part of their caseload. They found that client deaths were often sudden and unexpected, involving clients who had been progressing well in treatment, with staff often having a positive outlook for the client's future. Inevitably, though, their clients were decreasing their tolerance, making them vulnerable to overdose or suicide when they then relapsed. Such sudden unexpected deaths are typically more problematic and they pose a risk of trauma (see Chapter 11).

The most common grief reactions of staff were sadness, guilt, anger, thoughts about their own mortality and feeling helpless. Although individual staff reacted differently, those who often reported the most grief-related reactions were:

- Women more than men.

- Staff who felt 'somewhat or very close' to their client.

- Staff who had experienced more of these deaths in their career (two or more) did not appear to become more used to dealing with them, suggesting 'cumulative grief' where each new death potentially re-stimulated past incidents.

- Staff who sought more sources of support.

- Staff with larger caseloads (of 30 or more clients), hinting at increased worry about further deaths because of the challenge of a large caseload. These staff were proportionately more likely to report anger, helplessness, trouble sleeping and crying.

- Career experience and staff age had no significant bearing on grief responses.

Almost half of staff (49%) said that the death affected their relationships with their other clients 'somewhat or a lot'. Also, the majority said they would attend a specific drug-related death support group (69%) or one-on-one support (65%) if they were offered it following a death.

Their findings correspond with our experiences. We would add that grieving can be affected by the workplace.

A member of staff often learns of the death at work. We know of or have personally experienced less than ideal practice in this area, such as being told by another client while counselling them; through an email to all staff from senior management; hearing it casually mentioned in the office; and being told during the daily team meeting.

Staff keep encountering the same issues that were faced by their client who died. This can remind staff of their perceived failings and associated guilt. Staff could easily project their own judgements about these perceived failings on to colleagues and clients, as well as potentially experience judgements from them too.

Burnout and high staff turnover are a significant issue for the substance use treatment field (Poulopoulos and Wolff 2010). The sector has experienced significant and prolonged reductions in funding during the period of 'austerity' (Advisory Council on the Misuse of Drugs 2017). These bereavements typically occur within the context of workplace stress, large caseloads and working with a client group who typically have complex needs. Bereavement needs to be seen as a significant stressor that can contribute to staff burnout. Measures to prevent burnout, according to drug treatment staff in one study, were 'a fairer distribution of work overload, opportunities for training and supervision, more vacations, better management and improvement of the relationships between staff and management, and finding a balance between home and work life' (Poulopoulos and Wolff 2010, p.308).

This study concluded that a healthier workforce could be achieved through the systematic provision of continuous training, systematic clinical and administrative supervision, giving staff incentives and other ways to increase motivation, and seeing burnout as a legitimate issue. Good organisational practice for the symptomatic relief of burnout includes staff development interventions, such as in-service training, time management and peer support groups and exchanging resources (Lewis, Packard and Lewis 2007).

Supporting bereaved staff

The aim is to provide support for both bereavement and professional needs arising from the death, including how these influence each other. We consider the following needs to be organisational policy, despite time, money and resources often being very limited:

- **Basic training about bereavement**, ideally at staff induction, would include the particular characteristics described above. This would assist also in supporting bereaved clients and family members (see below).

- **Staff need to be sensitively informed of the death by a manager in a private setting.** Include information about how the client died and any other available circumstantial information. This is important for grieving, such as helping a staff member make sense of any part they may have had in the death.

- **Normalise** the significant impact that losing a client can potentially have on staff.

- **Provide extra support** to meet the personal and professional needs of the individual staff member(s), which includes consideration of events leading up to the death and their subsequent grief. This support could be time for self-reflection, debriefing and one-to-one support with a line manager or clinical supervisor, peer support, expressing grief emotions, allowing time out of the office, and going to the funeral. This is vital for a healthy and robust team.

- **Foster a culture of reflective learning.** This promotes learning for the benefit of future practice and deters a 'blame culture' (Mcauley and Forsyth 2011). Regular clinical supervision and informal peer supervision are ways to create this culture.

- **Recognise the particular needs associated with these bereavements**, such as working with perceived professional failings and associated guilt (see Chapter 14), unrealistic therapeutic expectations and helplessness. Despite their training and experience, staff are potentially as vulnerable to relationship dynamics as family members, e.g. taking too much responsibility for someone who is addicted and the death provoking the existential reality that 'I thought I was helping you, but you still didn't stop using'. Consider providing specific substance-related support, as well as using Employee Assistance Programme counsellors who specialise in bereavement.

- **Sensitively notice the impact on a staff member's work.** The death may have a positive effect, e.g. emphasising harm reduction to clients, or be negative, e.g. a staff member looking for approval, being traumatised (see Chapter 11), suffering a loss of confidence, and avoiding decisions involving 'positive risks', such as moving clients from supervised prescriptions to take-home dosages. Offer additional clinical supervision.

- **'Gallows humour'** is normal in professional and emotionally contained environments that encounter death (Young 1995). It can be a useful emotional release, as long as respect is maintained for everyone.

- **Desensitisation to death** can happen and is typically characterised by ambivalence: the member of staff feels sad for the loss while also feeling the need to keep going. It is important to recognise and accept both, and accept that it is okay to be conflicted (Kuczewski *et al.* 2014).

- **Relapse.** Staff can be in recovery from their own addictive substance use. The death of a client increases their risk of relapse, although this is unlikely to be the only reason if it happens.

- **Self-care.** Ultimately, the responsibility for self-care lies with the member of staff and this is considered an ethical professional standard (BACP 2018).

Substance use treatment services and bereaved families

Section by Rual Gibson and Peter Cartwright

This section considers how substance treatment services can help the family of their client who has died.[3]

This is a sensitive and challenging area of work. Staff normally feel conflicted about engaging with the family: although they can feel guilty for their perceived failings and fear being blamed, they also understand how the family feel and want to help them (Velleman 2014). Family members may or may not have an existing relationship with staff.

Following the death of a client, it is good practice for services to review what happened to improve future service delivery. Serious consideration should be given, on a case-by-case basis, to informing the bereaved family of the findings of this review. This information is important for the family members' grieving process and mitigates against them having unfinished business (see Chapter 12). Let families lead this conversation and aim to inform them as far as possible. Do not assume information has already been given to them by the police or hospital.

This obviously needs to be balanced by the confidentiality of the client who died. When little or no information can be shared, it is important to acknowledge how family members feel about that. Explain the confidentiality

---

3   For the minimum support a service needs to offer, see the guidance at: www.bath.ac.uk/ publications/bereaved-through-substance-use/attachments/bereaved-through-substance-use.pdf

policy and data protection laws, and how they help clients to trust and engage in treatment. Also, say if the deceased client had not given their consent for their family to be informed about their treatment.

Families typically value making sense of their loved one's treatment and of the substance-related aspects of the death (Cartwright 2019; Velleman 2014). Offer to explain to families the service's treatment, including the inevitable limitations on what can be achieved; also explain what is easily overlooked or taken for granted, such as what addiction is, how an overdose happens, the room where their loved one actually received treatment, etc. Families often value hearing about their loved one and this does not have to involve confidential information. For example, it can be as simple as hearing that you enjoyed their humour or they were supportive of other people using the service.

However, some family members can be angry with treatment services for not helping their loved one (Cartwright 2019; Velleman 2014) (see Chapters 4 and 6). Their anger may be entirely justified, or it may be deflecting blame on to the service that 'belongs' elsewhere (see Chapter 14). Good practice is for senior management to take this up with the family and thereby shield staff involved in service delivery (who may already be blaming themselves).

There is also the possibility of a staff member needing to give evidence at the coroner's court, during which it is likely that the family would be present. Occasionally, a worker is cross-examined by a family member in the coroner's court (Velleman 2014).

17

Later Bereavement, and How Far Can We Help?

The final chapter considers what later bereavement is like and how far we can help:

- the potential characteristics of long-term adaptation to substance-related bereavement

- existential aspects of bereavement

- concluding thoughts.

A client may not be ready for the ideas presented in this chapter. Also, there are limits on what is possible in substance-related bereavements, so it is important to avoid the idea of closure and 'getting over it'. Furthermore, '[often grieving] can be a long, slow, exceedingly painful process. It is a journey during which many bereaved people find themselves and their lives completely changed' (Ross 1996, p.7).

The outcome of these bereavements is often about integrating the loss into being a part of who someone is, rather than recovering from it.

Therefore, you need to be realistic and honest with clients about what counselling can achieve. Our desire to support a client to find something of benefit in their loss and have a satisfying new life can inadvertently miss the enormity of their loss and its impact on their life going forward. Last, you need to balance a recognition of the typically long-term, complex and severe nature of these bereavements with being aware of possible complexities and difficulties in grieving, particularly for clients with insecure attachment styles and/or traumatic bereavement (see Chapter 1).

Potential characteristics of long-term adaptation

Although bereavement is a highly individual journey, all clients ultimately need to adapt to their loss. Adaptation has typical potential characteristics, described below. These characteristics provide you with clues to how far clients have adapted to their bereavement and ideas about potential further support to offer, although the significance of each one will vary between clients. Recognise that these clients may need to use counselling on and off over a long time (Cartwright 2019), so may not complete all that is possible with you, and refer them on for needs beyond your capacity, available time or organisational role. A client has, as far as practical:

- **Adapted to bereavement, or, if not, integrated grief into their life going forward.** There is the recognition they may not 'get over it' and will probably always be sad when thinking of the deceased, but the bereavement now lacks the intensity and wrenching quality it had previously (Worden 2009). They have regained an interest in life, can feel more hopeful, experience gratification and adopt new life roles (Worden 2009). They have a new 'normal', mostly about life 'here and now'. This may include grief as a familiar and manageable part of who they now are (Jordan 2019).

- **Developed enough self- and social support** so that re-stimulated grief can be made sense of and feels manageable, including good enough ways to do loss- and restoration-orientated activities and can oscillate effectively between them.

- **Updated and reconstructed their assumptive world and identity** as necessary, including any gain from the death and the ability to be autonomous again.

- **Developed a coherent, compassionate and realistic narrative** of their life with the deceased, the death and its aftermath, which fits with who they are now.

- **Worked through any trauma** from before the death, the death itself and the aftermath. They recognise any re-stimulated trauma and have enough self- and social support to cope with that. They have possibly gained post-traumatic growth.

- **Worked through any unfinished business and associated emotions** about their relationship with the deceased, the death and its aftermath. Where things remain unknown, unresolved or unsatisfactory, they have a way to live with that.

- **Worked through shame and stigma**, as far as possible, and have developed ways to manage any future stigma.

- **Worked through anger, blame and guilt**, as far as possible.

- **Worked through any depression** from before the death, the death itself and the aftermath, and have developed the self- and social support to manage any recurrence of depression.

- **Reframed their loss and secondary losses as needs,** and are able to meet those needs as far as possible.

- **Developed a healthy continuing bond** (if that is meaningful to them) that fully recognises that the deceased has gone and is compatible with their future life and relationships with others.

- **Worked through the existential implications of the death,** e.g. a new way of living that is meaningful, has purpose and is satisfying, and that does not deny the existence of the deceased; revised their worldview and spirituality; and created meaning and gain from the loss.

Existential aspects of bereavement

He who has a 'why' to live can bear almost any 'how' [he lives]. (Friedrich Nietzsche)

In everyday life, the inevitability of death is easily denied or avoided, but the death of a loved one confronts bereaved people with this profoundly disturbing and anxiety-provoking existential reality. Often bereavement provokes other existential realities, such as the responsibility we have for our own choices and our associated freedom to choose, existential isolation and aloneness, and the intrinsic meaninglessness of life (Yalom 1980).

In the context of substance-related bereavements, this also might include the choices a client made about the care and support they gave to a loved one during their addiction, or the apparent meaninglessness of a loved one's life that was dominated by addiction, mental health difficulties and associated suffering, as well as the distressing and anxiety-provoking thought that their loved one somehow did this to themselves (Guy and Holloway 2007), which, when relevant, is not to imply that addictive use is a choice (see Chapter 3). Additionally, these bereavements often provoke particular existential realities about relationships with others: 'I cannot make you stop doing something if you are not inclined to do so', 'However much I care for you, I can't make you well' and 'How do I be both independent and healthily dependent on others?'

When fully experienced, these existential realities may deeply undermine a client's assumptive world and the meaning they give their lives (see page 26 and Chapter 17). It is difficult to find meaning in the face of suffering, and without meaning there is no hope. Indeed, clients often ask: 'What's the point in carrying on?' However, bereavement also offers the potential to face these existential realties, and through doing so, paradoxically, find a meaningful life by discovering what is now really of meaning in life (Yalom 1980). For example, bereaved people often find the death affirms their own being alive, how life is short, and are more able to see what really matters in life beyond their preoccupation with daily desires and concerns.

However, bereavement does not always require a reappraisal of life's meaning. Many clients find consolation in systems of secular and spiritual beliefs and practices that have served them well in the past (Neimeyer and Sands 2011).

Much of this work is not possible early in grieving, when emotions dominate. At this time, you will need to hold hope for a client and remind them that they have the potential for a meaningful life beyond their bereavement. As meaning-making becomes possible, explicitly invite them to consider the existential implications of the death. What can they live for now? What is their purpose in life now? Also:

> Transformations or life adjustments are often preceded by difficult and apparently impossible situations and the task is often just to find ways of tolerating the anxiety or hopeless feelings to allow a readjustment or working through, rather than finding a relief of the distress. (Joyce and Sills 2014, p.220)

This work is where philosophy, spirituality and counselling meet, and easily develops into considering clients' worldview and spirituality.

John

Sarah's death evoked an existential awakening of John's deep wish to live more fully and thereby not continue to miss out on being with others. As he said: 'I had to lose Sarah to find other people.' He then joined a bereaved parents' group.

Additionally, John formed a continuing bond with Sarah by giving the group members the care he had not given to Sarah, deciding not to add to the injustice in the world in how he behaved, and by donating money to her favourite charity.

Worldview and spirituality

The realities of existence, meaning and purpose are shaped in part by people's worldview and spirituality. This varies from a recognisable religious faith to less-defined forms of spirituality with minimal dogma and belief, which still retain a sense of awe and connection to something larger, to a secular or atheist worldview that informs morality, gives meaning and provides a sense of connection to others and the world. When bereavement challenges a client's assumptive world, this can damage their worldview and spirituality, and in turn they may then lose their meaning and purpose in life.

Clients may experience a range of associated difficulties: a loss of or questioning of their religious faith or a less-defined sense of something lost or missing; existential crisis, such as the meaninglessness of their life. Also, clients of dual heritage may potentially struggle with seemingly irreconcilable contradictions between different parts of their cultural and spiritual background.

Clients can be reluctant (even feel ashamed) about discussing metaphysical concepts, and feel the need to justify their spiritual beliefs or fear having them explained away (Bonanno 2009). Therefore, this work requires being able to meet across the differences there often are between us and our clients (see Chapter 7). It helps to ask whether your beliefs are important to them, and, if so, how. This work then requires exploring their worldview and spirituality, how significant it is to them, to what extent it has been damaged by the death, and how it may be meaningfully redefined or reconstructed.

Potential themes to explore include where a client believes a loved one is now, whether they believe a loved one is still addicted or suffering in some other way, whether they will meet a loved one again, whether their loved one will be reincarnated; a loss of or questioning of religious faith, the role of their god in what happened, and their faith's tenets about the death (such as seeing suicide as a sin).

Often, an objective, empirical or scientific approach lacks the evidence or cannot answer the questions a client has. Therefore, it is important to stay with their beliefs and subjective experience. The outcome of this work commonly includes doubt, mystery and perhaps ultimately an acceptance of not knowing. This can feel unsatisfactory, so explore how a client can live with that outcome. Conversely, it also can confirm fundamental truths about being human, such as the primary importance of love, of attachment, in our lives.

Where the work moves into the spiritual and religious realm, you need to consider your limits and whether to refer them to a faith leader. Recognise that clients can experience such people and their religious communities as both helpful and/or unhelpful.

▨ Mahi

Mahi found that she began questioning her Sikh faith following Jake's death and was deeply troubled by the prospect of losing it and, through that, her connection to her culture. Her counsellor suggested this was another aspect of her assumptive world that had been disrupted by her traumatic bereavement. This helped Mahi to make sense of the experience and gave her the confidence that she might be able to work this through in the same way she had other challenges to her assumptive world.

Mahi used counselling to identify the specific religious concerns she had about Jake's chemsex behaviour. However, through doing this both she and her counsellor agreed that he was not able to help her to consider these. Her counsellor proposed, and Mahi agreed, that he still support her to work this through. This involved Mahi exploring what she wanted and considering who to talk to at her gurdwara (temple), and providing opportunities to reflect after those conversations to establish what they meant for her faith.

Through this spiritual work and counselling support, Mahi began making presentations about the risks of drug use to local schools and to community meetings at her gurdwara. These presentations were her way of honouring both her faith and Jake's life, as well as giving his death meaning. An unexpected consequence was meeting other bereaved mothers, which enlarged her social support and broke down some of her sense of stigma. After several years Mahi decided to make a presentation at the DrugFAM annual conference (see page 304) to celebrate Jake's life.

Rituals and ceremonies

Meaning and spirituality can be expressed through ritual and ceremony. In our Western, secular, diverse society, traditional rituals and ceremonies can fall into disuse or lose their relevance and meaning (Imber-Black and Roberts 1998). For example, few people still observe Christianity's formal periods of mourning.

Where this happens for a client, or they have a need that traditional rituals or ceremonies do not meet, suggest they modify an existing ritual or ceremony or create something of their own. This can give a sense of control and personal expression at a time when both feel lacking, can mark a stigmatised death and disenfranchised grief in a helpful way, and can be a continuing bond through a loved one being present (despite their actual absence) in a ritual or ceremony. To work, rituals and ceremonies need a degree of letting go of rationality and literalness, and going with the spirit of them, because it is the meaning, symbolism and *experience* that matter (Bonanno 2009).

When creating these with clients, recognise that they need to serve a purpose and acknowledge what is significant; that they can be private, for the family or public; and that they need to be informed by a client's culture, identity, values and worldview or spiritual beliefs.

▌ Emma

In counselling, Emma created a ritual to use every day to remind herself of what she had gained from Steve's death and to honour his life. This involved saying: 'I am deeply distressed by what happened to you and I choose not to reduce your whole life to your death. Rather I choose to honour all of you, including the father of my children, and our life together.'

Emma and her counsellor spoke at length about how she could keep hold of this ritual and the valuable personal development she had made to support herself, especially when she became anxious or her grief was re-stimulated. Emma struggled with this because when she most needed to, she found it hard to remember the ritual. Her counsellor had a collection of different coloured, polished stones and invited Emma to pick the one she most wanted, and then gave it to her. He added: 'I propose that you keep your stone close at hand, such as in your bag, and when you feel distressed, take it out and hold it. The stone symbolises all that you have gained from our work together, such as your ability to calm and reassure yourself by calming breathing and self-talk, and your choice to honour Steve as a whole person and your life together.'

Emma really liked this idea. After the work had ended, holding her stone became a ritualised way to evoke these ideas and hold on to her counsellor's care of her.

FURTHER READING ON EXISTENTIAL MATTERS

May, R. (1983) *The Discovery of Being*. New York, NY: Norton.

Yalom, I. (2009) *Staring at the Sun: Overcoming the Terror of Death*. San Francisco, CA: Jossey-Bass.

FURTHER READING ON CREATING RITUALS

Imber-Black, E. and Roberts, J. (1998) *Rituals for Our Times: Celebrating, Healing, and Changing Our Lives and Our Relationships*. Lanham, MD: Jason Aronson.

Concluding thoughts

The wound is the place where the light enters you. (Rumi, Persian poet)

My view is that the best we can do is support a client to heal their 'wound' so it becomes a 'scar'; their loss is still there, it has left its mark, yet it no longer feels like a wound and becomes the path to new possibilities. This healing comes through not just enduring or tolerating the loss of a loved one, but, counterintuitively, by moving towards it and honouring it. Where a client allows themselves to be fully and deeply affected by their bereavement, accepting and embracing how they need to develop as a person and to adapt, they can really integrate the experience into their whole being. This honouring is not about what is 'good' or 'bad'; rather, it is the acceptance that each part of bereavement 'just is', be it negative, indifferent or welcome.

Through choosing this approach, there is the possibility of transforming suffering into something of benefit, by finding opportunities and personal meaning in the loss that simultaneously do not deny it. This is a familiar idea in religion and philosophical thought, such as the Buddhist idea of the second dart (see page 166), and was described by the Jewish existential therapist Viktor Frankl following his experiences of surviving the Nazi concentration camps:

> [E]verything can be taken from man but one thing: the last of the human freedoms – to choose one's attitude in any given set of circumstances, to choose one's own way... [H]uman potential at its best...to transform a personal tragedy into a triumph, to turn one's predicament into human achievement... When we are no longer able to change a situation...we are challenged to change ourselves. (Frankl 1969, pp.66, 135)

Put another way, this is a client moving from just being a survivor (whose identity is defined by past events) to being a whole person again (who has the right to a future). The loss becomes just one of their parts; there are new possibilities gained from it and there is also a meaningful life that is not associated with the loss.

Often this involves giving the loss meaning by creating something 'good' from something so 'bad'. This is frequently characterised by a pursuit of moral purpose and meaning (Guy and Holloway 2007), creative responses to stigmatising stereotypes and rebuilding identity (Valentine and Walter 2015), or creating a 'survivor mission' where meaning and gain are created following a traumatic event (Herman 2001, p.207). These can be seen as a form of continuing bond, often motivated by a deep love and attachment.

The three fictitious clients illustrate how support can facilitate this moving towards and honouring of grief, and transforming suffering into something of benefit. Emma developed the self-support to down-regulate her emotional experience and thereby be better able to work through her relationship with Steve and associated guilt and shame, from which she gained how to form healthier relationships and keep her children safe. John used counselling to develop his self-support to feel his emotions, eventually enabling him to forgive Sarah and to some extent himself, and, unexpectedly, to discover the benefit of connecting to other people and form a continuing bond with Sarah. Mahi needed to develop the self-support to engage with her traumatic bereavement, and so not avoid it, which enabled her to eventually work through her shame and the questioning of her faith; this in turn helped her create a way to honour both her faith and Jake, and give his death meaning.

Real life examples in this book are Philippa Skinner writing her book (page 15), Roger Kirby's existential choice to 'End the Struggle and Dance with Life' (pages 92–4), and the creation of the charity DrugFAM by bereaved mother Elizabeth Burton-Phillips (pages 302–5). Equally meaningful is this quotation from Claire Chambers, a bereaved sister, which captures this honouring of bereavement and the potential for transformation that it holds:

I want to live too and have always said that Paul never got the chance, so I want to live twice the life for him too. Life is so precious for us all.

Part 3

Examples of Good Practice

Part 3 offers examples of good practice in the United Kingdom of supporting people who are bereaved through a substance-related death, and ends with some examples from abroad.

The BEAD (Bereaved through Alcohol and Drugs) Project

Section by Fiona Turnbull, with Jane Shackman and Oliver Standing

This project was the result of a ground-breaking partnership between Cruse Bereavement Care and Adfam, the first at national level between the bereavement and substance use sectors.[1] It grew out of our recognition that the death of someone you love from substance use is *not* the same as any other bereavement and that there was nowhere near enough targeted support for people facing this kind of loss. In consultation,[2] people told us that shame, stigma and their often well-founded fear of judgement often stopped them from seeking out support.

This is why **peer support** – people who have faced the same adversity offering support to one another – was integral to the approach of the BEAD project.

---

1   Cruse Bereavement Care is the leading provider of bereavement support in England, Wales and Northern Ireland. Adfam is the UK charity dedicated to representing the needs of families affected by substance use. BEAD was funded by the Big Lottery Fund in England only from 2013 to 2017.

2   See BEAD consultation findings report published by Cruse and Adfam: www.cruse.org.uk/sites/default/files/default_images/pdf/Documents-and-fact-sheets/BEAD_ConsultationFindings_final_June%202015.pdf

All the support was delivered by trained peer support volunteers who were at a point in their own grief where they were ready to support others. The project ran from 2013 to 2017: some BEAD peer support volunteers now offer support via the Cruse Helpline and local branches.

The original project offered three pathways of support: an informal befriending service available for six months; up to eight sessions of structured telephone bereavement support; and peer support groups that ran periodically in London for eight sessions. In addition, we created a dedicated website providing information, advice and personal accounts (www.beadproject.org.uk) which is still live.

Peer support

Peer support was highly effective for this group of bereaved people (Turnbull and Standing 2016). Knowing that their BEAD volunteer had walked in their shoes enabled the bereaved person to talk freely, often for the first time, about their grief and the person who died. The BEAD volunteer could embody hope for the future, help the bereaved person to rebuild their confidence, and support them to access other support, such as Al Anon meetings.[3] BEAD support group members regularly reported that they felt less isolated by being with others with comparable experiences. Many have built up friendships and stayed in touch after the group sessions ended.

The BEAD volunteers also benefitted. Many describe how their involvement has enabled something positive to emerge from their own deeply painful experiences of grief. As well as the satisfaction of supporting others, they frequently attest that the work helped them process their own grief at a deeper level. One volunteer described how she has become more open about growing up as the child of an alcoholic parent. This work was challenging, so volunteers needed to be well supported (including in the recruitment, training and induction processes when their own personal grief may resurface). Each volunteer had regular supervision with a Cruse supervisor, an experienced practitioner who offered guidance and space to talk about the impact of the work.

We know there was more to do to meet the diverse needs of different groups. People from black and minority ethnic communities, men and younger people were under-represented among BEAD clients.[4] Others, such as homeless people or gay men bereaved as a result of chemsex, face additional barriers to accessing support. It was also challenging for BEAD volunteers to identify appropriate

---

3   Al Anon family groups support those affected by someone else's drinking, including when the person may no longer be part of their lives or has died.

4   The overwhelming majority of bereaved people who were supported by BEAD were white; nearly 80% were women; and nearly 70% were over the age of 45.

referral routes for BEAD clients with serious substance use or complex mental health issues that were beyond the role of BEAD volunteers.

Lessons from the BEAD project

Many reading this book may not have experienced a substance-related bereavement and are therefore unable to offer peer support. However, the following insights, drawn from our volunteers' experiences, are applicable whatever your role.

The majority of bereaved people need as much support to process the multiple losses and impact of having lived with their loved one's substance use as they do for the death itself. We would go so far as to say that it is impossible to talk solely about the bereavement. Support them to grieve *all* these losses, particularly the pain of losing someone to substance use before the death. Even the loss of chaos and unpredictability can take time to adjust to and add to feelings of emptiness.

Exploring the bereaved person's own understanding of their loved one's substance use is important. For some, it helps to think of it as an illness; for others, not. So explore what it means for them and support them to reflect on what was, and was not, within their control. The bereavement may also tap into fears about the bereaved person's own substance use, especially for those whose parents used substances. Even when there may have been previous near-death experiences such as overdoses, or a long drawn-out illness, the death itself is typically a shock and often leaves many unanswered questions.

Emphasise that you offer a confidential space where the bereaved person can talk freely. Often, they may have held on to secrets for fear of betraying their loved one and out of shame. Your consistency can be a powerful reparative relational experience. Many bereaved people have felt powerless and frightened in the face of their loved one's chaotic lifestyle, and have potentially been confronted with deeply distressing experiences, such as prostitution, needles in the house, offending behaviour, domestic abuse and threats from drug dealers. Many have been focused entirely on the person who used substances. Working with you may be the first time in a long time – or ever – that they have experienced someone putting *their* needs first and offering them a reliable and stable presence. You may need to encourage them to give themselves permission to receive support and take care of themselves, and to suggest how they can make the most of your support. When working by telephone, for example, suggest they find a quiet space away from interruption. Attune to their language and avoid jargon and labelling. If you talk about co-dependency (see page 130), for example, you may unwittingly exacerbate self-blame. Talk to them about who *they* are and support them to rediscover their identity in these new changed circumstances.

Bereaved people frequently find that others forget that they loved the person who died, no longer mention them and commonly make assumptions about how they might be feeling, perhaps imagining that they are relieved. Therefore, encourage the bereaved person to remember the person who died by showing genuine interest and allowing them to remember all aspects of who they were, because this can help them to integrate complex and seemingly contradictory emotions such as love and anger, sorrow and blame.

Among the most overwhelming emotions is crippling guilt, perhaps especially for parents. The bereaved person needs space to air this feeling without being unintentionally dismissed by comments such as 'It wasn't your fault', however well intended. Instead, the aim is to help them gain ownership of what genuinely belongs to them and to realise what was not in their control. For example, children of alcoholic parents commonly blame themselves, so it can be therapeutic to remind them gently that, as children, they could not be held responsible.

We hope bereavement services and drug and alcohol agencies will draw inspiration from BEAD to initiate informal and more structured opportunities for peer support. Given the intense isolation experienced by so many people bereaved through substance use, the more opportunities that exist to expand their networks of support, the better.

Bereavement through addiction

Section by Pete Weinstock

Bereavement Through Addiction (BTA) began in 2009 as the lone voice of Joan Hollywood, with her partner, Paul, who spoke out about her grief for the loss of her son, Paul. She highlighted the inadequate and unacceptable response from her community, including from the police and mental health services. She said: 'It shouldn't be like this; we need a different response,' and said it to anyone who would listen and many who would not. Sadly, Joan died in 2015, but by then things were changing, and she triggered and then contributed to the first large-scale research project into these bereavements (Valentine 2018).

Joan campaigned on the stigmatising social attitudes about people with problematic substance use and their families and friends. This stigma can be severely disabling and result in very real shame and hurt. Terms like 'junkie' and judgements about people's lives conflict with a sense that 'That's my child and I want to love and care for them'. People sometimes feel they are denied the right to grieve and the respect normally given to the bereaved. For example, the mother of a son who recently died through his occasional drug use did not know how to explain the death to her extended family because she feared their judgement.

BTA is for people in Bristol, the South-West and other parts of the country where this support is less well developed. It combines one-to-one and group support with a campaigning voice that challenges stigma. There is an annual memorial service to commemorate and celebrate the lives of people lost through substance use. This has been a great comfort to many people, some of whom do not use other support.

What we have found helps

BTA is available when nothing else is, at a time when nothing matters and nothing can possibly help with the pain of grief. People seek help and guidance with seemingly impossible feelings of loss, anger and deep sadness, and sometimes confusion, isolation, guilt, shame and trauma. Their trauma can be compounded by the response of services and others in the community who are poorly informed and stigmatising.

I think our initial response is of great significance. It may be the only response that is warm, supportive and encouraging. We also inform people about possible next steps that can give hope when the world appears to have ended. Sometimes we just write or call to acknowledge their loss and explain about our support. Just knowing support is available, even if not used, is useful sometimes.

We provide an opportunity to talk, be acknowledged and be witnessed. There is great therapeutic value for people to hear their own voice tell the story. Groups provide a space to sit with others who understand the pain, hear others' stories and see progress on the journey towards acceptance and self-compassion.

I observe that people often develop an active, continuing relationship with the individual who has died that is important and helps them to cope. One parent writes a letter each birthday and Christmas to their loved one; another has a continuing conversation with the person she has lost and imagines their responses.

The difficulties we encounter and how they are worked with

People are sometimes reluctant to reveal personal details because they may be ashamed or because of their illegal drug use. Anonymity gives a freedom to speak openly, so I do not ask if I think the conversation matters more than recording details.

There is an observable difference in views, attitudes and responses of each family member.

Often there is blame for other family members, the person who died and the services that failed. While someone was still alive, there can be a stereotypical divide between a father's angry, helpless and punitive response (largely a consequence of being unable to protect their family and solve the very real problems they have) and a mother's loyalty and refusal to give up on a child who uses, to the point of self-harm. Then, in bereavement, a father becomes angry and blames the mother for the way she responded to the individual using substances that reinforced problematic substance use, while sacrificing her own health. The emotional pressures that arise can be unmanageable and may lead to parental separation. Children may blame their parents. These deaths are often seen as someone's fault, be that parents, partners, overburdened services, a social class or ethnic group, or institutions and authorities that do not care enough. Perhaps anger is more familiar and feels freer to express than other emotions, such as deep sadness.

Then there are regrets about having let the person down, failing them in some crucial way, or having shown frustrated (even harsh) behaviour towards them while they were alive. There is often guilt for what now seems unforgivable and irredeemable. Generally, there is a shadow of 'failure' that hangs over these deaths. Our work helps with the recognition that these feelings are to some extent inevitable when mourning. Sometimes the goal is to help people turn the anger, blame and guilt into deep sadness, including their unmet expectations for the person's life.

Another obstacle is a limited understanding of addiction, the services that treat substance use, and how someone only stops using when they are ready within themselves. It can be very useful for bereaved people to have a clearer picture about these and it often helps them realise they did not let their loved one down.

Low participation in groups is a difficulty. I believe this can result from the emotional and physical effects of bereavement – hopelessness, being overwhelmed and fatigue – as well as childcare or financial difficulties.

We also see individuals suffering emotional exhaustion, mental health issues and feelings of rejection and abandonment. A significant number also have problematic substance use and bereavement feeds directly into their continued use. Their requests for support have been an area of recent expansion.

DrugFAM

Section by Elizabeth Burton-Phillips

When my son Nick tragically ended his own life in 2004, aged just 27, his twin brother Simon and I were determined that something positive should come from his untimely death.

In 2006, I founded DrugFAM, to provide a lifeline of safe, caring and professional support to those affected by someone else's substance use. Our core purpose is to ensure these families are understood, educated and supported. This includes supporting people who are bereaved through a substance-related death. We believe that offering bereaved clients a safe place to share their thoughts and feelings with others who have gone through similar experiences can help with grieving and alleviate any sense of shame and isolation. This is particularly true if there has been negative media coverage and when a death is particularly stigmatised (such as when someone died by suicide coupled with substance use). Our dedicated, trained bereavement team at DrugFAM offers a range of bereavement support. Our service is open to everyone, although we find that some communities try to deal with everything internally and hide the cause of bereavement.

Our bereavement support usually begins with telephone and email support. People receive a personal letter from me with a pack that includes our handbook and information about our support. Some clients come to us for one-to-one support and we are also able to organise local befriending visits. We work with our clients according to their individual emotional needs. This includes sharing their individual experiences of loss, gaining understanding about bereavement, and supporting them at an inquest when requested.

> I decided to take the huge step to call... I felt inadequate as a mother that I could not make my son better... I felt encouraged to talk and share the feelings and worries in a very safe environment... I wasn't judged or frowned upon and for the first time I felt I hadn't failed myself as a mother or indeed failed my son... I soon realised there were no quick answers to the complicated disease of addiction but there was great hope and understanding to be gained, knowledge of how to cope and how to move forward in what had seemed an impossible situation.

We are often the first port of call for professionals, family, friends and carers seeking to help and support those who are bereaved.

In response to increasing demand we have developed a very successful bereavement support group, which meets quarterly and attracts an average of 18 bereaved people. These are held on Sunday afternoons at the request of our clients. The afternoon is planned to offer support to everyone who participates, regardless of where they are in their bereavement, and is split into two sessions. The first offers structured support around a particular theme, such as making sense of addiction, coping with grief or working through guilt, and is facilitated by Peter Cartwright (who also trains our team). The second session is unstructured and is an opportunity for people to talk and share their memories of the person they have lost. DrugFAM places great value on remembering, honouring and grieving for the whole of who someone was, not just their substance use. Clients are encouraged to bring along pictures, videos, music or anything else that is special about the person they lost that they would like to share with others.

> It was very moving and cathartic for us to be there and we were really impressed with the presentation. It gave us a new perspective on coping with bereavement.

Running concurrently with this group we also offer 'The Nicholas Mills Memorial Project' for young people, aged 18 to 30 years, who are bereaved by a substance-related death. These sessions are creative in content and are led by young professionals for this particular age group. They have proved to be very successful because young people enjoy being together to talk about the person they have lost in a smaller group and value being creative around the memories they have of the person they have lost. They are always given a voice at our annual conference and we usually show a video of the work they have produced.

> Showed me that even if I don't like the 'sitting in a circle talking about yourself' style…there are many other ways to express how I feel.

Since 2009, DrugFAM has run an annual Bereaved by Addiction Conference, which has a different theme every year. The conference is open to anyone and brings together mostly bereaved families, but also practitioners, campaigners and volunteers from both the UK and overseas. Over the years we have developed a successful structure that balances the personal stories of our clients with professional guidance and emotional support. This special day provides an opportunity to share experiences and knowledge with others who have experienced a similar loss; develop friendships outside of DrugFAM; and meet with a range of stakeholders including counsellors, therapists and family practitioners.

> It was a day that I could share my brother's memory without feeling judged and knowing that no one would have the thought or desire to describe him as being 'just a Dirty Junkie' that deserved to die… Yesterday was the first day since his death that I felt his memory was embraced and his plight fully understood. He became real again.

We have developed our bespoke 'Bereaved by Addiction' handbook, written in large part by the bereaved, which aims to help anyone who has been bereaved through a substance-related death. Our clients often find it offers ways to manage this extremely difficult time a little more easily and to realise they are not alone. It has become a leading text for practitioners supporting the bereaved, and is used and promoted by organisations such as Cruse Bereavement Care and Adfam.

In 2015 DrugFAM became a member of the National Suicide Prevention Alliance because sadly some of our bereaved clients feel they can no longer cope, or wish to be with their loved one who died, and call when they are contemplating suicide.

FASS (Family Addiction Support Service)

Section by Marlene Taylor

The charity I work for was set up in 1986 by family members coming together because of their concern about the growing drug and alcohol problem in Glasgow.[5] These families led the way in campaigning for support, not only for themselves but also for people experiencing alcohol/drug problems. FASS is unique in that it offers kinship, family and bereavement support.

Scotland's first bereavement group was started at FASS in 1995 by two mothers who lost their sons that same year. We now host several peer bereavement groups.

These mothers also started a beautiful Quilt of Remembrance. We find families appreciate the opportunity to add patches to the quilt. These patches enable mothers, fathers, children, partners and siblings to channel their grief creatively into a lasting tribute to their loved one. When FASS has visits by those in authority, such as politicians, we hold meetings where the quilt is hung, as a visual and stark reminder of the lives lost and the families devastated, to bring the statistics to life.

We also offer individual support. This is offered by two practitioners, both of whom are mothers who have lost a child in this way and so can directly relate to and empathise with clients, and also have counselling skills and bereavement training. We find many of those seeking individual support feel more able and willing to open up to those who have been in a similar position.

We have an annual trip to a tranquil place located outside Glasgow, which those who are bereaved find beneficial. It is run by German nuns, has a small chapel (although it's for people of all faiths and none) and is a very spiritual place set in beautiful grounds. While here, some people find it helpful to write a letter to their loved one and pour out their feelings.

Our bereavement services are accessed mostly by parents. To date we have not had much success in attracting referrals from some of the BAME communities and believe this is due to the cultural sensitivities around not only drugs but also alcohol. We have links with BAME support organisations and know they can also struggle to break down these barriers.

---

5   Since writing this account, Marlene Taylor has retired from FASS. There has also been changes in personnel that means the family support workers role is no longer being delivered by two bereaved mothers.

We find it hugely helpful with both engaging and then supporting someone if the person offering support is also bereaved in this way and that they had the same relationship with the person who died, such as a mother. This seems important, whether it is one of our workers or a peer offering the support, because people believe their pain and grief will be truly understood. A local newspaper article about a bereaved FASS worker led to an immense number of phone calls asking for that person. Also, it is important that people have access to support soon after seeking it, and where possible that there is no limit on the number of appointments.

Aspects of drug- and alcohol-related bereavements that people find particularly difficult include them feeling disenfranchised (often not supported by the public and their communities); that these deaths can often be seen as self-inflicted (with families feeling guilt, despair and isolation, as well as judged); and that no parent expects to bury their child. We find it is vital that these bereaved families can come together and offer each other support.

As well as the emotional aspects of bereavement, people often have to deal with officials, such as the police and the procurator fiscal. This can greatly exacerbate what is already a very traumatic time: professionals' attitudes can seem uncaring, clinical and confusing; having police in the home can be intimidating; sometimes a family cannot make the usual funeral arrangements until they receive permission from the procurator fiscal; and clothing and personal effects of their loved may be removed and can take up to a year to be returned.

Therefore, in 2012 FASS started working with the police and procurator fiscal to look at better ways of working. We held a conference where many of our support group members, the police and the procurator fiscal came together. It gave the police and procurator fiscal an opportunity to explain their processes and for family members to give their viewpoint.

FASS commissioned a short drama for the conference, titled *Chap at the Door*, which shows the lead-up to and impact of a drug-related death on a family. This is still performed and receives rave reviews. It is all the more remarkable because the people who took part have all been affected in this way and their experiences were used to produce this powerful and emotive piece of work. Since then we have used the drama to train the police, and following recording by Greater Glasgow and Clyde NHS, it has been used by FASS to raise awareness in a variety of settings, particularly for workforce development. This Bereavement Resource Pack is now available to other providers to use.

FASS and the police jointly produced an information leaflet that officers give to a family when attending a suspected substance-related death. It briefly explains the processes involved and provides a point of contact. The police in Glasgow now have a dedicated team who make direct contact with the 'significant other' the day after a death and give them a name and direct line for any future questions and information. Together, these changes are a massive improvement and can make a huge difference. We are very grateful to the police for their willingness to improve.

For the past 25 years, FASS has held an annual ecumenical service of remembrance for all faiths and none, supported by a beautiful choir. People come together and remember in a place where they are supported and know they are not alone. This special service includes a part titled 'Family Reflection', where a family member shares their story and their loved one's life, which really remembers and honours that precious life. We also read out loved ones' names, and a candle is lit for all these names, as well as one for every other soul who died in Glasgow that year. The turnout is always fantastic, and it is a very humbling and moving service. It is so important that these people who died are remembered, with all the love and respect they deserve, because they are so much more than a statistic or a person with an alcohol/drug problem.

Scottish Families Affected by Alcohol & Drugs – Bereavement Support Service

Section by Justina Murray and Scott Clements

Scottish Families Affected by Alcohol & Drugs was set up in 2003 by families themselves, who came together to support each other and form a united voice for recognition and change. This formed the beginnings of the organisation we have become. Our new strategic plan acknowledges our roots, recognising and championing the strength of families with a clear framework of five outcomes – that families are supported, included, recognised, connected to communities and a movement for change. These outcomes relate directly to family members bereaved after a substance-related death.

In August 2012 we hosted a press conference reporting the 584 drug-related deaths in Scotland in 2011, and highlighting that behind each death is a hidden grieving family. This, along with active representation on Scotland's National Forum on Drug-related Deaths, led to us directly engaging with bereaved family members who shared their stories, including experiences of seeking support. They highlighted their need for support, when they need it, and that the individual providing support should help them understand their grief and develop strategies to cope with their loss. Two key themes emerged in relation to accessing bereavement counselling:

1. The length of time to access counselling was excessive due to organisational policies or waiting lists.

> I contacted [service providing counselling] and they told me I must wait six months; I need help now.

2. The counsellor should be compassionate and have knowledge of addiction and related issues.

> Where can I find a counsellor who will understand about addiction and my son dying and who won't judge me? Everyone is judging me…other family members and so-called professionals…

The Bereavement Support Service was launched in spring 2014 with support and funding from the Scottish Government. It is available throughout Scotland to anyone aged over 16 who has been bereaved through a drug-related death. It can be directly accessed through the Scottish Families helpline, providing immediate listening/emotional support and, where appropriate, access to free bereavement counselling within a week. We fund six sessions of local, face-to-face counselling. All counsellors who join our affiliated counsellor list must have knowledge of addiction and related issues.

We work in partnership with Police Scotland and other services that regularly come into contact with bereaved families. These partners are crucial in ensuring families are made aware of the service, and with the family's permission a referral can be made on their behalf.

As of 31 March 2019, our bereavement service has run for four years and provided counselling and support to 271 bereaved family members. We have also developed practitioners' and policymakers' awareness, increased empathy and responsiveness around the unique nature of drug-related bereavement, and raised public and media awareness.

Feedback from family members has identified that we are filling a gap in support, in particular through offering counselling at no charge, and having links with local counsellors right across Scotland – a truly national service.

The counselling sessions are giving people space, time and hope:

> It gave me the space to fully experience my guilt, giving me time to understand why I feel the way I do.

> I can see my life is beginning to have hope, I can live life the way I want without feeling guilty.

Family members are given permission to feel as they do, and not to feel guilty for past actions, current emotions, or even for still being alive:

> It's okay to miss her.

> I can now wake up in the morning and keep busy and know it's okay to laugh.

Using the CORE-ISMs outcomes tool (which measures impact on mental health, risk and wellbeing), we have identified a 40% reduction in the symptoms individuals experience between their intake screening and completion of counselling.

Practitioners too have noted an increase in their own understanding, following our training, workshops and conference presentations:

I have more awareness of the issues of stigma and the practical difficulties encountered. Knowing key overdose risks will also help me to be more aware of these when working with families.

I have greater awareness of the additional factors facing families who have experienced a drug-related death, which will allow me to take a more empathetic approach.

Looking ahead (based on a 'glass-half-full' assumption that we will secure ongoing funding for the core service), we are planning to extend the service to include alcohol-related deaths, support for practitioners impacted by service user deaths, and a new commitment to ensure we actively connect with all families across all of the equality groups, with a particular focus on reaching young people, men, minority ethnic groups and the LGBTQI community.

We are keen to increase awareness of and access to the bereavement service. We know there is a significant gap between the 867 drug-related deaths in Scotland in 2016 and the 60 referrals we received. We are reviewing our initial contact with those accessing the service to make sure they are better prepared for formal counselling and feel confident and comfortable participating in their counselling.

We are commissioning an external evaluation of our first three years' experience and learning. Also we are planning 'storytelling' work to capture the voices and perspectives of those using the service. We are working with Police Scotland and FASS (see above) to review the formal letter given to families at the time of a sudden or unexplained death, and we are co-producing a new booklet with families to replace an earlier Scottish Government publication *Overdose: Bereavement – What Happens Now?* (2009).

We know that families act as a protective factor in reducing drug-related deaths, playing a key role in keeping their loved ones alive in the most difficult circumstances. It is only right that we respond with time, care and compassion when they need our support most:

It was really helpful to have had the opportunity of the counselling. The atmosphere was relaxed. I know I have some time to go to feel 100% but I feel so much better already.

How creative writing can benefit people bereaved through a substance-related death

Section by Christina Thatcher

In July 2013 I lost my father to a drug overdose. Following his death, the sense of isolation made it difficult to do ordinary things like go to work, buy groceries and sleep. I researched how to deal with these feelings but found academic and community resources limited. So, instead, I wrote poetry, read memoirs and learned, slowly, that I was not alone. I realised then that I wanted to support others who were bereaved. So, just three months after my father died, I decided to set up the first Death Writing workshops in Cardiff and have since run 17 sessions.

The aim of each free two-hour workshop is to provide a safe space for bereaved people to speak and write about their experiences in an environment where the usual taboos about death are temporarily lifted. Every workshop focuses on a different topic, from family and funeral politics to memories and resilience. These workshops:

- **Are open to all members of the community** who are bereaved or soon-to-be bereaved, and are advertised through Facebook, emails and posters.

- **Provide a welcoming, inclusive space** for a maximum of ten participants. The windows and doors of the café workshop space are blacked out to create a private environment.

- **Begin with ensuring that everyone knows what to expect by:**
    - introducing myself, my background, bereavement experience and reasons for starting Death Writing
    - explaining the aims, culture and format of the workshops
    - providing information on local bereavement services
    - giving participants permission to be upset, have privacy, and share only if they want to.

- **Create opportunities for writing, discussion and reflection by:**
    - creating a familiar structure that includes a free write, poem prompt to write, break, another prompt to write and a reading opportunity
    - choosing exercises and poetry that are accessible
    - providing voluntary opportunities for participants to share their thoughts, feelings and writing.

Due to the workshops' sensitive nature, participants are asked to sign up in advance. They tend to book up within one hour of going live online and frequently have a long waiting list. To date 81 people have taken part in the sessions; some have participated in multiple workshops resulting in a total of 156 participants.

Participants come from a variety of socioeconomic, religious and ethnic backgrounds. Their experiences of bereavement vary, from those newly bereaved to those bereaved more than 30 years ago; from those who have been bereaved by 'natural' deaths to those bereaved by more 'complex' deaths. To accommodate this diversity, the workshops are person-centred. Poems are printed in a large font and read aloud before discussions begin in case anyone has difficulty reading. Discussions are welcome, but silence is, too. Writing is optional – everyone is also given the opportunity to draw, sit quietly, meditate, walk outside or do anything else that feels right for them.

Those who have been bereaved by complex deaths – such as substance-related deaths – often express that family, friends and organisations do not understand their grief, so they did not receive the support they needed to reintegrate into the non-grieving community. The stigma and taboos associated with these deaths are regular topics of conversation in Death Writing sessions. To me, this lack of community support for disenfranchised grief means something crucial: those bereaved by addiction, suicide and other complex deaths need more opportunities to reflect on their grief, express their feelings and rebuild their confidence.

This, I feel, is where creative writing can help, by:

- being used as a tool for self-reflection

- acting as an emotional outlet where private and/or publicly stigmatised feelings can be expressed openly

- providing a way of 'communicating' with lost loved ones in order to alleviate guilt, regret and loss

- giving many people an insight into feelings and thoughts they did not know they had.

These observations are backed by academic research from scholars such as Pennebaker (1985) and Lepore (1997) that links expressive writing to improved mental health and wellbeing.

Every Death Writing workshop opens with a 'free write' that allows participants to put their insecurities aside, forget about spelling and grammar, and just write on a topic for five or ten minutes. The invitation to write might be like this:

'Describe your grief – how do you feel? What effect has it had on you? You can use metaphors (i.e. my grief is a river or a mountain) or you can simply write a description. Don't worry about the spelling, grammar, or style. Just write freely for the next ten minutes.'

To check in with them and learn more about their experience, I then ask participants how it went for them, if they found the task challenging, and whether anything they wrote surprised them.

Once participants have got their pen moving with a free write, I find it useful to share some contemporary poetry. These narrative and accessible poems often evoke a feeling, spark a memory or introduce an idea that would have not otherwise come up – for example, the poem 'Late' by Christopher Reid (2009), where the author remembers the feeling of his wife coming home, putting on her pyjamas and sliding into bed with him. I then give a prompt which responds to this poem:

'Write about a positive memory of the person you lost. What do you remember? What was happening? Describe the memory, your thoughts and feelings. You can write a poem, piece of prose, dialogue, whatever feels right to you. Take 15 minutes to write.'

Managing the feelings that arise in these groups can be delicate, so it is important to remain open, engaged and empathetic.

The advantage of creative writing is that anyone can do it, anywhere – in the comfort of their home, the privacy of their therapist's office, on a train or in a workshop. Those who lack confidence in writing often gain it in a group setting where they can start slowly, with even just a few words, and learn that everyone's stories and experiences are valued. Those who are illiterate or dyslexic can draw or have their words transcribed for them into poetry or prose.

For anyone who would like to bring creative writing into their practice, my tips are:

- **Have a five-minute free write at the start and a further ten minutes** (or more) for further writing.

- **Use specific writing prompts** that ask concrete questions or give clear instructions:

'Where do you think most about the person you lost? What is that place like? How do you feel when you're there? Take 15 minutes to write about this.'

'Write about an object that reminds you of someone you lost. Think about the way the object looks and feels, where it is and what meaning it has for you. Take 15 minutes to write about this.'

These can be adapted easily and interpreted widely to ensure each participant can work on something important for them in that moment. However, leave plenty of room for them to explore the topic(s) in their own way.

- **Provide an opportunity to share or read out their work aloud, but do not make this compulsory.** Sometimes listening to others or having the chance to think through what they have just written is equally valuable.

Examples from abroad

Section by Lorna Templeton

We have already seen in this chapter that support for people bereaved through a substance-related death is improving across the UK, but what about elsewhere in the world? There are two levels of support to consider: generic and specific.

In terms of generic support, someone bereaved through substance use can access generic bereavement counselling and other forms of support such as group-orientated, telephone or online. The Compassionate Friends offers peer support for bereaved parents in many countries including Australia, Belgium, Canada, France, Germany, the Netherlands, South Africa and the United States of America (USA). If the death was, for example, a suicide or a homicide, then bereaved people could access help from support organisations in their country.

In terms of specific support, it has been very hard to find much that is available in other countries, although it is impractical to undertake a comprehensive global search and searching has been limited to the English language. A rare example of specific support is the National Family Support Network[6] in the Republic of Ireland, which runs an eight-week group programme and also holds an annual national service of commemoration for those who have died. In the USA, numerous websites offer various resources and forms of online and other support for those who have experienced this kind of loss. GRASP[7] (Grief Recovery After a Substance Passing), which is part of the website Broken No More, has a range of resources including a network of local meetings, online resources, recommended books and tributes and reflections by bereaved people. Another example is Cathy Taughinbaugh's website,[8] offering online support and a listing of other generic and specific resources including a memorial page, groups and books. Other examples of online support are New Beginnings,[9]

---

6   www.fsn.ie/news-events/news/bereavement-support-programme
7   grasphelp.org
8   https://cathytaughinbaugh.com/when-addiction-wins-support-for-grieving-families
9   www.newbeginningsdrugrehab.org/guide-to-dealing-with-death-of-addict

which offers a guide to coping with these bereavements, and Addiction Campuses,[10] which also has an online guide and offers telephone support.

Finally, on a global level, International Overdose Awareness Day[11] held on 31 August each year, provides opportunities for those who have been bereaved through addiction to post online tributes. There are also social media communities of people bereaved this way, such as on Facebook.

Overall, however, examples of specific support are few and far between. There is a particular lack of evidence-based services or interventions for the bereaved, who are growing in number and who often have a very particular experience of bereavement. We can only speculate as to the reasons behind this lack of support and why the bulk of the support seems to be in the UK, the Republic of Ireland and the USA. It is possible that stigma around substance use and death is keeping the need hidden, with only relatively small successes in tackling that stigma seen in some countries. Furthermore, certainly in the UK and the USA, the majority of identified support has developed through courageous individuals who have experienced this type of bereavement campaigning for more support and starting services or other forms of support. Finally, the support available in some countries (e.g. Scotland and the Republic of Ireland) is associated with increased government backing of the issues and of events such as annual memorial services.

---

10 www.addictioncampuses.com/blog/dealing-with-the-loss-of-a-loved-one-from-drugs-or-alcohol

11 www.overdoseday.com

References

Adfam (2011a) 'Learning from loss: drug-related bereavement.' *Families UpFront*. London: Adfam. Accessed on 17/2/2018 at www.adfam.org.uk/cms/fuf/doc/Adfam_Families_UpFront_Issue_3.pdf

Adfam (2011b) *Working with Grandparents Raising Their Grandchildren Due to Parental Substance Use*. London: Adfam.

Adfam (2012a) *Challenging Stigma: Tackling the Prejudice Experienced by the Families of Drug and Alcohol Users*. London: Adfam.

Adfam (2012b) 'Social Return on Investment Briefing. Supporting families affected by substance misuse: the economic case for investment.' Accessed on 23/9/2017 at www.adfam.org.uk/cms/docs/Adfam_Briefing_-_The_social_return_of_investing_in_drug_and_alcohol_family_support_services.pdf

Adfam (2012c) 'Between a rock and a hard place: How parents deal with children who use substances and perpetrate abuse.' Accessed on 12/6/2018 at www.adfam.org.uk/files/docs/Between_a_rock_and_a_hard_place_-_Project_report.pdf

Advisory Council on the Misuse of Drugs (2003) *Hidden Harm: Responding to the Needs of Children of Problem Drug Users*. London: The Home Office.

Advisory Council on the Misuse of Drugs (2011) *Hidden Harm*. London: ACMD. Accessed on 28/12/2018 at https://assets.publishing.service.gov.uk/government/uploads/system/uploads/attachment_data/file/120620/hidden-harm-full.pdf

Advisory Council on the Misuse of Drugs (2016) *Reducing Opioid-Related Deaths in the UK*. London: ACMD. Accessed on 2/6/2019 at www.gov.uk/government/uploads/system/uploads/attachment_data/file/576560/ACMD-Drug-Related-Deaths-Report-161212.pdf

Advisory Council on the Misuse of Drugs (2017) *Commissioning Impact on Drug Treatment*. London: Advisory Council on the Misuse of Drugs. Accessed on 27/6/2019 at https://assets.publishing.service.gov.uk/government/uploads/system/uploads/attachment_data/file/642811/Final_Commissioning_report_5.15_6th_Sept.pdf

Agabi, C. and Wilson, J. (2005) 'Trauma, PTSD, and resilience: A review of the literature.' *Trauma Violence and Abuse 6*, 195–216.

Alexander-Passe, N. (2015) 'Investigating post-traumatic stress disorder (PTSD) triggered by the experience of dyslexia in mainstream school education?' *Journal of Psychology and Psychotherapy 5*, 6, 1–6.

Allen, J.G. (2013) *Restoring Mentalizing in Attachment Relationships: Treating Trauma with Plain Old Therapy*. Arlington, VA: American Psychiatric Publishing.

Amnesty International (2017) *'If You Are Poor, You Are Killed': Extrajudicial Executions in the Philippines' 'War on Drugs'*. Accessed on 5/11/2019 at www.amnesty.org/download/Documents/ASA3555172017ENGLISH.PDF

Anderson M., Hawkins L., Eddleston M., Thompson J.P., Vale, A. and Thomas, S.H.L. (2016) 'Severe and fatal pharmaceutical poisoning in young children in the UK.' *Archives of Disease in Childhood 101*, 7, 653–656.

Armstrong, D. and Shakespeare-Finch, J. (2011) 'Relationship to the bereaved and perceptions of severity of trauma differentiate elements of posttraumatic growth.' *Omega – Journal of Death and Dying 63*, 2, 125–140.

Australian Bureau of Statistics (2015) *National Health Survey: First Results, 2014–15: Alcohol Consumption.* Canberra: ABS. Accessed on 26/12/2017 at www.abs.gov.au/ausstats/abs@.nsf/Lookup/by%20Subject/4364.0.55.001~2014-15~Main%20Features~Alcohol%20consumption~25

Australian Bureau of Statistics (2018) *Deaths Due to Harmful Alcohol Consumption in Australia.* Canberra: ABS. Accessed on 2/6/2019 at www.abs.gov.au/ausstats/abs@.nsf/Lookup/by%20Subject/3303.0~2017~Main%20Features~Deaths%20due%20to%20harmful%20alcohol%20consumption%20in%20Australia~4

Barker, M.-J. (2017) *BACP Good Practice across the Counselling Professions 001: Gender, Sexual, and Relationship Diversity (GSRD).* Lutterworth: British Association for Counselling and Psychotherapy.

Bartholomew, K. (1990) 'Avoidance of intimacy: An attachment perspective.' *Journal of Social and Personal Relationships 7*, 2, 147–178.

Beattie, M. (1992) *Codependent No More* (2nd edition). Center City, MN: Hazelden.

Beck, A.T. and Steer, R.A. (1989) 'Clinical predictors of eventual suicide: A 5- to 10-year prospective study of suicide attempters.' *Journal of Affective Disorders 17*, 3, 203–209.

Beisser, A.R. (1970) 'The Paradoxical Theory of Change.' In J. Fagan and I. Shepherd (eds) *Gestalt Therapy Now.* Palo Alto, CA: Science and Behavior Books.

Bogdanowicz, K.M., Stewart, R., Chang, C.-K., Shetty, H. *et al.* (2018) 'Excess overdose mortality immediately following transfer of patients and their care as well as after cessation of opioid substitution therapy.' *Addiction 113*, 5, 946–995.

Bonanno, G. (2009) *The Other Side of Sadness: What the New Science of Bereavement Tells Us About Life After Loss.* New York, NY: Basic Books.

Boss, P. (2000) *Ambiguous Loss: Learning to Live with Unresolved Grief.* Cambridge, MA: Harvard University Press.

Boss, P. (2006) *Loss, Trauma, and Resilience: Therapeutic Work with Ambiguous Loss.* New York, NY: Norton.

Boss, P. (2010) 'The trauma and complicated grief of ambiguous loss.' *Pastoral Psychology 59*, 137–145.

Bowlby, J. (1969) *Attachment and Loss. Volume 1: Attachment.* London: Hogarth Press.

Bristowe, K., Marshall, S. and Harding, R. (2016) 'The bereavement experiences of lesbian, gay, bisexual and /or trans* people who have lost a partner: A systematic review, thematic synthesis and modelling of the literature.' *Palliative Medicine 30*, 8, 730–744.

British Association for Counselling and Psychotherapy (2018) *Ethical Framework for the Counselling Professions.* Lutterworth: BACP.

Browne, S. (2008) 'The therapy maze.' *Therapy Today*, June 2008, 9–18.

Burns, D.D. (2000) *Feeling Good: The New Mood Therapy.* New York, NY: HarperCollins.

Canadian Drug Policy Coalition (2013) *Opioid Overdose Prevention and Response in Canada.* Vancouver: CDPC Accessed on 26/12/2017 at www.documentcloud.org/documents/1200721-cdpc-overdose-prevention-policy-web-final.html

Cartwright, P. (2015) 'Bereaved through substance use: Guidelines for those whose work brings them into contact with adults after a drug or alcohol-related death.' Accessed on 1/9/2019 at www.bath.ac.uk/publications/bereaved-through-substance-use/attachments/bereaved-through-substance-use.pdf

Cartwright, P. (2019) 'How helpful is counselling for people bereaved through a substance-related death?' *Bereavement Care 38*, 1, 23–32.

Cavanagh, J.T., Carson, A.J., Sharpe, M. and Lawrie, S.M. (2003) 'Psychological autopsy studies of suicide: A systematic review.' *Psychological Medicine 33*, 3, 395–405.

Centres for Disease Control and Prevention (CDC) (2008) 'Alcohol-Attributable Deaths and Years of Potential Life Lost among American Indians and Alaska Natives – United States, 2001–2005.' Accessed on 5/4/2018 at www.cdc.gov/mmwr/preview/mmwrhtml/mm5734a3.htm

Centres for Disease Control and Prevention (CDC) (2018) 'Fact Sheets – Alcohol Use and Your Health.' Accessed on 2/6/2019 at www.cdc.gov/alcohol/fact-sheets/alcohol-use.htm

Centres for Disease Control and Prevention (CDC) (2019) 'Drug and Opioid-Involved Overdose Deaths – United States, 2013–2017.' Accessed on 2/6/2019 at www.cdc.gov/mmwr/volumes/67/wr/mm675152e1.htm?s_cid=mm675152e1_w

Chapple, A. and Ziebland, S. (2010). 'Viewing the body after bereavement due to a traumatic death: Qualitative study in the UK.' *British Medical Journal 340*, c2301.

Chapple, A., Ziebland, S. and Hawton, K. (2015) 'Taboo and the different death? Perceptions of those bereaved by suicide or other traumatic death.' *Sociology of Health & Illness 37*, 4, 610–625.

Chaudoir, S.R. and Fisher, J.D. (2010) 'The disclosure processes model: Understanding disclosure decision-making and post-disclosure outcomes among people living with a concealable stigmatized identity.' *Psychological Bulletin 136*, 2, 236–256.

Childress, A. (2006) 'What Can Human Brain Imaging Tell Us about Vulnerability to Addiction and to Relapse?' In W.R. Miller and K.M. Carroll (eds) *Rethinking Substance Abuse: What the Science Shows, and What We Should Do about It*. New York, NY: Guilford Press.

Cleiren, M.P.H.D. (1993) *Bereavement and Adaptation: A Comparative Study of the Aftermath of Death*. Philadelphia, PA: Taylor & Francis.

Clemmens, M.C. and Matzko, H. (2005) 'Gestalt Approaches to Substance Use/Abuse/Dependency: Theory and Practice.' In A.L. Woldt and S.M. Toman (eds) *Gestalt Therapy: History, Theory, and Practice*. Thousand Oaks, CA: SAGE Publications.

College of Occupational Therapists, National Association of Paediatric Occupational Therapists (2003) *'Doubly Disadvantaged': Report of a Survey on Waiting Lists and Waiting Times for Occupational Therapy Services for Children with Developmental Coordination Disorder*. London: COT. Accessed on 1/11/2019 at www.rcot.co.uk/practice-resources/rcot-publications/downloads/doubly-disadvantaged

Conner, K.R., Pinquart, M. and Gamble, S.A. 'Meta-analysis of depression and substance use among individuals with alcohol use disorders.' *Journal of Substance Abuse and Treatment 37*, 2, 127–137.

Connors, G.J., DiClemente, C.C., Velasquez, M.M. and Donovan D.M. (2013) *Substance Abuse Treatment and the Stages of Change: Selecting and Planning Interventions* (2nd edition). New York, NY: Guilford Press.

Copello, A., Templeton, L., Orford, J. and Velleman, R. (2010) 'The 5-Step Method: Evidence of gains for affected family members.' *Drugs: Education, Prevention and Policy 17*, s1, 86–99.

Copello, A., Velleman, R. and Templeton, L. (2005) 'Family interventions in the treatment of alcohol and drug problems.' *Drug and Alcohol Review 24*, 4, 369–385.

Crawford, R. (1998) *How High Can You Bounce? Turn Setbacks into Comebacks*. New York, NY: Bantam Books.

Crisp, A.H., Gelder, M.G., Rix, S., Meltzer, H.I. and Rowlands, O.J. (2000) 'Stigmatisation of people with mental illnesses.' *British Journal of Psychiatry 177*, 4–7.

Currie, N. (2014) 'Aboriginal Health Council of Western Australia Submission Response Inquiry into the harmful use of alcohol in Aboriginal and Torres Strait Islander communities.' Aboriginal Health Council of Western Australia. Accessed on 5/4/2018 at www.aph.gov.au/DocumentStore. ashx?id=0a0eb432-8c8e-4e0d-876e-1cb604e4c73bandsubId=251874

Dana, D. (2018) *The Polyvagal Theory in Therapy: Engaging the Rhythm of Regulation*. New York, NY: Norton.

Da Silva, E.A., Noto, R.A. and Formigoni, M.L.O.S. (2007) 'Death by drug overdose: Impact on families.' *Journal of Psychoactive Drugs 39*, 3, 301–306.

DiClemente, C.C. (2003) *Addiction and Change: How Addictions Develop and Addicted People Recover*. New York, NY: Guilford Press.

Doka, K. (1989) *Disenfranchised Grief: Recognizing Hidden Sorrow*. Lexington, MA: Lexington Books.

Doka, K. (2002a) 'Disenfranchised Grief.' In Kenneth J. Doka (ed.) *Living with Grief: Loss in Later Life*. Washington, DC: The Hospice Foundation of America.

Doka, K. (2002b) 'How We Die: Stigmatised Death and Disenfranchised Grief.' In K. Doka (ed.) *Disenfranchised Grief*. Champaign, IL: Research Press.

DrugFAM (2013) *Bereaved by Addiction: A Booklet for Anyone Bereaved Through Drug or Alcohol Use*. High Wycombe, England: DrugFAM.

DrugWise (2018) 'Deaths.' Accessed on 4/6/2019 at www.drugwise.org.uk/deaths

Emmons, R.A. (2007) *Thanks! How the New Science of Gratitude Can Make You Happier*. New York, NY: Houghton Mifflin Harcourt.

European Monitoring Centre for Drugs and Drug Addiction (2015) *European Drug Report 2015.* Lisbon: EMCDDA. Accessed on 10/6/2017 at www.emcdda.europa.eu/edr2015

European Monitoring Centre for Drugs and Drug Addiction (2017) *European Drug Report 2017.* Lisbon: EMCDDA. Accessed on 10/6/2017 at www.emcdda.europa.eu/edr2017

European Monitoring Centre for Drugs and Drug Addiction (2019) *European Drug Report 2019.* Lisbon: EMCDDA. Accessed on 9/8/2019 at www.emcdda.europa.eu/edr2019

Feeney, B. and Collins, L. (2001) 'Predictors of caregiving in adult intimate relationships: An attachment theoretical perspective.' *Journal of Personality and Social Psychology 80*, 6, 972–994

Feigelman, W., Gorman, B. and Jordan, J. (2009) 'Stigmatization and suicide bereavement.' *Death Studies 33*, 7, 591–608.

Feigelman, W., Jordan, J. and Gorman, B. (2011) 'Parental grief after a child's drug death compared to other death causes: Investigating a greatly neglected bereavement population.' *Omega – Journal of Death and Dying 63*, 4, 291–316.

Feigelman, W., Jordan, R., McIntosh, J. and Feigelman, B. (2012) *Devastating Losses: How Parents Cope with the Death of a Child to Suicide or Drugs.* New York, NY: Springer.

Flores, P.J. (2004) 'Addiction as an Attachment Disorder: Implications for Group Psychotherapy.' In B. Reading and M. Weegmann (eds) *Group Psychotherapy and Addiction.* London: Whurr Publishers.

Fonagy, P., Gergely, G., Jurist, E.L. and Target, M. (2004) *Affect Regulation, Mentalization, and the Development of the Self.* London: Karnac Books.

Ford, A., McKell, J., Templeton, L. and Valentine, C. (2018) 'The Impact of a Substance-Related Death.' In C. Valentine (ed.) *Families Bereaved by Alcohol or Drugs: Research on Experiences, Coping and Support.* London and New York, NY: Routledge.

Foundation for a Drug-Free World (2017) *The Truth About Alcohol: International Statistics.* Los Angeles, CA: Foundation for a Drug-Free World. Accessed on 2/6/2019 at www.drugfreeworld.org/drugfacts/alcohol/international-statistics.html

Frankl, V.E. (1969) *Man's Search for Meaning: An Introduction to Logotherapy.* London: Hodder & Stoughton.

Fuchs, B. (1999) 'Betrayal, Revenge and Forgiveness – A Life Initiation.' In H. Jackson (ed.) *Creating Harmony: Conflict Resolution in Community.* East Meon: Permanent Publications.

Fuld, S. (2018) 'Autism spectrum disorder: The impact of stressful and traumatic life events and implications for clinical practice.' *Clinical Social Work Journal 46*, 3, 210–219.

Gerbarg, P.L. and Brown, R.P. (2016) 'Neurobiology and neurophysiology of breath practices in psychiatric care.' *Psychiatric Times*, 30 November. Accessed on 15/8/2019 at www.psychiatrictimes.com/special-reports/neurobiology-and-neurophysiology-breath-practices-psychiatric-care

Goleman, D. (1996) *Emotional Intelligence: Why It Can Matter More Than IQ.* London: Bloomsbury Publishing.

Gray, A. (1994) *An Introduction to the Therapeutic Frame.* London: Routledge.

Gross, J.J. (ed.) (2014) *Handbook of Emotion Regulation* (2nd edition). New York, NY: Guilford Press.

Gulbenkoglu, H. (2007) *Supporting People with Disabilities Coping with Grief and Loss: An Easy-to-Read Booklet.* Melbourne: Scope (Vic) Ltd.

Guy, P. (2004) 'Bereavement through drug use: Messages from research.' *Practice 16*, 1, 43–54.

Guy, P. and Holloway, M. (2007) 'Drug-related deaths and the "special deaths" of late modernity.' *Sociology 41*, 1, 83–96.

Hammersley, D. (2013) 'What have antidepressants got to do with depression?' *Private Practice Journal*, Summer 2013, 15–17.

Hanson, R. and Mendius, R. (2009) *Buddha's Brain: The Practical Neuroscience of Happiness, Love, and Wisdom.* Oakland, CA: New Harbinger Publications.

Hansson, R.O. and Stroebe, M.S. (2003) 'Grief, Older Adulthood.' In T.P. Gullotta and M. Bloom (eds) *Encyclopedia of Primary Prevention and Health Promotion.* New York, NY: Kluwer Academic.

Harding, M. (2014) 'Suicide risk assessment and threats of suicide.' *Patient.* Accessed on 4/8/2019 at https://patient.info/doctor/suicide-risk-assessment-and-threats-of-suicide#ref-8

Harris, E.C. and Barraclough, B. (1997) 'Suicide as an outcome for mental disorders: A meta-analysis.' *British Journal of Psychiatry 170*, 3, 205–228.

Herman, J.L. (2001) *Trauma and Recovery*. London: Pandora.

Hindmarch C. (2009) *On the Death of a Child* (3rd edition). Oxford: Radcliffe.

Hockenhull, J., Murphy, K.G. and Paterson, S. (2017) 'An observed rise in γ-hydroxybutyrate-associated deaths in London: Evidence to suggest a possible link with concomitant rise in chemsex.' *Forensic Science International 270*, 93–97.

Holland, J.M., Currier, J.M. and Neimeyer, R.A. (2006) 'Meaning reconstruction in the first two years of bereavement: The role of sense-making and benefit-finding.' *Omega – Journal of Death and Dying 53*, 3, 175–191.

Holland, J.M. and Neimeyer, R.A. (2011) 'Separation and traumatic distress in prolonged grief: The role of cause of death and relationship to the deceased.' *Journal of Psychopathology and Behavioural Assessment 33*, 2, 254–263.

Home Office (2013) *Information for Local Areas on the Change to the Definition of Domestic Violence and Abuse*. Accessed on 22/7/2017 at www.gov.uk/government/uploads/system/uploads/attachment_data/file/142701/guide-on-definition-of-dv.pdf

Home Office (2018) *Drug Misuse: Findings from the 2015/16 Crime Survey for England and Wales* (2nd edition). London: Home Office. Accessed on 2/4/2018 at www.gov.uk/government/uploads/system/uploads/attachment_data/file/564760/drug-misuse-1516.pdf

Houston, G. (2003) *Brief Gestalt Therapy*. London: SAGE Publications.

Human Rights Watch (2018) 'Philippines.' Accessed on 2/4/2018 at www.hrw.org/asia/philippines

Idsoe, T., Dyregrov, A. and Idsoe, E.C. (2012) 'Bullying and PTSD symptoms.' *Journal of Abnormal Child Psychology 40*, 6, 901–911.

Imber-Black, E. and Roberts, J. (1998) *Rituals for Our Times: Celebrating, Healing, and Changing Our Lives and Our Relationships*. Lanham, MD: Jason Aronson.

Janoff-Bulman, R. (1988) 'Victims of Violence.' In S. Fisher and J. Reason (eds) *Handbook of Life Stress, Cognition and Health*. Chichester: Wiley.

Jeffers, S. (2007) *Feel the Fear and Do It Anyway*. New York, NY: Fawcett Books.

Jerath, R., Crawford, M.W., Barnes, V.A. and Harden, K. (2015) 'Self-regulation of breathing as a primary treatment for anxiety.' *Applied Psychophysiology and Biofeedback 40*, 2, 107–115. Accessed on 16/8/2019 at www.ncbi.nlm.nih.gov/pubmed/25869930

Johnson, J.G., Zhang, B. and Prigerson, H.G. (2008) 'Investigation of a developmental model of risk for depression and suicidality following spousal bereavement.' *Suicide and Life-Threatening Behavior 38*, 1, 1–12.

Joiner, T. (2005) *Why People Die by Suicide*. Cambridge, MA: Harvard University Press.

Joint Formulary Committee (2017) *British National Formulary* (74th edition). London: British Medical Association and Royal Pharmaceutical Society.

Jordan, J.R. (2012) 'Guided Imaginal Conversations with the Deceased.' In R.A. Neimeyer (ed.) *Techniques of Grief Therapy: Creative Practices for Counseling the Bereaved*. New York, NY: Routledge.

Jordan, J.R. (2019) 'Addressing Bereavement after Traumatic Loss.' Webinar by J.R. Jordan and P.S. Kosminsky, 15/5/2019, NScience.

Jordan, J.R. and McIntosh, J.L. (2010) *Grief After Suicide: Understanding the Consequences and Caring for the Survivors*. New York, NY: Taylor & Francis.

Jordan, J.R. and Neimeyer, R.A. (2003) 'Does grief counseling work?' *Death Studies 27*, 9, 765–786.

Joyce, P. and Sills, C. (2014) *Skills in Gestalt Counselling and Psychotherapy* (3rd edition). London: SAGE Publications.

Kabat-Zinn, J. (1994) *Wherever You Go, There You Are*. New York, NY: Hyperion.

Kauffman, J. (2002a) 'Safety and the Assumptive World: A Theory of Traumatic Loss.' In J. Kauffman (ed.) *Loss of the Assumptive World: A Theory of Traumatic Loss*. New York, NY: Brunner-Routledge.

Kauffman, J. (2002b) 'The Psychology of Disenfranchised Grief: Liberation, Shame, and Self-Disenfranchisement.' In K.J. Doka (ed.) *Disenfranchised Grief: New Directions, Challenges, and Strategies for Practice*. Champaign, IL: Research Press.

Kelly, J.F. (2016) *How Addiction Occurs*. Boston, MA: Harvard Medical School. Accessed on 2/2/2018 at www.recoveryanswers.org/media/harvard-professor-john-kelly-how-addiction-occurs

Kelly, J.F. and Westerhoff, C.M. (2010) 'Does it matter how we refer to individuals with substance-related conditions? A randomized study of two commonly used terms.' *International Journal of Drug Policy 21*, 3, 202–207.

Kessler, R.C., Borges, G. and Walters, E.E. (1999) 'Prevalence of and risk factors for lifetime suicide attempts in the National Comorbidity Survey.' *Archives of General Psychiatry 56*, 7, 617–626.

Klass, D., Silverman, P.R. and Nickman, S.L. (eds) (1996) *Continuing Bonds: New Understandings of Grief*. Philadelphia, PA: Taylor & Francis.

Korb, M.P., Gorrell, J. and Van De Riet, V. (1989) *Gestalt Therapy: Practice and Theory* (2nd edition). Boston, MA: Allyn and Bacon.

Kosminsky, P.S. (2019) 'Addressing Bereavement after Traumatic Loss.' Webinar by J.R. Jordan and P.S. Kosminsky, 15/5/2019, NScience.

Kosminsky, P.S. and Jordan, J.R. (2016) *Attachment-Informed Grief Therapy: The Clinician's Guide to Foundations and Applications*. New York, NY: Routledge.

Kristensen, P., Weisæth, L. and Heir, T. (2012) 'Bereavement and mental health after sudden and violent losses: A review.' *Psychiatry 75*, 1, 76–97.

Krpan, K.M., Kross, E., Berman, M.G., Deldin, P.J., Askren, M.K. and Jonides, J. (2013) 'An everyday activity as a treatment for depression: The benefits of expressive writing for people diagnosed with major depressive disorder.' *Journal of Affective Disorders 150*, 3, 1148–1151.

Kuczewski, M.G., McCarthy, M.P., Michelfelder, A., Anderson, E.E., Wasson, K. and Hatchett, L. (2014) '"I will never let that be OK again": Student reflections on competent spiritual care for dying patients.' *Academic Medicine 89*, 1, 54–59.

Kunreuther, E. and Palmer, A. (2018) *Drinking, Drug Use, and Addiction in the Autism Community*. London: Jessica Kingsley Publishers.

Kuykendall, J. (2001) 'Disorders of Fluency Special Interest Group.' Workshop, London.

Laurie, A. and Neimeyer, R.A. (2008) 'African Americans in bereavement: Grief as a function of ethnicity.' *Omega – Journal of Death and Dying 57*, 2, 173–193.

Lawton, H., Gilbert, J. and Turnbull, F. (2016) 'Bereavement through drugs and alcohol.' *Bereavement Care 35*, 2, 48–51.

Leahy, R.L., Tirch, D.D. and Napolitano, L.A. (2011) *Emotion Regulation in Psychotherapy: A Practitioner's Guide*. New York, NY: Guilford Press.

Lee, R.G. and Wheeler, G. (eds) (1996) *The Voice of Shame: Silence and Connection in Psychotherapy*. San Francisco, CA: Jossey-Bass, for the Gestalt Institute of Cleveland.

Lehman, D.R., Wortman, C.B. and Williams, A.F. (1987) 'Long-term effects of losing a spouse or child in a motor vehicle crash.' *Journal of Personality and Social Psychology 52*, 1, 218–231.

Leick, N. and Davidsen-Nielsen, M. (1991) *Healing Pain: Attachment, Loss and Grief Therapy*. London: Routledge.

Lemma, A. (1996) *Introduction to Psychopathology*. London: SAGE Publications.

Lepore, S.J. (1997) 'Expressive writing moderates the relation between intrusive thoughts and depressive symptoms.' *Journal of Personality and Social Psychology 73*, 5, 1030–1037.

Levine, P.A. (2008) *Healing Trauma*. Boulder, CO: Sounds True.

Levine, S. (1986) *Who Dies? An Investigation of Conscious Living and Conscious Dying*. Dublin: Gill and Macmillan.

Lewis, J.A., Packard, T. and Lewis, M.D. (2007) *Management of Human Services Programs* (5th edition). Belmont, CA: Brooks/Cole.

Lloyd, C. (2010) *Sinning and Sinned Against: The Stigmatisation of Problem Drug Users*. London: UK Drugs Policy Commission.

Mackenbach, J., Kulhánová, I., Bopp, M., Borrell, C. *et al.* (2015) 'Inequalities in alcohol-related mortality in 17 European countries: A retrospective analysis of mortality registers.' PLOS Medicine. Accessed on 26/12/2017 at htttps://journals.plos.org/plosmedicine/article?id=10.1371/journal.pmed.1001909

Main, M. (1996) 'Introduction to the special section on attachment and psychopathology: 2. Overview of the field of attachment.' *Journal of Consulting and Clinical Psychology 64*, 2, 237–243.

Mammen, G. and Faulkner, G. (2013) 'Physical activity and the prevention of depression: A systematic review of prospective studies.' *American Journal of Preventive Medicine 45*, 5, 649–657.

Marlatt, G.A. and Gordon, J.R. (eds) (1985) *Relapse Prevention: Maintenance Strategies in the Treatment of Addictive Behaviors*. New York, NY: Guilford Press.

Martin, T.L. and Doka, K.J. (2011) 'The Influence of Gender and Socialization on Grieving Styles.' In R.A. Neimeyer, D.L. Harris, H.R. Winokuer and G.F. Thornton (eds) *Grief and Bereavement in Contemporary Society: Bridging Research and Practice*. New York, NY: Routledge.

Masferrer, L. (2017) 'Is complicated grief a risk factor for substance use? A comparison of substance-users and normative grievers.' *Addiction Research and Theory 25*, 5, 361–369.

Masferrer, L., Garre-Olmo, J. and Caparros, B. (2015) 'Is there any relationship between drug users' bereavement and substance consumption?' *Heroin Addiction and Related Clinical Problems 17*, 6, 23–30.

Mearns, D., Thorne, B. and McLeod, J. (2013) *Person-Centred Counselling in Action* (4th edition). London: SAGE Publications.

Mcauley, A. and Forsyth, A.J. (2011) 'The impact of drug-related death on staff who have experienced it as part of their caseload: An exploratory study.' *Journal of Substance Use 16*, 1, 68–78.

McGregor Hepburn, J. (2012) 'A problem of guilt: An exploration of feelings of guilt as an obstacle to psychic change.' *British Journal of Psychotherapy 28*, 2, 188–200.

Miles, M.S. and Demi, A.S. (1991–1992) 'A comparison of guilt in bereaved parents whose children died by suicide, accident, or chronic disease.' *Omega – Journal of Death and Dying 24*, 3, 203–215.

Miller, W.R. and Rollnick, S. (2002) *Motivational Interviewing: Preparing People for Change* (2nd edition). New York, NY: Guilford Press.

Miniati, M., Callari, A. and Pini, S. (2017) 'Adult attachment style and suicidality.' *Psychiatria Danubina 29*, 3, 250–259.

Murphy, S.A., Johnson, L.C. and Lohan, J. (2003) 'Finding meaning in a child's violent death: A five-year prospective analysis of parents' personal narratives and empirical data.' *Death Studies 27*, 5, 381–404.

Najavits, L.M., Weiss R.D. and Shaw S.R. (1997) 'The link between substance abuse and posttraumatic stress disorder in women: A research review.' *American Journal on Addictions 6*, 4, 273–283.

National Health Service (2019) 'Can I drink alcohol if I'm taking antidepressants?' Accessed on 1/11/2019 at www.nhs.uk/chq/pages/863.aspx?categoryid=73andsubcategoryid=103

National Institute for Health and Care Excellence (NICE) (2018) 'Depression in adults: recognition and management.' Clinical guideline [CG90]. Accessed on 23/8/2019 at www.nice.org.uk/guidance/cg90/ifp/chapter/depression

National Records of Scotland (2019) *Drug-related Deaths in Scotland in 2018*. Edinburgh: NRS. Accessed on 9/8/2019 at www.nrscotland.gov.uk/files//statistics/drug-related-deaths/2018/drug-related-deaths-18-pub.pdf

Neimeyer, R.A. (ed.) (2012) *Techniques of Grief Therapy: Creative Practices for Counseling the Bereaved*. New York, NY: Routledge.

Neimeyer, R.A. and Jordan, J.R. (2002) 'Disenfranchisement and Comparative Failure: Grief Therapy and the Co-construction of Meaning.' In K.J. Doka (ed.) *Disenfranchised Grief: New Directions, Challenges, and Strategies for Practice*. Champaign, IL: Research Press.

Neimeyer, R.A. and Sands, D.C. (2011) 'Meaning Reconstruction in Bereavement: From Principles to Practice.' In R.A. Neimeyer, D.L. Harris, H.R. Winokuer and G.F. Thornton (eds) *Grief and Bereavement in Contemporary Society: Bridging Research and Practice*. New York, NY: Routledge.

New York Times, The (2019) 'Top executives of Insys, an opioid company, are found guilty of racketeering.' 2 May. Accessed on 1/11/2019 at www.nytimes.com/2019/05/02/health/insys-trial-verdict-kapoor.html

Northern Ireland Statistics and Research Agency (2017) *Drug Related and Drug Misuse Deaths 2006–2016*. Belfast: NISRA. Accessed on 2/6/2019 at www.nisra.gov.uk/publications/drug-related-and-drug-misuse-deaths-2006-2016

O'Connor, R.C. (2010) 'Psychological Perspectives on Suicidal Behaviour.' In U. Kumar and M.K. Mandal (eds) *Suicidal Behaviour: Assessment of People-at-Risk*. London: SAGE Publications.

O'Connor, M.F., Wellisch, D.K., Stanton, A.L., Eisenberger, N.I., Irwin, M.R. and Leiberman, M.D. (2008) 'Craving love: Enduring grief activates brain's reward center.' *NeuroImage 42*, 2, 969–972.

Office for National Statistics (2015) *Deaths Related to Drug Poisoning in England and Wales: 2014 Registrations*. London: ONS. Accessed on 11/4/2018 at www.ons.gov.uk/peoplepopulation andcommunity/birthsdeathsandmarriages/deaths/bulletins/deathsrelatedtodrugpoisoning inenglandandwales/2015-09-03

Office for National Statistics (2016) *Deaths Involving Legal Highs in England and Wales: Between 2004 and 2013*. London: ONS. Accessed on 1/9/2019 at www.ons.gov.uk/peoplepopulationandcommunity/ birthsdeathsandmarriages/deaths/articles/deathsinvolvinglegalhighsinenglandandwales/ between2004and2013

Office for National Statistics (2018a) *Alcohol-Specific Deaths in the UK: Registered in 2017*. London: ONS. Accessed on 2/6/2019 at www.ons.gov.uk/peoplepopulationandcommunity/healthandsocialcare/ causesofdeath/bulletins/alcoholrelateddeathsintheunitedkingdom/registeredin2017

Office for National Statistics (2018b) *Deaths Related to Drug Poisoning in England and Wales: 2017 Registrations*. London: ONS. Accessed on 2/6/2019 at www.ons.gov.uk/peoplepopu- lationandcommunity/birthsdeathsandmarriages/deaths/bulletins/deathsrelatedtodrugpoisoning inenglandandwales/2017registrations

Office for National Statistics (2019) *Drug-Related Deaths and Suicides in Prison Custody in England and Wales: 2008 to 2016*. London: ONS. Accessed on 9/8/2019 at www.ons.gov.uk/ peoplepopulationandcommunity/birthsdeathsandmarriages/deaths/articles/drugrelateddeathsand suicideinprisoncustodyinenglandandwales/2008to2016

Office for National Statistics (2019) *Deaths Related to Drug Poisoning in England and Wales: 2018 Registrations*. London: ONS. Accessed on 9/8/2019 at www.ons.gov.uk/peoplepopu- lationandcommunity/birthsdeathsandmarriages/deaths/bulletins/deathsrelatedtodrugpoisoningin englandandwales/2018registrations

Ogden, P., Minton, K. and Pain, C. (2006) *Trauma and the Body: A Sensorimotor Approach to Psychotherapy*. London: Norton.

Ohlmeier, M.D., Peters, K., Te Wildt, B.T., Zedler, M. *et al.* (2008) 'Comorbidity of Alcohol and Substance Dependence With Attention-Deficit/Hyperactivity Disorder (ADHD).' *Alcohol and Alcoholism, 43*, 3, 300–304.

Orford, J. (2001) *Excessive Appetites: A Psychological View of Addictions*. Chichester: Wiley.

Orford, J., Natera, G., Copello, A., Atkinson, C. *et al.* (2005) *Coping with Alcohol and Drug Problems: The Experiences of Family Members in Three Contrasting Cultures*. Hove: Routledge.

Orford, J., Velleman, R., Natera, G., Templeton, L. and Copello, A. (2013) 'Addiction in the family is a major but neglected contributor to the global burden of adult ill-health.' *Social Science and Medicine 78*, 1, 70–77.

Osterweis, M., Solomon, F. and Green, M. (eds) (1984) *Bereavement: Reactions, Consequences, and Care*. Washington, DC: National Academy Press.

Palmer, B.R., Gignac, G., Ekermans, G. and Stough, C. (2007) 'A Comprehensive Framework for Emotional Intelligence.' In R.J. Emmerling, V.K. Shanwal and M.K. Mandal (eds) *Emotional Intelligence: Theoretical and Cultural Perspectives*. New York, NY: Nova Science.

Parkes, C.M. (2001) *Bereavement: Studies of Grief in Adult Life* (3rd edition). Philadelphia, PA: Taylor & Francis.

Parkes, C.M. (2004) 'Depression and Helplessness: What Helps?' Lecture, 6 October 2014, St Christopher's Hospice, London.

Parkes, C.M. (2009) *Love and Loss: The Roots of Grief and Its Complications*. Hove: Routledge.

Parkes, C.M., Laungani, P. and Young, B. (eds) (2015) *Death and Bereavement Across Cultures* (2nd edition). London and New York, NY: Routledge.

Parkes, C.M. and Prigerson, H.G. (2010) *Bereavement: Studies of Grief in Adult Life* (4th edition). London: Penguin Books.

Paul, C. (2006) 'Guilt and blame in the grieving process.' *Bereavement Care 25*, 3, 50–52.

Pearlman, L.A., Wortman, C.B., Feuer, C.A., Farber, C.H. and Rando, T.A. (2014) *Treating Traumatic Bereavement: A Practitioner's Guide*. New York, NY: Guilford Press.

Pennebaker, J.W. (1985) 'Traumatic experience and psychosomatic disease: Exploring the roles of behavioural inhibition, obsession, and confiding.' *Canadian Psychology 26*, 2, 82–95.

Perls, F., Hefferline, R.F and Goodman, P. (1972) *Gestalt Therapy: Excitement and Growth in the Human Personality.* London: Souvenir Press.

Piers, G. and Singer, M.B. (1972) *Shame and Guilt: A Psychoanalytic and a Cultural Study.* New York, NY: Norton.

Poelmans, G.J.V. (2011) 'Genes and Protein Networks for Neurodevelopmental Disorders.' PhD thesis, Donders Instituut, Nijmegen.

Porges, S.W. (2011) *The Polyvagal Theory: Neurophysiological Foundations of Emotions, Attachment, Communication, and Self-Regulation.* New York, NY and London: Norton.

Poulopoulos, C. and Wolff, K. (2010) 'Staff perceptions about stress and staff burnout in drug treatment organisations: A comparative qualitative study in Greece and the UK with implications for training.' *Therapeutic Communities 31*, 3, 298–311.

Power, A. (2013) 'Working with Attachment Theory.' Training course, 23 March 2013, Psychotherapy UK, London.

Prigerson, H.G., Horowitz, M.J., Jacobs, S.C., Parkes, C.M. *et al.* (2009) Prolonged grief disorder: Psychometric validation of criteria proposed for DSM-V and ICD-11. *PLOS Medicine 6*, 8, e1000121.

Public Health Agency of Canada (2016) *The Chief Public Health Officer's Report on the State of Public Health in Canada 2015: Alcohol Consumption in Canada.* Ottawa: PHAC. Accessed on 11/4/18 at http://healthycanadians.gc.ca/publications/department-ministere/state-public-health-alcohol-2015-etat-sante-publique-alcool/alt/state-phac-alcohol-2015-etat-aspc-alcool-eng.pdf

Public Health England (2015) *New Psychoactive Substances in Prisons: A Toolkit for Prison Staff.* London: PHE. Accessed on 1/4/2018 at https://assets.publishing.service.gov.uk/government/uploads/system/uploads/attachment_data/file/669541/9011-phe-nps-toolkit-update-final.pdf

Public Health England (2017) *Better Care for People with Co-occurring Mental Health and Alcohol/Drug Use Conditions: A Guide for Commissioners and Service Providers.* London: PHE. Accessed on 3/3/2019 at https://assets.publishing.service.gov.uk/government/uploads/system/uploads/attachment_data/file/625809/Co-occurring_mental_health_and_alcohol_drug_use_conditions.pdf

Rando, T.A. (1993) *Treatment of Complicated Mourning.* Champaign, IL: Research Press.

Rando, T.A., Doka, K.J., Fleming, S., Franco, M.H. *et al.* (2012) 'A call to the field: Complicated grief in the DSM-5.' *Omega – Journal of Death and Dying 65*, 4, 251–255.

Reid, C. (2009) *A Scattering.* Oxford: Areté.

Renn, P. (2012) *The Silent Past and the Invisible Present.* New York, NY: Routledge.

Riches, G. and Dawson, P. (1998) 'Spoiled memories: Problems of grief resolution in families bereaved through murder.' *Mortality 3*, 2, 143–159.

Riches, G. and Dawson, P. (2000) *An Intimate Loneliness: Supporting Bereaved Parents and Siblings.* Buckingham: Open University Press.

Robson, P. (2009) *Forbidden Drugs* (3rd edition). Oxford: Oxford University Press.

Room, R., Rehm, J., Trotter, R.T., Paglia, A. and Ustun, T.B. (2001) 'Cross-Cultural Views on Stigma, Valuation, Parity, and Societal Values Towards Disability.' In T.B. Üstün, S. Chatterji, J.E. Bickenbach, R.T. Trotter *et al.* (eds) *Disability and Culture: Universalism and Diversity.* Seattle, WA: Hogrefe & Huber Publishers.

Rosenberg, S. (2017) *Accessing the Healing Power of the Vagus Nerve.* Berkeley, CA: North Atlantic Books.

Ross, E. (1996) 'Alcohol and bereavement.' *Bereavement Care 15*, 1, 5–7.

Rosenblatt, P. (1993) 'Grief: The Social Context of Private Feelings.' In M. Stroebe, W. Stroebe and R. Hansson (eds) *Handbook of Bereavement Research: Theory, Research and Intervention.* Cambridge: Cambridge University Press.

Rothschild, B. (2000) *The Body Remembers: The Psychophysiology of Trauma and Trauma Treatment.* New York, NY: Norton.

Rothschild, B. (2017) *The Body Remembers Volume 2: Revolutionizing Trauma Treatment.* New York, NY: Norton.

Roubal, J. (2007) 'Depression – A Gestalt theoretical perspective.' *British Gestalt Journal 16*, 1, 35–43.

Royal Society for Public Health (2016) *Taking a New Line on Drugs.* London: RSPH. Accessed on 10/5/2019 at www.rsph.org.uk/uploads/assets/uploaded/36dfae8b-7b10-4b28-9f6776743003e1a1.pdf

Rynearson, E.K. and Salloum, A. (2011) 'Restorative Retelling: Revising the Narrative of Violent Death.' In R.A. Neimeyer, D.L. Harris, H.R. Winokuer and G.F. Thornton (eds) *Grief and Bereavement in Contemporary Society: Bridging Research and Practice.* New York, NY: Routledge.

Rynearson, E.K., Schut, H. and Stroebe, M. (2013) 'Complicated Grief After Violent Death: Identification and Intervention.' In M.S. Stroebe, H. Schut and J. van den Bout (eds) *Complicated Grief: Scientific Foundations for Health Care Professionals.* New York, NY: Routledge.

Scheper-Hughes, N. (1992) *Death Without Weeping: The Violence of Everyday Life in Brazil.* Berkeley, CA: University of California Press.

Schore, A. (2012) *The Science and Art of Psychotherapy.* London: Norton.

Schut, H., Stroebe, M.S., van den Bout, J. and de Keijser, J. (1997) 'Intervention for the bereaved: Gender differences in the efficacy of two counselling programmes.' *British Journal of Clinical Psychology 36*, 1, 63–72.

Schwartz, A. (2019) 'Somatic Psychology as Integrated into Evidence Based Trauma Treatment.' Training course, 13–14 June 2019, NScience UK.

Scottish Government (2009) *Overdose: Bereavement. What Happens Now?* Edinburgh: Crown Copyright. Accessed on 10/11/2017 at www.gov.scot/Publications/2009/01/30140842/0

Seligman, M.E.P. (1975) *Helplessness.* San Francisco, CA: Freeman.

Siegel, D.J. (2012) *The Developing Mind: How Relationships and the Brain Interact to Shape Who We Are* (2nd edition). New York, NY: Guilford Press.

Simonsen, G. and Cooper, M. (2015) 'Helpful aspects of bereavement counselling: An interpretative phenomenological analysis.' *Counselling and Psychotherapy Research 15*, 2, 119–127.

Skinner, P. (2012) *See You Soon: A Mother's Story of Drugs, Grief and Hope.* Presence Books in partnership with Spoonbill Publications.

Spittle, B., Bragan, K. and James, B. (1976) 'Risk-taking propensity, depression and parasuicide.' *Australian and New Zealand Journal of Psychiatry 10*, 3, 269–273.

Stanton, M., Dunkley, C. and Melly, S. (2008) 'Emotion Regulation Treatment.' Workshop, Brunel University, London.

Stedeford, A. (1994) *Facing Death: Patients, Families and Professionals* (2nd edition). Oxford: Sobell.

Steger, M.F. and Kashdan, T.B. (2009) 'Depression and everyday social activity, belonging, and well-being.' *Journal of Counselling Psychology 56*, 2, 289–300.

Stern, D. (1985) *The Interpersonal World of the Infant.* New York, NY: Basic Books.

Stewart, S.H. (1996) 'Alcohol abuse in individuals exposed to trauma: A critical review.' *Psychological Bulletin 120*, 1, 83–112.

Stroebe, M. and Schut, H. (1999) 'The Dual Process Model of coping with bereavement: Rationale and description.' *Death Studies 23*, 3, 197–224.

Stroebe, M. and Schut, H. (2010) 'The Dual Process Model of coping with bereavement: A decade on.' *Omega – Journal of Death and Dying 61*, 4, 273–289.

Stroebe, M., Schut, H. and Boerner, K. (2010) 'Continuing bonds in adaptation to bereavement: Toward theoretical integration.' *Clinical Psychology Review 30*, 2, 259–268.

Stroebe, M. and Stroebe, W. (1993) 'The Mortality of Bereavement: A Review.' In M. Stroebe, W. Stroebe and R. Hanson (eds) *Handbook of Bereavement.* New York, NY, and Cambridge: Cambridge University Press.

Tedeschi, R.G. and Calhoun, L.G. (2007) 'Beyond the concept of recovery: Growth and the experience of loss.' *Death Studies 32*, 1, 27–39.

Templeton, L. McKell, J., Velleman, R. and Hay, G. (2018a) 'The Diversity of Bereavement through Substance Use.' In C. Valentine (ed.) *Families Bereaved by Alcohol or Drugs: Research on Experiences, Coping and Support.* London and New York, NY: Routledge.

Templeton, L., Valentine, C., McKell, J., Ford, A. *et al.* (2016) 'Bereavement following a fatal overdose: The experiences of adults in England and Scotland.' *Drugs: Education, Prevention and Policy 24*, 1, 58–66.

Templeton, L. and Velleman, R. (2018) 'Families Living with and Bereaved by Substance Use.' In C. Valentine (ed.) *Families Bereaved by Alcohol or Drugs: Research on Experiences, Coping and Support.* London and New York, NY: Routledge.

Templeton L., Yarwood, G.A., Wright S. and Galvani S. (2018b) 'Experiences of families, friends and carers: End of Life Care for People with Alcohol and Drug Problems.' Manchester Metropolitan University Research Briefing No. 4. Accessed on 2/11/2018 at https://endoflifecaresubstanceuse. files.wordpress.com/2018/08/family-strand-briefing-31-july-2018-final.pdf

Turnbull, F. and Standing, O. (2016) 'Drug and alcohol-related bereavement and the role of peer support.' *Bereavement Care 35*, 3, 102–108.

United Nations Office on Drugs and Crime (2007) *A Participatory Handbook for Youth Drug Prevention Programmes: A Guide for Development and Improvement.* Vienna: United Nations. Accessed on 23/4/2017 at www.unodc.org/pdf/youthnet/handbook.pdf

United Nations Office on Drugs and Crime (2017) *World Drug Report 2017.* Vienna: United Nations. Accessed on 2/6/2019 at www.unodc.org/wdr2017.

United Nations Office on Drugs and Crime (2019) *World Drug Report 2018.* Vienna: United Nations. Accessed on 9/8/2019 at www.unodc.org/wdr2018

Valentine, C. (ed.) (2018) *Families Bereaved by Alcohol or Drugs: Research on Experiences, Coping and Support.* London and New York, NY: Routledge.

Valentine, C. and Bauld, L. (2018) 'Researching Families Bereaved by Alcohol or Drugs.' In C. Valentine (ed.) *Families Bereaved by Alcohol or Drugs: Research on Experiences, Coping and Support.* London and New York, NY: Routledge.

Valentine, C. and Templeton, L. (2018) 'Remembering a Life that Involved Substance Use.' In C. Valentine (ed.) *Families Bereaved by Alcohol or Drugs: Research on Experiences, Coping and Support.* London and New York, NY: Routledge.

Valentine, C. and Walter, T. (2015) 'Creative responses to a drug- or alcohol-related death: A sociocultural analysis.' *Journal of Illness, Crisis and Loss 23*, 4, 310–322.

van Boekel, L.C., Browers, E.P., van Weeghel, J. and Garretsen, H.F. (2013) 'Stigma among health professionals towards patients with substance use disorders and its consequences for healthcare delivery: Systematic review.' *Drug and Alcohol Dependence 131*, 23–35.

van der Kolk, B. (2014) *The Body Keeps the Score.* London: Penguin Books.

van Deurzen, E. (2002) *Existential Counselling and Psychotherapy in Practice.* London: SAGE Publications.

Velleman, R. (2014) 'When our clients die: effects on family members, on our services, and how (if) we respond.' Report from a workshop delivered at the Aquarius Annual Conference, 17 July 2014.

VicHealth and Foundation for Alcohol Research and Education (2014) 'Alcohol kills more than 5,500 every year new figures show.' Accessed on 26/12/2017 at www.vichealth.vic.gov.au/media-and-resources/media-releases/alcohol-kills-15-australians-a-day

Vlasto, C. (2010) 'Therapists' views of the relative benefits and pitfalls of group work and one-to-one counselling for bereavement.' *Counselling and Psychotherapy Research 10*, 1, 60–66.

Walker, P. (2013) *Complex PTSD: From Surviving to Thriving.* N.P.: Azure Coyote.

Walker, R. (2014) *The Shame of Poverty.* Oxford: Oxford University Press.

Walter, F., Carr, M.J., Mok, P.L.H., Astrup, A. *et al.* (2017) 'Premature mortality among patients recently discharged from their first inpatient psychiatric treatment.' *JAMA Psychiatry 74*, 5, 485–492.

Walter, T. (1996) 'A new model of grief: Bereavement and biography.' *Mortality 1*, 1, 7–25.

Walter, T. (1999) *On Bereavement: The Culture of Grief.* Buckingham: Open University Press.

Walter, T. (2005) 'Mediator deathwork.' *Death Studies 29*, 5, 383–412.

Walter, T. and Ford, A. (2018) 'Managing Stigma.' In C. Valentine (ed.) *Families Bereaved by Alcohol or Drugs: Research on Experiences, Coping and Support.* London and New York, NY: Routledge.

Walter, T., Ford, A., Templeton, L., Valentine, C. and Velleman, R. (2015) 'Compassion or Stigma? How adults bereaved by alcohol or drugs experience services.' *Health and Social Care in the Community* 25, 6, 1714–1721.

Wegscheider-Cruse, S. (1981) *Another Chance: Hope and Health for the Alcoholic Family.* Paolo Alto, CA: Science & Behavior Books.

Wertheimer, A. (2001) A *Special Scar: The Experiences of People Bereaved by Suicide* (2nd edition). Hove: Brunner-Routledge.

Wheaton, B. (1990) 'Life transitions, role histories, and mental health.' *American Sociological Review* 55, 2, 209–223.

Wilcox, H.C., Conner, K.R. and Caine, E.D. (2004) 'Association of alcohol and drug use disorders and completed suicide: an empirical review of cohort studies.' *Drug and Alcohol Dependence 76,* Supplement 7, S11–S19.

Williams, J. and O'Donovan, M.C. (2006) 'The genetics of developmental dyslexia.' *European Journal of Human Genetics 14,* 6, 681–689.

Worden, J.W. (2009) *Grief Counselling and Grief Therapy: A Handbook for the Mental Health Practitioner* (4th edition). Hove, East Sussex: Routledge.

World Health Organization (1992) *The ICD-10 Classification of Mental and Behavioural Disorders: Clinical Descriptions and Diagnostic Guidelines.* Geneva: WHO. Accessed on 2/2/2018 at www.who.int/classifications/icd/en/bluebook.pdf

World Health Organization (1994) *Lexicon of Alcohol and Drug Terms.* Geneva: WHO. Accessed on 2/2/2018 at http://apps.who.int/iris/bitstream/10665/39461/1/9241544686_eng.pdf

World Health Organization (2000) *Preventing Suicide: A Resource for Primary Health Care Workers.* Geneva: WHO. Accessed on 16/4/2019 at www.who.int/mental_health/media/en/59.pdf

World Health Organization (2014) *Global Status Report on Alcohol and Health 2014.* Geneva: WHO. Accessed on 2/6/2019 at www.who.int/substance_abuse/publications/alcohol_2014/en

World Health Organization (2018) 'Fact sheet on alcohol consumption, alcohol-attributable harm and alcohol policy responses in European Union Member States, Norway and Switzerland.' Accessed on 2/6/2019 at www.euro.who.int/__data/assets/pdf_file/0009/386577/fs-alcohol-eng.pdf?ua=1

Wyllie, C., Platt, S., Brownlie, J., Chandler, A. *et al.* (2012) *Men, Suicide and Society: Why Disadvantaged Men in Mid-Life Die by Suicide.* Surrey: Samaritans.

Yalom, I. (1980) *Existential Psychotherapy.* New York, NY: Basic Books.

Yates, R. (2013) 'Bad mouthing, bad habits and bad, bad, boys: An exploration of the relationship between dyslexia and drug dependence.' *Mental Health and Substance Use 6,* 3, 184–202.

Yontef, G. (1993) *Awareness, Dialogue and Process: Essays on Gestalt Therapy.* Highland, NY: Gestalt Journal Press.

Yontef, G. (1996) 'Shame and Guilt in Gestalt Therapy: Theory and Practice.' In R.G. Lee and G. Wheeler (eds) *The Voice of Shame.* San Francisco, CA: Jossey-Bass, for the Gestalt Institute of Cleveland.

Young, M. (1995) 'Black humour: Making light of death.' *Policing and Society 5,* 2, 151–167.

Zador, D., Kidd, B., Hutchinson, S., Taylor, A. *et al.* (2005) *National Investigation into Drug Related Deaths in Scotland, 2003.* Edinburgh: Scottish Executive. Accessed on 26/4/2019 at www.scotland.gov.uk/Publications/2005/08/03161745/17507

Zandvoort, A. (2012) 'Living and laughing in the shadow of death: Complicated grief, trauma and resilience.' *British Journal of Psychotherapy Integration 9,* 2, 33–44.

Zandvoort, A. and Zandvoort, M. (2012) 'Trauma and the use of co-operative inquiry to develop a "survivor mission".' *British Journal of Psychotherapy Integration 9,* 2, 45–55.

Subject Index

United Kingdom 82–4
USA 85
stigma
    assumptions and 100, 222
    good practice around 128–32
    impact on bereavement 113–4
    internalised as shame 222–3
    overview 89–90
stimulants 50
stress 197–9
substance treatment service 17, 285–6
substance use
    co-occurring difficulties 57–9
    experimental use 53
    knowledge of 102–4
    problematic use 53
    range of behaviours 51–4
substance use by client
    addictive use 277–81
    client in recovery 279–81
    counselling dynamics 271–2
    death of the client 282–5
    ethical boundaries 272
    increased use 269–70
    joint working 277–8
    referring to specialist 274–5
    substances used 270–1
substances
    definition 49–50
    types of 50–1
sudden deaths 202–3
suicide deaths 74–5, 110–2, 241
support
    being with the client 149–51
    for family 75–6
    groups 116, 126, 127, 298–9
    identifying/developing client's 153–6, 208–11
    lack of 115–6
    self-support 156–9, 187, 208–11,
        226–7, 263–4, 288
    what everyone can do 147–9

survivor guilt 184, 243
sympathetic nervous system (SNS) 197

termination stage of change 59, 61
terminology 19–20, 130–1
therapeutic relationship 207
time/space for grief 148
tobacco 50
trauma
    definition 201–2
    signs/symptoms 205–6
traumatic bereavement
    assessing for trauma 204–6
    characteristics of 202–4
    counselling for 206–8, 288
    definition 109
    overview 199–202
    post-traumatic growth 204, 288
'trip' 50
twin studies 55–6
'two-chair work' 177–8

uncertainty 217–8
unexpected deaths 202–3
unfinished business 67, 104–7, 188, 189, 213–8, 288
United Kingdom statistics 82–4
up-regulating emotions 170–1
'uppers' 50
USA statistics 85

values, client's 180
viewing the body 117, 184

window of tolerance 142–3, 167, 168,
    171, 201, 205, 207, 208
women 82, 84, 86, 116, 164, 234, 298
worldview 156, 173, 190, 206, 289, 290–2

Author Index

Peter Cartwright has over twenty years of experience of both counselling bereaved people and supporting families affected by a loved one's drug or alcohol use. He has brought these two strands together to develop a specialism in substance-related bereavements through his work as a counsellor, trainer, researcher and author. This includes being author of 'How helpful is counselling for people bereaved through a substance-related death?', published by Bereavement Care journal in 2019; co-author of Chapter 7 – 'Improving the Response of Services, in Families Bereaved by Alcohol and Drugs: Research on Experiences, Coping and Support', published by Routledge in 2018; being primary author and the chair of the national working group that produced 'Bereaved through substance use: Guidelines for those whose work brings them into contact with adults after a drug or alcohol-related death', published by the University of Bath in 2015; and being co-author of 'Bereaved by Addiction: A Booklet for Anyone Bereaved Through Drug or Alcohol Use' published by DrugFAM in 2013. He lives in London, where he also trained as a counsellor at The Gestalt Centre.

CPI Antony Rowe
Eastbourne, UK
April 04, 2025